ETHNODRAMA

CROSSROADS IN QUALITATIVE INQUIRY

Series Editors
Norman K. Denzin, University of Illinois, Urbana-Champaign
Yvonna S. Lincoln, Texas A&M University

ABOUT THE SERIES
Qualitative methods are material and interpretive practices. They do not stand outside politics and cultural criticism. This spirit of critically imagining and pursuing a more democratic society has been a guiding feature of qualitative inquiry from the very beginning. The Crossroads in Qualitative Inquiry series will take up such methodological and moral issues as the local and the global, text and context, voice, writing for the other, and the presence of the author in the text. The Crossroads series understands that the discourses of a critical, moral methodology are basic to any effort to re-engage the promise of the social sciences for democracy in the 21st Century. This international series creates a space for the exploration of new representational forms and new critical, cultural studies.

SUBMITTING MANUSCRIPTS
Book proposals should be sent to Crossroads in Qualitative Inquiry Series, c/o Norman K. Denzin, Institute for Communication Studies, 810 S. Wright Street, University of Illinois, Champaign, Illinois 61820, or emailed to n-denzin@uiuc.edu.

BOOKS IN THIS SERIES
Volume 1: *Incarceration Nation: Investigative Prison Poems of Hope and Terror*, by Stephen John Hartnett (2003)

Volume 2: *9/11 in American Culture*, edited by Norman K. Denzin and Yvonna S. Lincoln (2003)

Volume 3: *Turning Points in Qualitative Research: Tying Knots in the Handkerchief*, edited by Yvonna S. Lincoln and Norman K. Denzin (2003)

Volume 4: *Uprising of Hope: Sharing the Zapatista Journey to Alternative Development*, Duncan Earle and Jeanne Simonelli (2005)

Volume 5: *Ethnodrama: An Anthology of Reality Theatre*, edited by Johnny Saldaña (2005)

ETHNODRAMA

An Anthology of
Reality Theatre

Edited by
JOHNNY SALDAÑA

ALTAMIRA
PRESS

A Division of
ROWMAN & LITTLEFIELD PUBLISHERS, INC.
Walnut Creek • Lanham • New York • Toronto • Oxford

Fronticepiece: Chris Marley as the poet Mack in Saldaña, Finley, and Finley's *Street Rat*.

AltaMira Press
A division of Rowman & Littlefield Publishers, Inc.
1630 North Main Street, #367
Walnut Creek, CA 94596
www.altamirapress.com

Rowman & Littlefield Publishers, Inc.
A wholly owned subsidiary of The Rowman & Littlefield Publishing Group, Inc.
4501 Forbes Boulevard, Suite 200
Lanham, MD 20706

PO Box 317
Oxford
OX2 9RU, UK

British Library Cataloguing in Publication Information Available

Library of Congress Cataloging-in-Publication Data

Ethnodrama : an anthology of reality theatre / edited by Johnny Saldaña.
    p. cm. — (Crossroads in qualitative inquiry ; v. 5)
Includes bibliographical references.
ISBN 0-7591-0812-9 (cloth : alk. paper) — ISBN 0-7591-0813-7 (pbk. : alk. paper)
    1. Social problems—Drama. 2. American drama—21st century. 3. Ethnology—
Research—Drama. 4. Social sciences—Research—Drama. I. Saldaña, Johnny.
II. Series.

PS627.S63E86 2004
812'.60803556—dc22   2004018673

Printed in the United States of America

♾™ The paper used in this publication meets the minimum requirements of American National Standard for Information Sciences—Permanence of Paper for Printed Library Materials, ANSI/NISO Z39.48–1992.

ISBN 978-0-7591-08134

Contents

Acknowledgments

Thanks are extended to the following:

Norman K. Denzin, Yvonna S. Lincoln, Mitch Allen, and AltaMira Press for supporting this publication project and acknowledging the legitimacy of arts-based research.

Kristina Razmara, Terry Fischer, Monica Riley, and the production staffs of Rowman & Littlefield and AltaMira Press.

The Arizona State University Katherine K. Herberger College of Fine Arts (J. Robert Wills, Dean), Institute for Studies in the Arts, and Department of Theatre; the University of Alberta's International Institute for Qualitative Methodology; the University of Victoria Department of Theatre; the International Drama in Education Research Institute; and the American Educational Research Association's Arts-Based Educational Research Special Interest Group, for financially supporting the editor's ethnotheatrical productions.

Brian Schlemmer, Harry F. Wolcott, Charles Vanover, Susan Finley, and Macklin Finley, for allowing the editor to adapt their stories and research into ethnodramatic form.

Selected material from the editor's introduction originally appeared in Johnny Saldaña's "Dramatizing Data: A Primer," *Qualitative Inquiry*, volume 9, number 2, 2003, pp. 218–36, copyright © 2003 Sage Publications.

Selections from *Finding My Place: The Brad Trilogy* originally appeared in Harry F. Wolcott's *Sneaky Kid and Its Aftermath: Ethics and Intimacy in Fieldwork* (AltaMira Press, 2002).

Series Editors' Foreword

By Norman K. Denzin
and Yvonna S. Lincoln

The performative turn has been taken in the social sciences. We have moved from textual ethnographies to performative [auto] ethnographies. "Performance-sensitive ways of knowing" (Conquergood, 1998, p. 26) contribute to an epistemological and political pluralism that challenges existing ways of knowing and representing the world. Such formations are more inclusionary and better suited than existing ways for thinking about postcolonial or "subaltern" cultural practices (Conquergood, 1998, p. 26). Performance approaches to knowing insist on immediacy, and involvement. They consist of partial, plural, incomplete, and contingent understandings, not the analytic distance of detachment, the hallmarks of the textual and positivist paradigms (Pelias, 1999, pp. ix, xi; 2004, p. 1).

A hallmark of this series is the belief that the performance-based human disciplines can contribute to radical social change, to economic justice, to a cultural politics that extends the "principles of a radical democracy to all aspects of society" (Giroux, 2003, pp. x, 25). We understand that the discourses of a critical, moral methodology are basic to any effort to re-engage the promise of the social sciences for democracy in the twenty-first century. Thus does this international series create a space for new representational forms that are at the crossroads of critical, qualitative inquiry.

Enter Johnny Saldaña's wonderful book, *Ethnodrama: An Anthology of Reality Theatre*. This book is long overdue. Those of us committed to the performance paradigm have not had in a single source a collection of ethnodramas that could be used for teaching and instruction. Saldaña's anthology gives us this book. Anchored in the arts-based tradition of qualitative inquiry, his *ethnotheatre* employs the "traditional craft and artistic techniques of theatre production to mount for an audience a live performance event of research participants' experiences." An *ethnodrama*, the written script, consists of dramatized selections of narratives collected through interviewing and participation observation.

Ethnodrama: An Anthology of Reality Theatre is an international collection of play scripts, performance works, and works of "creative nonfiction" that exemplify Saldaña's assessment of the very best of this new genre of arts-based research. The anthology is divided into three parts: ethnodramatic monologue, ethnodramatic dialogue with monologue, and ethnodramatic extensions. An appendix offers a valuable guide of current works that can serve as dramatic models for ethnodrama. Saldaña's magnificent Introduction locates this field in its proper literatures, gives the reader a vocabulary of terms (plot, story line, dramatic structure, character, scenography) and a typology of forms.

Saldaña shows how ethnodrama, as a form of ethnographic theatre, involves "participant and audience empowerment through forum reconstruction and 'dialogical interactions' " (Mienczakowski, 1995, p. 361). Ethnodramas are a form of public voice ethnography, organized by the proposition "that performed ethnography may provide more accessible and clearer public explanations of research than is frequently the case with traditional, written report texts" (Mienczakowski, 2001, p. 471). Ethnodramas differ from other forms of performance ethnographic practice "because it is their overt intention . . . to be a form of public voice ethnography that has emancipatory and educational potential" (Mienczakowski, 2001, p. 469).

Ethnodramas can help enact a politics of resistance and possibility by giving a voice to the previously silenced, by creating a space for audiences and performers to actually engage in meaningful dialogue and discourse (Madison, 2003). Such performances enact a performance-centered pedagogy. This fusion of critical pedagogy and performance praxis uses performance as a method of investigation, as a way of doing evaluation ethnography, as a method of understanding, as a way of collaboratively engaging the meanings of experience, as a way of mobilizing persons for action in the world. This form of critical, collaborative inquiry privileges the primacy of experience, the concept of voice, and the importance of turning inquiry sites into spaces where democratic public discourse can take place. In this way ethnodramas help create the conditions for an emancipatory democratic politics.

Johnny Saldaña and his collaborators are to be thanked for giving us the platform from which this new form of critical qualitative inquiry can be launched.

Prologue: *the theatre*

BY MONICA PRENDERGAST

Editor's Introduction

Prendergast's (2001) award-winning thesis examined adolescent audience development and education through an adjunct program connected with a Canadian professional theatre company. Unique to her research was the analysis and display of qualitative data in poetic form (Glesne, 1999, pp. 183–87; Prendergast, 2003), culled from her participants' written survey responses. One of the initial poems in her document reveals her personal philosophy toward theatre as an art form, and it is presented here as a prologue to the anthology and as an exemplar of arts-based research.

the theatre

the theatre

must never
be boring

indeed
must be
the opposite
of boring

so it may
delight and arouse
the senses
and the mind

may soothe
and shake
and shock

dig deep
really and
truly deep

in the earning
of a single clap
or bravo

* * *

my father
dying
complained little
to me
but that it
(dying)
was boring

the theatre
was his life
and is mine

if theatre
is boring
it is both
bad and wrong

there is much
of theatre
which bores

but a moment
a memory

(Lear cradling
Cordelia

Salieri grieving
Mozart

Godot waiting
offstage

Courage moving
on)

more than
counteract
that which bores

. . .

the actor
steps into
the light

and we
the audience
concentrate

transfix and transform
what is performed
with our collective
gaze

create in community
the space
of the stage

cooperate in believing
this temporary (suspended)
reality

ask only that
our actor help us

(by being always
and ever
open
honest
and true)

trust this journey

make the trip worthwhile

An Introduction to Ethnodrama

BY JOHNNY SALDAÑA

ermit me to begin with some detailed but necessary definitions, constructed from my own perspective and experiences. As clinical and precise as these descriptions may appear, they serve as important criteria for what's included in this unique anthology of plays, and as understandings for the reader before reviewing these dramatic works. Also, the intended audiences for this book come from a variety of academic disciplines ranging from the fine arts to the social sciences. So it's helpful if we're all on the same page from the beginning.

Ethno*theatre* employs the traditional craft and artistic techniques of theatre production to mount for an audience a live performance event of research participants' experiences and/or the researcher's interpretations of data. This research—meaning, to investigate, in its broadest sense—can be conducted by artists, scholars, or even by the participants themselves in such diverse fields of study as sociology, anthropology, psychology, education, health care, women's studies, justice studies, ethnic studies, cultural studies, political science, journalism, human communication, performance studies, and theatre. The goal is to investigate a particular facet of the human condition for purposes of adapting those observations and insights into a performance medium. Simply put,

1

this is preparatory fieldwork for theatrical production work. An ethno*drama*, the written script, consists of dramatized, significant selections of narrative collected through interviews, participant observation field notes, journal entries, and/or print and media artifacts such as diaries, television broadcasts, newspaper articles, and court proceedings. Simply put, this is dramatizing the data. *(artifacts)*

What makes ethnotheatre an appropriate presentational mode for ethnographic research? Performance critic Sylvia Drake challenges writers to consider the appropriateness of a story's medium, and whether a tale would be best told through live theatre, television, or film. Just as some theatrical and media works are adapted from literary sources (e.g., Tom Wolfe's *The Right Stuff* [1979]; Studs Terkel's *Working* [1974]), selected research reports lend themselves to adaptation for the stage, television/video, or film. Several studies have already been transformed or possess exciting possibilities for the intimacy of the stage (e.g., Harry F. Wolcott's "Sneaky Kid," 1994, 2002), the documentary flavor of television/video (e.g., Jonothan Kozol's *Savage Inequalities*, 1991), or the magnitude of film (e.g., Jennifer Toth's *The Mole People: Life in the Tunnels beneath New York City*, 1993). There are times when the need to document one's research theatrically simply "feels right." J. Taylor (2003) prefaces her autobiographical ethnodrama by noting that her initial writing shifted between essay and performance: "By the third draft, the text itself began to exceed the limitations of the page, demanding props, lights, a slide show, music, performance" (p. 192). A key question to discern the most appropriate mode of representation and presentation for ethnographic research is: Will the participant's story be credibly, vividly, and persuasively told for an audience through a traditional written report, video documentary, photographic portfolio, website, poetry, dance, music, visual art installation, or ethnodrama? If it's the latter, then a qualitative researcher playwrites with data.

Ethnotheatre is not intended as a "clever" presentation medium to replace the academician's scholarly report traditionally delivered behind a podium. Nor is it intended as a didactic form of theatre that employs visual novelty to present dry nonfiction on stage for purposes of educating an audience on current issues and affairs. Ethnotheatre is just one of several forms available to present and represent a study of people and their culture—ethnography. Depending on your values system, ethnodrama can be perceived as a legitimate and credible form of research documentation, or as an "alternative," "experimental," lesserthan mode of fieldwork reporting. Naturally, I support the former perspective and find advocacy from van Maanen's (1988) classification of ethnodrama as a variant of the "impressionist tale" which highlights the episodic, complex, and ambivalent realities . . . perhaps made too pat and ordered by realist or confessional conventions. Impressionist tales, with their silent disavowal of grand theorizing, their radical grasping for the particular, eventful, contextual, and unusual, contain an important message. They protest the ultimate superficiality of much of the published research in social sciences—ethnographic or otherwise. (p. 119)

Lincoln and Denzin (2003) focus the purpose of art form further through the dramas' examination of "crises and moments of epiphany in the culture. Suspended in time, they are liminal moments. They open up institutions and their practices for critical inspection and evaluation" (p. 377). Depending on the particular goals of the ethnodramatist and production company, the artistic project is not only aesthetic, it possesses "emancipatory potential" for motivating social change within participants and audiences (Mienczakowski, 1995; Mienczakowski & Morgan, 2001). Ethnotheatre is a manifesto that exposes oppression and challenges the existing social order through an artistic rendering of moral and political discourse (Denzin, 2004). From feminist perspectives, "The act of women speaking their own stories publicly . . . radically challenges traditional notions of agency, spectacle, and spectatorship as female performers move their voices and bodies from the background to the foreground" (Carver, 2003, p. 16).

Ethnodrama: An Anthology of Reality Theatre is an international, multicultural collection of play scripts and documented performance works that exemplify the editor's assessment of the best of a relatively new genre of arts-based research and a noticeable trend in the field of theatre production itself.[1] The traditional western canon of dramatic literature consists primarily of literary and commercial works whose content is more generally fiction than fact. Ethnodrama differs by maintaining close allegiance to the lived experiences of real people while presenting their stories through an artistic medium—"creative nonfiction," as some genres of qualitative inquiry have been labeled. These works are comparable in intent to the performances of interviews collected by Anna Deavere Smith (2000); to Anne Nelson's (2002) gripping tribute to the heroes of September 11, 2001, in *The Guys*; or to Moisés Kaufman and Members of the Tectonic Theater Project's (2001) celebrated drama *The Laramie Project*. But this anthology's plays are more local in their content, more particular in their focus, and more intimate in their experience. Nevertheless, these ethnodramas also capture verisimilitude and universality through their primary sources for monologue and dialogue: reality.

All Playwrights Are Ethnodramatists

Theatre in the western world has been telling stories for over 2,500 years and, more often than not, representing social life on stage—interpreted artistically by playwrights and actors with perceptive insight into the human condition. Playwrights are and always have been ethnodramatists, for what other source for a drama *is* there besides social life? Ancient Greek tragedies and comedies such as *The Trojan Women* and *Lysistrata* included their playwrights' commentary, through choral episodes and protagonists, on the ravages of war to their civilization. Though it's doubtful that Euripides or Aristophanes systematically gathered their fellow citizens' perspectives on current conflicts, theatre served as both a forum and medium for expressing the sociopolitical climate of the times.

Depending on the nature of their vision, contemporary artists employ traditional ethnographic methods to gather informative data for their plays. William H. Hoffman's (1985) groundbreaking drama on AIDS, *As Is*, incorporated preparatory fieldwork: "I did my research. I visited friends who had the disease; I talked with a hospice worker; I went to support groups; I attended lectures; I made field trips to the Gay Men's Health Crisis. . . . I spent hours eavesdropping in gay bars, taking the public pulse" (p. xiii). Many people are unaware that one of the most popular, Pulitzer Prize–winning American musicals, *A Chorus Line*, includes character monologues and lyrics derived from interview transcripts. In the book's preface, Samuel G. Freedman writes,

> On January 18, 1974, some 24 dancers met with [director/choreographer Michael] Bennett in a rehearsal studio on East 23rd Street. For the next twelve hours, and again a few weeks later, they danced and talked and ate and talked and drank and talked, with a tape recorder capturing every revelation. . . . Still, it diminishes the achievement of *A Chorus Line* to imply, as theatre legend often has, that creating the show simply involved editing a few transcripts and setting them to song. More than specific anecdotes, the gypsies [a slang term for musical chorus dancers] supplied verisimilitude . . . the realities of their lives. And by remaining faithful to the peculiarities of that narrow world, Bennett and his collaborators let true universality emerge. "There is *truth* on that stage," he later would say. "Nothing monumental or astounding, but truth nevertheless." (Bennett et al., 1995, p. viii)

When film, television, or theatre adapts a nonfiction literary work, or examines current social reality in natural contexts, these art forms are dramatizing data. Michael Moore's 2002 Academy Award–winning documentary *Bowling for Columbine* is a collage of on-camera interviews, news footage, and statistical data that examine and comment on the high school shooting tragedy in Littleton, Colorado, and the broader implications of violence in the United States. His *Fahrenheit 9/11*, a film critiquing American President George W. Bush and the war in Iraq, received the 2004 Cannes Film Festival's coveted top prize, the Palme d'Or—an anomaly for a documentary. At the awards ceremony, Moore noted that "Nonfiction is taking itself out of its own ghetto." Chinese theatre and film director Zhang Yang casts the actor Jia Hongsheng and his actual parents to portray themselves in *Quitting*, a 2001 cinematic ethnodrama. Hongsheng's rise to fame as a performer is cut short by his drug abuse, hallucinations, depression, and consequent institutionalization by his mother and father. The screenplay, based on six months of interviews with the actor and his family and friends, literally re-creates their tumultuous life stories from the 1990s. Television news programs such as *60 Minutes, Dateline,* and *20/20* construct and present many of their stories as if they were short two- or three-act plays, complete with characters with whom we identify, an intermission of commercials, and a suspenseful build to a climactic revelation. Even the convoluted texts of news briefings by U.S. Defense Secretary Donald Rumsfeld have been used for poetic verse adaptations and lyrics for operatic songs by musician Bryant Kong (Hinds, 2004).

Chicago's Lookingglass Theatre Company in 2003 staged an adaptation of the nonfiction classic *Race: How Blacks and Whites Think and Feel about the American Obsession* by Studs Terkel (1993), while Steppenwolf Theatre produced investigative journalist Barbara Ehrenreich's *Nickel and Dimed: On (Not) Getting by in America* (2002). Eve Ensler's (2000) *The Vagina Monologues* evolved from her conversations and interviews with over 200 women about their vaginas, and staging the play has become a global, national phenomenon—V-Day, an event to protest violence against women. Ensler's monologues vary from near-verbatim interview text to composite interviews to inspired, original pieces. One of New York City's most recent critical successes is Jessica Blank and Erik Jensen's *The Exonerated* (2004), a staged reading of interview transcripts and court proceedings from the true stories of six innocent survivors who served time on death row. In 2004, the Pulitzer Prize and Broadway's Tony Award for best play were awarded to Doug Wright's (2004) *I Am My Own Wife,* a biographical ethnodrama based on extensive interviews with gay transvestite Charlotte von Mahlsdorf, who lived in Germany during its oppressive twentieth century regime. "Reality theatre" is only a minor trend within the live art form (professional theatre *is* a commercial venture, after all, and needs to produce appealing entertainments to generate sufficient audiences and revenue). But it does complement what is happening more prominently in the national media, and these trends are a natural outcome of a current social need: the need of everyday citizens to transcend their normative status and gain significant social acknowledgment through revelatory, performative participation in a public venue.

On Reality TV

PBS's 1973 television miniseries *An American Family* offered the viewing public, at that time, a progressively painful and sometimes shocking weekly glimpse at the deterioration of a marriage. But the twelve-episode program was not fictional soap opera. Cameras followed the Loud family in their California home and on their travels to document their natural lives with uncensored honesty. This pioneering reality TV show was both hailed and criticized in the 1970s for its stark portrayal of human truth. I recall watching the series as a teenager when it originally aired and remember the discomfort it caused me when I heard the family members' coarse language and watched their uninhibited actions at home. It was gripping drama because I knew that what I was watching had actually happened to real people.

By today's standards of shock value, *An American Family* is moderately tame. The general public, through television, now has access to the live or videotaped reality of the courtroom, the operating and autopsy tables, and the lives of prostitutes, drug addicts, and drag queens in such programs as *America Undercover*. Commentator James Pinkerton (2002) observes how our nation's emergent cultural permissiveness now interplays with electronic media and cyberspace technology, generating "new styles of confession and revelation" (p. V2). The 2004 internationally broadcast Superbowl halftime show sparked national debate for its notorious, one-second, "unintentional" (according to fellow performer Justin Timberlake) display of Janet Jackson's breast. Virtual strangers on sex-oriented, Internet chat rooms can e-mail each other digital photographs of their naked bodies. Everyday citizens on talk shows hosted by such moderators as Rikki Lake and Jerry Springer disclose with unabashed honesty the intimate problems and details of their private lives. Viewers can become voyeurs of celebrities' daily lifestyles through such programs as *The Osbournes* and *The Anna Nicole Show*, which offer us their reality (albeit edited) as entertainment and, questionably, enlightenment.

Made-for-television movies based on actual people's stories have always been a mainstay of programming, but at the beginning of the twenty-first century, reality TV exploded as a media phenomenon. Network programming of this genre blurred fiction and nonfiction as both entertainment and representation through everyday people competing on national television for some sort of prize, ranging from a potential marriage partner to a million dollars to a lucrative performance contract. Several social critics focused on negative issues inherent in these shows, such as the sadistic degradation of human dignity through the producers' secret twists-of-plot (e.g., in *Boy Meets Boy*, out of three male finalists from which the gay protagonist had to choose, one finalist was straight), or the cutthroat rules of contestant comparison, secret voting, and elimination from the "game" (e.g., *Survivor, Big Brother, The Apprentice*). Competition is a major facet of American culture, and television producers skew reality with a competitive twist to make this type of programming pseudo-gladiatorial and thus more engaging for television audiences—and to compete for higher Nielsen ratings. Though the reality TV trend is still strong as of 2004, it may one day overstay its welcome. The only reason networks develop such shows is their potential for high ratings and thus higher advertising revenue. Once the audience demand and market for this genre wane, reality TV will no longer be produced and broadcast.

But as a theatre practitioner, I noticed other, more interesting phenomena at work during the reality TV movement. Television became more than interactive with its viewers—it became participatory. *America's Funniest Home Videos* encouraged the public to submit clips from those humorous moments in their lives captured on tape for broadcast on national television. On such series as *Fame* and *American Idol* (karaoke with magnitude, as I call it), virtually anyone, not just trained performers, could audition for possible casting in several of these programs. Not everyone made the cut, but most everyone had the opportunity. The average citizen could now be transformed into a celebrity—literally overnight. And in addition to everyday citizens achieving more than their fifteen minutes of fame by becoming active participants on network or cable television, some programs included related websites and toll-free phone numbers in which the viewing public could vote to sway the outcome (e.g., voting for the funniest comedian in *Last Comic Standing*). A final example is not television-related but an interesting hybrid of film and theatre and a form of participatory entertainment ("Karaoke," 2004). In a New York City nightclub called the Den of Cin, a cinematic version of karaoke is now available in which customers replicate famous scenes from major films by substituting their own voices in place of the original motion picture soundtrack. Through "movieoke," the common human fantasy of being a movie star can now be fulfilled through technology.

I was interviewed once by my university's fine arts publicist about my ethnodramatic productions. The goal was to develop a story that could be circulated to national print media in hopes of being published, thus bringing higher visibility to our department. Since the competition for limited print space is fierce, news items need a "spin" to motivate an editor to include a story in a magazine or newspaper. The publicist asked me a standard question from her interview repertory in order to learn what was unique about ethnodrama and to find some facet of the genre the general public could relate to: "Why should my 83-year-old grandmother in New Jersey care about the work you're doing?" I replied without hesitation, "Because your 83-year-old grandmother in New Jersey could become the subject of my next ethnodrama."

I've heard it forecast that, with the advent of technology, people would need more actual human touch to compensate for the electronic, distancing effects of the computer. When we feel that we have become tired of or jaded by the superficiality of mediated interaction, we seek more fulfilling social interaction, a connection to authenticity (Piccalo, 2003). In addition to these premises, the unforeseen events of the stark reality of 9/11 jolted the United States back to the present, back to the day-to-day, back to finding more significant meaning to life. Though not everyone is thinking meta-ontologically, reality seems to have become more prevalent and fascinating than fiction. Reality is the current novelty; reality is the trend.

On Reality Theatre

There is also a trend in educational and community-based theatre in which the development of original work, rather than the remounting of established classics, is in vogue. These productions address issues that are personal, local, contextual, and immediate—signature works by particular artists examining a particular issue for a particular audience. One example is a high school educator facilitating improvisationally developed scenes by her students on topics ranging from peer cruelty to teenage drinking. Another example is a professional theatre company commissioned to develop a theatrical event based on a community's concern with escalating racial conflicts. The goal is not to create a commercial Broadway hit, but to provide a forum for artists with social vision and audiences with social need (Boal, 2002). It is rare that an original work developed by a group devoted to such causes will be remounted by another theatre company. These performance pieces sacrifice mainstream canonicity in exchange for socially conscious merit and higher social purpose. Those who participate in these ventures can be meaningfully fed through this dramatic rant at our sense of injustice in the world. Accompanying trends have been labeled "theatre of the oppressed," "theatre for social change," "theatre for development," "popular theatre," "applied theatre," "playback theatre," "sociodrama," and "grassroots theatre"—modes with a participatory component and social or therapeutic purposes (see Denzin, 2003; P. Taylor, 2003). "Ethnodrama" and "ethnotheatre" are now two more terms to add to the list of current theatrical movements.[2]

Ethnodrama is the theatrical distant cousin of reality TV. But by no means is the edited, commercially interrupted, prime time media fare of reality TV authentic. Though film and television are nothing more than chemical, electronic, and digital forms of live theatre, theatre is generally more honest in what it's up to. Reality TV portrays everyday people in conflict or competition with each other in prepackaged, sometimes covert circumstances. Unfortunately, "reality TV is base," according to Michael Rohd, one of the contributors to this anthology. "It asks us to enjoy the stripping of dignity, the false monologue, edited into shame and pandering as a true voice. If we do our jobs right with [ethnotheatre], we are exploring, restoring, achieving dignity, and asking questions." Real people's real stories, told in artistically crafted ways by a sensitive production company, are genres of storytelling that rise above the current popular trend of reality TV. Mienczakowski, another contributor and pioneer of the genre, asserts that "the ethnographic construction of dramatic scripts, validated by contributors, peers, and informed others, is potentially able to achieve vraisemblance and cultural ingress as effectively, if not more effectively, than some traditional means of research reporting" (2003, p. 421). Noted sociologist Norman K. Denzin (1997) supports this and even goes so far as to claim that ethnotheatre has become "the single, most powerful way for ethnography to recover yet interrogate the meanings of lived experience" (pp. 94–95).

Recent plays like *I Am My Own Wife*, *The Exonerated*, and *The Laramie Project*, plus the solo performance work of Anna Deavere Smith (*Twilight: Los Angeles, 1992*; *Fires in the Mirror*) demonstrate that gathering the voices of real people and transferring them onto the stage in aesthetically sound ways can become riveting theatre. Historically, the time is right to formally disseminate a collection of ethnodramas.

The Scholarly and Commercial Legacy of Ethnodrama

Selected writers in theatre and the social sciences have examined and theorized about the disciplines' blurred genres and their implications for interpretation, performance, and everyday life (Barone, 2002; Barranger, 2004; Berg, 2001, chap. 4; Conquergood, 1991; Dening, 1996; Denzin, 2001b, 2003; Geertz,

1983; Goffman, 1959; Goodall, 2000; Kalb, 2001; Landy, 1993; Mienczakowski, 1995, 2001; Rex et al., 2002; Saldaña, 1999, 2003; Schechner, 1985; Turner, 1982; Turner & Turner, 1982).[3] Ethnotheatre represents a fairly recent movement in the field of qualitative inquiry to experiment with arts-based modes of research representation (Bagley & Cancienne, 2002; Barone, 1997; Denzin, 1997; Diamond & Mullen, 1999, 2000; Eisner, 1997; Ellis & Bochner, 1996; Finley & Knowles, 1995; Jipson & Paley, 1997; Sparkes, 2002; Spry, 2001). Prominent methodologists in qualitative inquiry have constructed research representation and presentation—if not social life itself—as "performance" (in its broadest sense), and have encouraged experiments with narrative form and genre (Denzin, 2001a). Some scholars in the social sciences may employ the term "performance" in casual ways that irk the sensibilities of those deeply involved in the culture of theatre, for mounting a theatrical production, regardless of its magnitude, is hard work. Nevertheless, theatre is one of the artistic media through which fictionalized and nonfictionalized social life—the human condition—can be portrayed symbolically and aesthetically for spectator engagement and reflection. Examples of qualitative, ethnographic, and autoethnographic work presented in dramatic form have increased exponentially over the past decade, and include diverse content from multiple disciplines:[4]

Education

- a typical day in teacher's lives at school (Walker, Pick, & MacDonald, 1991)
- novice teachers struggling with and reflecting on their practices (Boran, 1999; Chávez, Adams, & Araujo, 2004; Rogers, Frellick, & Babinski, 2002; Vanover & Saldaña, 2002)
- nonheterosexual physical education teachers (Sykes, Chapman, & Swedberg, 2002; Chapman, Sykes & Swedberg, 2003)
- a tough but inspiring Chicago high school English teacher (Vanover, 2004)
- power struggles and control issues in school administration (Meyer, 1998, 2001a, 2001b)
- the Oregon state public school system (Rohd, 2004)
- the writing processes of middle schoolers (Donmoyer & Yennie-Donmoyer, 1995)
- doctoral fieldwork in agricultural education (Thorp, 2003)
- assessment dilemmas (Donovan, 2004)
- a multicultural arts education project (Burge, 2000)
- evaluation of a state fine arts program (Cozart et al., 2003)

Vocation and Occupation

- the artistic development of an adolescent actor (Saldaña, 1998a, 1998b)
- the audition process for professional actors and directors (Jackson, 1993)
- theatrical community organization and life (Becker, McCall, Morris, & Meshejian, 1989; McCall, Becker, & Meshejian, 1990)
- personal stories of jazz musicians (Kotarba, 1998)
- a taxicab driver's perspectives on his job (Snow, 2002)
- an African American female's professorship (Jones, 2003)
- a cafeteria workers' strike and labor culture on a university campus (Madison, 2003)
- the Flint, Michigan, 1936–1937 autoworkers' sit-down strike (Nethercott & Leighton, 1990)
- a musical adaptation of Studs Terkel's *Working* (Schwartz & Faso, 1978)
- an adaptation of Barbara Ehrenreich's *Nickel and Dimed* (Holden, 2004)

Health

- communications between a physician and a cancer patient (Paget, 1995)
- women's metastatic breast cancer (Gray & Sinding, 2002)
- a woman's diagnosis and treatment of breast cancer (Park-Fuller, 2003)
- prostate cancer's effects on men and their spouses (Gray & Sinding, 2002)
- attitudes toward schizophrenia (Mienczakowski, Smith, & Morgan, 2002).
- Alzheimer's disease (Cole, McIntyre, & McAuliffe, 2001)
- alcohol and drug abuse, and detoxification (Mienczakowski, 1996, 1997)
- aging, autonomy, and mental health of older persons (McLean, 2004)
- HIV/AIDS awareness and people with HIV/AIDS (Corey, 1993)
- cross-cultural health work in Australia (Preisinger, Schroeder, & Scott-Hoy, 2000)

Ethnic/Racial Identity and Racism

- a Vietnamese American female reclaiming her voice after a racist incident (Bui, 2001)
- Latina identity and voice (De la Garza, 2000)
- the daily lives of women in Lebanon (Farah, 2003)
- predicaments of a biracial and mixed heritage woman (Hunter, 2004)

- racial identity and conflict in high school settings (Goldstein, 2001a, 2001b, 2002; Rohd, 2001)
- racism in rural and urban communities (Pifer, 1999; Rohd & Eason, 2002)
- community reactions to the 1991 Crown Heights and 1992 Los Angeles riots (Smith, 1993, 1994)
- immigration and borderlands issues between the United States and Mexico (Casas, 2003)

Gender and Sexual Identity

- adolescent female gender identity development (Collins, 2001)
- breasts and female identity (Gannon, 2004)
- the vagina and female identity (Ensler, 2000)
- women in academia (Spore & Harrison, 2000)
- adolescent masculinities in drama programs at an all-boys school (Sallis, 2003)
- hegemonic masculinity in the culture of university physical education (in Sparkes, 2002)
- a lesbian's reflections on her family and academia (J. Taylor, 2003)
- a gay man's reflections on AIDS and a pride parade (Gingrich-Philbrook, 1997)
- the life of gay German transvestite Charlotte von Mahlsdorf (Wright, 2004)
- the struggles of queer street youth (Bowles, 1997)

Homelessness

- homeless youth in New Orleans (Finley & Finley, 1998; Saldaña, Finley, & Finley, 2004)
- homeless youth and adults in Tempe, Arizona (Armijo & Lindemann, 2002)

Intrapersonal Reflections and Interpersonal Relationships

- a visual artist's cultural research and reflections on death (Montano, 2003)
- conversations between intimate couples (Crow, 1988)
- social dynamics and peer cruelty among teenagers (Norris, 2000)
- a theatre scholar's fieldwork in Tanzania and her relationship with a "native" lover (Ajwang' & Edmondson, 2003)

- a father's strained relationship with his adult son (Pelias, 2002)
- an African American scholar's reconciliation with his father's status as a garbage man (Alexander, 2000)
- mother-daughter communication (Miller, 1998)
- a woman's reflections on the death of her mother and its personal consequences (Spry, 2003)
- a woman's reflections on her daughter's birth and mother's death (Pineau, 2000)
- a gay man awaiting the death of his partner from AIDS (Dillard, 2000)
- the disintegration of a marriage (Foster, 2002)
- a couple experiencing the abortion of their child (Ellis & Bochner, 1992)

Anthropology

- fieldwork from Nigeria with the Yoruba (Jones, 1996, 2002)
- community life and relationships in Allen County, Ohio (Rohd, 2002)
- cotton mill workers' lives in the Carolina Piedmont region (Pollock, 1990)
- American identity (Community-Based Arts Collaborative Course, 2004)
- an adaptation of a cultural ethnographer's investigations (Welker & Goodall, 1997)
- a young man's emergent paranoid schizophrenia and his relationship with an educational anthropologist (Saldaña & Wolcott, 2001; Saldaña, 2002; Wolcott, 2002)
- anthropologist Colin Turnbull and director Peter Brook's collaboration with *The Ik* (Grinker, 2000; Higgins, Cannan, & Turnbull, 1984)

Justice Studies

- incarcerated African American males (Keck, 1996)
- incarcerated 12–18-year-old male offenders (D. Conrad, personal communication, October 13, 2003)
- a prison psychiatrist treating a troubled, special needs adolescent (Rollheiser, 2004)
- former gang members (Roberts, 2002)
- sexual assault recovery (Mienczakowski & Morgan, 2001)
- perspectives on Matthew Shepherd's murder (Kaufman & Members of the Tectonic Theater Project, 2001)
- stories of exonerated men and women (Blank & Jensen, 2004)

9/11

- educators reflecting on the aftermath of 9/11 (Lincoln, 2004)
- a New York City journalist and fire captain writing eulogies for deceased firefighters (Nelson, 2002)

Most of the ethnodramas I've read have been written by researchers, sometimes in collaboration with their participants. Several of these plays have been created by educators, anthropologists, or sociologists,[5] but with virtually no theatre or playwriting background, some of their work often exhibits didactic dialogue and a lack of staging potential. Also, several of these works have been written as textual representations for reading purposes only ("closet dramas," as they are called in dramatic literature) and have never been performed in front of a live audience.

The art of writing for the stage is similar to yet different from creating a dramatic narrative for qualitative reports, because ethnotheatre employs the media and conventions of theatrical production. A researcher's criteria for excellent ethnography in article or book formats don't always harmonize with an artist's criteria for excellent theatre. This may be difficult for some to accept but, to me, theatre's primary goal is neither to educate nor to enlighten. *Theatre's primary goal is to entertain—to entertain ideas as it entertains its spectators.* With ethnographic performance, then, comes the responsibility to create an entertainingly informative experience for an audience, one that is aesthetically sound, intellectually rich, and emotionally evocative. Ethnotheatre reveals a living culture through its character-participants, and if successful, the audience learns about their world and what it's like to live in it.

My own ethnotheatrical production work was influenced by my initial education and subsequent practice as a playwright, director, actor, designer, and instructor of theatre. This type of artistic training generates research perspectives different from colleagues first educated in social sciences who later in their academic careers explore drama as a genre of research representation. Examples from several ethnodramas will be used below to illustrate selected playwriting concepts and staging techniques—fundamental "technical skills" critical to the arts (Eisner, 2001, p. 144). These principles are addressed to those with minimal theatre production experience but with a basic knowledge of qualitative inquiry. There are no established or standardized criteria for what constitutes "good" ethnodrama. The success of a work is jointly constructed and determined by the participants, the artistic collaborators, and their audiences.

Plotting—The Conceptual Framework of Ethnodrama

Most writers label the progression of events in a story its plot. But in dramatic literature, *plot* is the overall structure of the play; *story line* refers to the progression of events within the plot. Dramatic structures include the number of acts, scenes, and vignettes (*units* to most theatre practitioners); whether the time line of events is chronological or randomly episodic; and whether monologue, dialogue, and/or lyric are the most appropriate narrative forms for its characters. The story line is the sequential arrangement of units within the plot.

These terms are differentiated because plotting and story lining in ethnodrama and conventional plays are initially separate but eventually interwoven processes. For example, in *Transforming Qualitative Data*, Harry F. Wolcott (1994) separated the three articles of "The Brad Trilogy" under the chapters "Description," "Analysis," and "Interpretation." This organizational arrangement stimulated the plot construction of its ethnodramatic adaptation, *Finding My Place: The Brad Trilogy* (Saldaña & Wolcott, 2001; Wolcott, 2002), into three separate scenes, also subtitled "Description," "Analysis" and "Interpretation." The addition of a prologue and epilogue provided a contextual framing and reflection, respectively, about the story. Since another plot choice was chronological linearity, the story line of the play follows a traditional beginning-middle-end design to portray events as they occurred between Harry, the anthropologist, and Brad, a young man with emergent paranoid schizophrenia, during the 1980s.

Jean Luc Godard is attributed with a plotting maxim: "A story should have a beginning, a middle, and an end—but not necessarily in that order." My first ethnodrama, *"Maybe someday, if I'm famous . . .",* which portrays the artistic development of an adolescent actor over two and a half years, did not follow strict chronological linearity. The initial analysis of this study's data reduced the 150-page corpus to one-third its length for core content examination (Seidman, 1991); linked multiple participant data for triangulation (Miles & Huberman, 1994); and used in vivo codes (codes derived from the actual language used by the participant) for category development (Strauss, 1987). This process generated eight distinct categories of participant meanings to form eight separate scenes. The plot was a linear collage loosely sequenced by chronology and progressive reflexivity. The play begins with the actor's past and ends with his projected future. But in-between is a series of scenes that advance from his public performances to his more personal, private thoughts (Saldaña, 1998b). I recommend in vivo coding for the data analytic process leading to ethnodrama.

Since monologue and dialogue (discussed later) are two fundamental components of playwriting, in vivo codes may highlight particular passages from transcripts and field notes worth including in the script.

There's a folk saying among theatre practitioners: "A play is life—with all the boring parts taken out." Comparable advice for those interested in scripting their research is: "An ethnodrama is the data corpus—with all the boring parts taken out." The basic content for ethnodrama is the reduction of field notes, interview transcripts, journal entries, etc., to salient, foreground issues—the "juicy stuff" for "dramatic impact" (Saldaña, 1998a, pp. 184–185). The results are a participant's and/or researcher's combination of meaningful life vignettes, significant insights, and epiphanies. This process generates the material from which the structure and content—its plot and story line—are constructed. Though this advice may sound highly prescriptive, most professional playwrights attest to the necessity of a solid framework, regardless of how the idea for a drama was first inspired.

Participants as Characters in Ethnodrama

Characters in an ethnodrama are generally the research participants portrayed by actors, but the actual researcher and participants themselves may be cast members. The total cast size consists of the minimum number of participants necessary to serve the story line's progression and includes those whose stories are potentially engaging for an audience. Characters serve multiple purposes in plays, but each individual should be rendered with dimensionality, regardless of length of time onstage. Most directors and actors approach the analysis of a character by examining (a) what the character says, overtly or covertly, about her life or objectives; (b) what the character does to achieve those objectives; (c) what other characters say about her and how they support or prevent the character from achieving her objectives; (d) what the playwright offers about characters in stage directions or supplementary text; and (e) what dramatic criticism and personal life experience offer about the characters. These conventions can be adapted for data analysis and function as guidelines to promote a three-dimensional portrayal of a participant in ethnodrama: (a) from interviews: what the participant reveals about his perceptions or constructed meanings; (b) from field notes, journal entries, or other written artifacts: what the researcher observes, infers, and interprets from the participant in action; (c) from observations or interviews with other participants connected to the primary case study: perspectives about the primary participant or phenomena; and (d) from research literature: what other scholars offer about the phenomena under investigation.

The majority of traditional plays are told from the protagonist's point of view, which serves as a model for retelling an individual participant's story as a case study. For example, some autoethnographies, such as Tillman-Healy's (1996) personal struggle with bulimia, suggest a one-person narrative plot. Even though friends, parents, and teachers are present in her story, I can envision one woman on stage portraying Tillman-Healy and all other roles, similar to Lily Tomlin alternating between over twenty characters in Jane Wagner's (1986) *The Search for Signs of Intelligent Life in the Universe*, or the solo performances of Anna Deavere Smith's (2000) interviews with various political figures, writers, and American citizens.[6] Some plays feature two characters in traditional protagonist and antagonist roles, or two characters, both flawed, who attempt to resolve their interpersonal conflicts. The interactions between the ethnographer and case study are suggested here, such as Brad and Harry F. Wolcott's relationship in his "Trilogy," or Elissa Foster's (2002) interactions with her husband in *Storm Tracking: Scenes of Marital Disintegration*.

Several newer dramas feature multiple characters in multiple vignettes presenting a series of monologues and/or small group scenes that portray significant moments from their lives—*ensemble plays* or a "polyphonic narrative" (Mienczakowski & Morgan, 2001, p. 220) with a spectrum of voices and no leading roles. Pifer's (1999) ethnodrama on race relations features a Ku Klux Klansman in full regalia describing the significance of a burning cross, though the actual character-participant was never encountered during fieldwork itself. The inclusion and brief monologue of the Klansman provide stunning counterpoint to the White participants' attitudes toward Blacks. Rollheiser (2004) interviewed five learning disabled adolescents during fieldwork, yet combined their stories and perceptions about education into a three-dimensional composite characterization—a troubled teenager named Daniel. Though some may take issue with this technique (a standard data analytic process, actually), a credibility check is in place: Mienczakowski and Morgan (2001) recommend that "*no* fictional characters, dialogue or scenarios are permitted [in the ethnodrama] unless they can be validated by informants and researchers as reasonable, likely, typical and representative of the range of behaviours and outcomes experienced in the setting" (p. 221).

Small or large group studies with contradictory perspectives from multiple participants suggest an ensemble play, of sorts. Conflicting agendas from students, parents, teachers, and administrators in education studies can be highlighted through juxtaposition (see Boran, 1999; Meyer, 1998). Finley and Finley's (1998) community of homeless youth in New Orleans is another ensemble. Both the formal research article (Finley & Finley, 1999) and its artistic representation through poetry (Finley, 2000) are rich material to adapt and portray onstage (Saldaña, Finley & Finley, 2004).

A problematic choice is the researcher's inclusion as a character-participant in an ethnodrama. Does the principal investigator have a role to play, one just as essential as the primary participants? In a fieldwork context, yes; but depending on the purpose of the research, is she a *major or minor character*? To apply some of the most common types of characters in dramatic literature, is the ethnographer (a) a leading character with extensive monologues composed of field notes and journal entries like some Brechtian narrator; (b) the leading character's best friend, a secondary but nevertheless important role because the lead confides her innermost secrets to you; (c) a chorus member (as in Greek tragedy), offering supplemental reflections and insights on human life, sug-

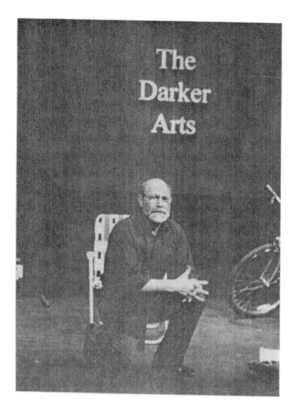

David Vining as Harry F. Wolcott addresses the audience in the prologue to Saldaña and Wolcott's *Finding My Place: The Brad Trilogy*

gested by the major characters' dilemmas; (d) an offstage voice, physically absent yet ever-present like some omniscient being; (e) a servant whose primary function is to announce the arrival of guests, deliver exposition, and sometimes function as comic relief; (f) an extra who stands with the background crowd, not commenting but merely reacting peripherally to issues detailed by the leads; or (g) an unnecessary character cut from the play all together? To adapt a popular folk saying from the culture of theatre, "There are no small parts, only small ethnographers." Sometimes the researcher's best positionality is offstage.

Most researchers have been taught to never let the data speak for itself, but I question that directive's applicability to ethnodrama. Many participants *can* speak on their own behalf without interpretive intervention from a fieldworker. Just as an ethnographer asks, "What is this research about?" ethnodramatists must ask, "Whose story is it?" Reflexivity is a common component in qualitative narratives, but in ethnotheatre, the researcher's onstage presence and commentary could detract from rather than add to the principal participants' stories. In *"Maybe someday, if I'm famous . . ."* my presence in scenes between the adolescent actor and his classroom theatre teachers was unnecessary. But my field note monologues of his rehearsal and performance processes were critical pieces of evidentiary data for the audience. Wolcott's intimate relationship with Brad requires that the researcher become a leading character-participant in the ethnodrama. But my contribution as the adapter of the script did not, to me, require my presence onstage. Doug Wright's personal dilemmas as a playwright are included in his drama *I Am My Own Wife* (whose sole actor portrays up to thirty-five characters). The story of how he got the story of Charlotte von Mahlsdorf is an intriguing journey worth sharing with an audience.

Monologue and Dialogue—Dramatizing the Data

Monologue

An autoethnographic prose narrative, with its central protagonist's perspective, lends itself to scripted adaptation as a one-person ethnodrama if the original story suggests playable stage action for a performer (Saldaña, 2003, p. 222). Solo performances in professional theatre, colloquially known as "one-woman" or "one-man shows," range in purpose from overtly political documentaries (Kalb, 2001) to confessional performance artworks (Bonney, 2000) to autobiographical and self-congratulatory entertainments (Horwitz, 2002). A solo performance—one actor with an extended monologue—is the theatrical cousin of the individual case study in ethnography. Solo performance also benefits the artist through opportunities to realize aesthetic visions, to voice sociopolitical commentary, and to exorcise personal demons through performative catharsis (Horwitz, 2002, p. 33). Spry (2003) notes that autobiographical performance "offers a thick description of an individual's engagement with cultural codes. . . . In the fieldwork, writing and performing of autoethnography, text and body are redefined, their boundaries blurring dialectically" (p. 170).

Monologues are extended passages of text spoken by one character and (a) addressed to another character listening on stage; (b) addressed directly to the audience; or (c) used to reveal inner thoughts spoken aloud—a soliloquy— for the audience (see Prendergast, 2001). A playwright of ethnodrama is not just a storyteller; she's a story-*reteller*. You don't compose what your participants tell you in interviews, but you can creatively and strategically edit the transcripts, assuming you wish to maintain rather than "restory" their narratives. Interviews with one participant generate transcript data suitable for transformation into one-person reflections. Company members of the ethnotheatre project *To Be American: A Work in Progress* (Community-Based Arts Collaborative Course, 2004) interviewed local citizens from varying backgrounds to gather their perceptions and thus data for the dramatic text. The questions consisted of such prompts as, "How do you see your upbringing, religion, race, gender, family status, organizational memberships, etc., as contributing to your American identity?" "Who/what taught you about being American?" "At what times in your life have you felt most aware of your American-ness? Why? [possible follow-up: Have you ever been accused of being un-American? What does that mean?]"

Anna Deavere Smith (2000) encourages the search for participants' rhythms, passions, and "the very moment that language fails them. In the very moment that they have to be more creative than they would have imagined in order to communicate. It's the very moment that they have to dig deeper than the surface to find words" (p. 53). And since a play is life—with all the boring parts taken out—and one of the playwright's functions is to use an economy of words to tell a story, the verbatim transcript is reduced to the "juicy stuff" for "dramatic impact." Lengthy sentences or extraneous passages within an extended narrative, whose absence will not affect the quality of the data or their intent, could be edited. Below is the original text from a portion of an interview with Barry, a high school actor. He recalls his past theatre viewing and research participant experiences in elementary school and speculates on their influence:

BARRY: And I remember going to see the shows. I remember the interviews afterwards, sitting out on the grass, talking about what we thought about the shows, and what we thought about the longitudinal study. I remember always having interns sitting in the back of the class, watching us do drama.

JOHNNY: What shows do you remember?

BARRY: I remember a lot of the Childsplay stuff. *[Childsplay is a local professional touring theatre company for young audiences]*

JOHNNY: Any particular titles or images come to mind?

BARRY: I remember *Clarissa's Closet*, which was interesting because I performed that last year. And I was thinking, "You know I've seen this, I've seen this, it was Childsplay came did it." And I also remember one about, I recall an Oriental setting, there were masks, uh, I don't know much about it, like journeying something.

JOHNNY: Any other images?

BARRY: I remember them coming out and taking their bows and then talking to us after the show, and the energy they had, and just the raw energy and everything. They were answering questions and they seemed to be having so much fun just being there, and I think that's when I first decided I wanted to be an actor. So I saw that and it was an amazing feeling, there was just energy, you could see it, it was emanating from them, and just from having done this show. And it was just a show for a bunch of elementary kids, and yet it was still, it was a show, you know? And it was, that was when it first, I first started thinking, "Hm, this is something I want to look into."

Following is the reduction of the data to what I considered essential and salient exposition for a brief monologue in *"Maybe someday, if I'm famous . . .":*

BARRY: And I remember going to see the shows, a lot of Childsplay stuff. I remember them coming out and taking their bows and then talking to us after the show. And the energy they had! They were answering questions and they seemed to be having so much fun just being there. And I think that's when I first decided I wanted to be an actor. It was an amazing feeling! That was when I first started thinking, "Hm, this is something I want to look into." (Saldaña, 1998b, p. 92)

A monologue showcases a character through a snapshot portrait of his life taken from a particular angle. Solo narratives reveal both personal and social insight with carefully selected detail and, if successfully written and successfully performed, generate emotional connection with audiences. The most engaging monologues reveal a discovery or retell an epiphany in a character-participant's life. In this excerpt from *Finding My Place: The Brad Trilogy*, Brad reflects on the alienation from his family and his sense of isolation. Like the example above, this monologue was assembled from various interview excerpts found in Wolcott's "Trilogy." The in vivo slide titles highlight key phrases from Brad's narrative for the audience. Stage directions note how the two actors interpreted the action in performance:

> *(BRAD turns on his radio; music:* Drive *{The Cars}, followed by* Millworker *{Bette Midler}). . . . (SLIDE: "a big difference")*
>
> BRAD: I saw a guy a few weeks ago who's the same age as me. He lived in a house behind us when I was in fifth grade. He still lives with his parents in the same place. I think about what he's been doing the last nine years and what I've been doing the last nine years and it's a big difference. He went to high school. Now he works in a gas station, has a motorcycle, and works on his truck. I guess that's all right for him, so long as he's mellow with his parents.
> *(SLIDE: "I've never really held a job.")*
> *(crosses to HARRY, sits on the lawn chair)*
> I've worked for my dad for a while—helped him wire houses and do light construction. I scraped paint for one company. I worked for a graveyard for about eight months, for a plumber awhile, planted trees for a while. Dishwashing. I've never really held a job. I wouldn't want to have to put up with a lot of people on a job that didn't make me much money. Like at a checkout counter—I don't want to be in front of that many people. I don't like a job where everyone sees you do it.
> *(SLIDE: "a loner")*
> I guess that I'm sorta a loner, maybe a hermit. I've had close friends, but I don't have any now. *(fighting back tears)*
> HARRY: *(to BRAD)* Shall I turn the tape recorder off for a while?
> BRAD: *(shakes his head "no"; tries to put up a brave front)* You've got what you've got. It doesn't make any difference what anybody else has. You can't wish you're somebody else, there's no point in it. Being by myself doesn't make all that much difference. No one knows who I am anyway.

Miranda Lilley as Genie and Jess Sari as Tigger dialogue at their homeless squat in *Street Rat*

(HARRY puts his hand comfortingly on BRAD's knee; BRAD remains still, looks as if he's about to reach for HARRY's hand, then pulls away, gets a wrench and starts working on his bike) (Saldaña, 2002, pp. 186–88)

Dialogue

Dialogue occurs when two or more characters exchange thoughts or confront an interpersonal conflict. Dialogue in the data can be found in a transcript's conversational interviews between the researcher and participant, a focus group interview, or participant observation field notes. But playwright Doug Wright (2004) cautions that an ethnodrama "is, after all, more than a series of interview exchanges: question, answer, question, answer, question, answer" (p. xix). Artistry enters when dialogue is artificially constructed from several sources of data gathered from different sites, different participants, and across different time periods (Finley & Finley, 1999). Participant voices from two or more data sources can be interwoven to: (a) offer triangulation; (b) highlight disconfirming evidence through juxtaposition; (c) exhibit collective story creation through multiple perspectives; and/or (d) condense "real time" data for purposes of dramatic economy.

In Scene 2 ("I Was Completely Empty") from *"Maybe someday, if I'm famous . . .",* three participants tell their own versions of the same event in Barry's life. In the excerpt below, Sandy is his mother; Derek is his high school theatre teacher. The three voices provide triangulation of data and contribute collectively to the storyline. When one participant quotes another, the two voices speak simultaneously. Note how the participants' brief monologues and dialogue vary in point of view. At times they speak directly to the audience, or to another character-participant, or to oneself:

> *(SLIDE: "2: I Was Completely Empty")*
> BARRY: *(to audience)* There was a period during junior high when I had
> no theatre in my life, didn't have any exposure to it, and
> *(SLIDE: "I got really heavy into drugs")*
> I got really heavy into drugs. I was hanging out with the wrong crowd.
> *(crosses to side of stage, puts school materials in his backpack)*
> SANDY: *(crossing forward, to audience)* He was never anti-social, but mak-
> ing the statement—the way he dressed, the way he looked.
> *(SLIDE: {picture of BARRY at junior high school age})*
> In fact, some of his junior high teachers would call me and say, "I
> noticed that he's hanging out with some unsavory characters and
> I think . . .", you know, that kind of stuff. It was kind of like teach-
> ing the dog not to run in the street by getting hit by a car. It was a
> horrible, painful, awful time. And yet,
> *(SLIDE: "If it doesn't kill you, it'll make you stronger")*
> if it doesn't kill you, it'll make you stronger. That's what's happened
> to Barry.
> *(crosses to side of stage)*
> *(SLIDE: DEREK)*
> DEREK: *(holding a cast list, crosses to audience)* When Barry came to
> University High School he was on the point of either being a doper
> or doing something. And I worked really hard with him to get him
> to stop smoking pot, to develop a sense of, *(to BARRY)* "Hey, you've
> got something to work with instead of working against."
> *(crosses to projection screen, posts the cast list on it)*
> BARRY: *(backpack slung on his shoulder, crosses to cast list, to audience)*
> When I came to University High I saw theatre was something that
> I knew, something that I was interested in. *(sees his name on the
> cast list)*
> *(SLIDE: "I got cast in my first show")*

So I came and I got cast in my first show. I got a lead for my first show which made me think, "Whoa—maybe there's something I'm good at here." *(to audience)* And I was in the position where there wasn't anything standing in-between me and theatre because there wasn't anything in my life. Drugs had taken up my whole life. And so as soon as I was ready to get out of that, I mean—
(SLIDE: "Theatre helped draw me out of drugs")
Theatre helped draw me out of drugs and, in a way, drugs helped draw me into theatre, in that they voided my life of everything else so I was completely empty—completely open towards picking up on theatre. . . .
SANDY: *(to audience)* I'll never forget the day Barry said to me,
BARRY AND SANDY: *(BARRY speaks to SANDY)* "You know, mom, you don't have to buy me all gray and black clothes anymore."
(SLIDE: "I started cleaning up my act")
BARRY: *(to audience)* I started cleaning up my act, and that had a lot to do with drama because I had something else, and it was almost intoxicating in and of itself. It gave me the strength to get away from that stuff. (Saldaña, 1998b, pp. 92–94)

Dialogue is the playwright's way of showing character interaction and interplay, terms found regularly in the qualitative research literature. Through dialogue we not only advance the action, we reveal character *reaction*, the symbolic interactionist's playing field. Actual conversational exchanges are virtually nonexistent in Wolcott's "Brad Trilogy." In the first article of the series, Brad's interview data are assembled into categories. Wolcott relies primarily on narration to share his own perspectives, but offers little dialogue spoken directly to Brad. As the adapter (Saldaña & Wolcott, 2001; Wolcott, 2002), I had to fictionalize possible conversations held between the two men and seek Wolcott's approval as a "participant check." Monologue narration to the audience was employed, when necessary, for exposition:

> *(music up:* Heart of Glass *by Blondie)*
> *(HARRY finds a bow saw on the ground, picks it up, looks at it curiously)*
> HARRY: Literally as well as figuratively, I discovered Brad in my own backyard, unannounced and uninvited.
> *(SLIDE: BRAD's cabin)*
> *(BRAD enters, carrying a sapling, stops when he and HARRY see each other; BRAD sets the sapling down, shuts radio music off; they look at each other warily)*

A 19 year-old had managed to construct a crude but sturdy 10 by 12 foot cabin at a remote corner of my densely wooded, 20-acre home-site, which my partner Norman has shared with me since 1968. He didn't know on whose property he had built his cabin, perhaps hoping he had chosen public land next to mine.

(hands BRAD the saw, which he grabs)

BRAD: *(defensively, to HARRY)* Can I stay?

(SLIDE: Early Encounters)

HARRY: *(beat, as HARRY looks BRAD over; to audience)* I attach great importance to first impressions. *(HARRY stares at BRAD; BRAD starts packing up his tools)* At the moment of our first and unexpected meeting, I felt hesitant about allowing him to remain on my land; yet I felt an even greater reluctance in insisting that he leave.

BRAD: *(to HARRY)* I needed some place to get out of the wind and keep dry. The rent ran out. I knew winter was coming and I'd have to do something.

HARRY: *(to audience)* He had no money, no job, and no place to go. I couldn't see how I could claim to be any kind of humanitarian and throw him off my property.

(SLIDE: Courtesy and Common Sense)

(HARRY picks up the sapling and examines it; to BRAD) I guess if you're going to be here, I need to know something about you: Where you're from? What kind of trouble you're in?

BRAD: *(takes sapling, saws into it)* I'm not in any trouble. I'm not that stupid. I used to live at this end of town; my father still lives here but I never see him. And I've lived in a lot of different places, like California, Portland, out in the country; different places in town, like The Mission—you had to sing for Jesus before they'd feed you there—a halfway house, *(slightly mumbling)* reform school.

HARRY: Reform school?

BRAD: *(defensively)* Yeah, but it wasn't really my fault. (Saldaña, 2002, pp. 173–75)

A playwright must also consider the effects of her text on other ethnotheatre collaborators. For the performer, central criteria are whether he or she "feels right" interpreting another's words, and finds a flow, logic, or justification for the monologues and dialogue. All ethnodramatists should hear their scripts read aloud before publishing or formally mounting the work to assess how the play *sounds*, and to solicit honest feedback from the readers on their experiences with speaking the text. Though not always possible to obtain when we stage real life, playwright José Rivera (2003) encourages us to "strive to create roles that actors you respect would kill to perform" (p. 23). For the audience, who must be engaged throughout the event, the central criterion is, "Do I care what these characters have to say?" Again, Rivera advises:

> Theatre is the explanation of life to the living. We try to tease apart the conflicting noises of living and make some kind of pattern and order. It's not so much an explanation of life as it is a recipe for understanding, a blueprint for navigation, a confidante with some answers—enough to guide you and encourage you, but not to dictate to you. (p. 23)

It is difficult to articulate and over-systematize the creative processes employed when constructing monologues and dialogue since playwriting is both a craft and an art. But always remember: the ultimate sin of theatre is to bore, and only a self-indulgent playwright refuses to edit lengthy text from initial and post-performance drafts.

Scenography—"Think Display"

Plays are not meant for reading only; scripts are written specifically for performance in front of an audience. Just as the late qualitative researchers Miles and Huberman coined, "Think display" for data analysis and presentation, a popular playwriting adage for ethnodramatists to consider is "Don't tell it, show it." If the consequent monologue and dialogue consists of people merely talking, then why bother using the visual medium of the stage? Why not convert it to radio drama or reader's theatre—both valid modes, but whose focus is on language (e.g., "teacher talk"), not action. And since ethnography analyzes participants in action, there are things to show on stage: descriptive replication with subtextual inferences of the way participants facially react, walk, gesture, pose, dress, vocally inflect, and interact with others. These nonverbal cues reveal much about characters and real people. Granted, reader's theatre is more portable and less expensive than a fully mounted theatrical production, particularly at conferences where the venues are breakout rooms of unpredictable size. But this mode presents primarily what we *heard* in the field, not what we *saw*.

Scenography refers to the total visual and aural conception for theatrical productions and includes the constituent elements of scenery, set and hand

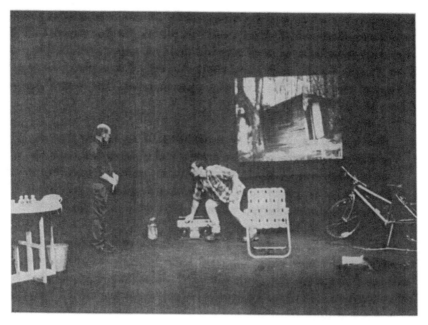

David Vining as Harry F. Wolcott and Charles Banaszewski as Brad on the unit set with a projection screen for *Finding My Place: The Brad Trilogy*

properties, costumes, makeup, lighting, sound, and technology. Scenography establishes time and place of a play, evokes mood, and serves the required action of the characters. This introduction cannot discuss in depth the potential of costumes (participant clothing), hand properties (artifacts), or scenery, lighting, and sound (the fieldwork environment) to enhance the ethnodramatic performance. But from my own experience I offer the classic design adage for guidance: "Less is more." A projected slide of Brad's cabin in Harry's woodlands is easier to create than rebuilding the actual cabin to scale and mounting it onstage.

Though the latter would be ideal for a production with an unlimited budget, the former is sufficient and much less expensive and time-consuming—especially for a tour. More accessible and inexpensive technology has led to the integration of projections and multimedia into recent ethnodramatic performance. But like all design choices, the use of technology should be carefully considered. Sometimes the actor alone is the only visual spectacle necessary to tell the story effectively.

I prioritize two scenographic elements in my ethnotheatrical work because they're the most accessible to produce and the most revealing about characters: hand properties and costumes. The artifacts participants handle in the field are rich visual material for transfer onto the stage: Barry's play scripts, his theatre teacher's clipboard, Brad's hand tools and broken bicycle, Harry's notepad and index cards. All of these items are central to these people's actual ways of working. The artifacts' presence and use by actors portraying the character-participants provide small-scale visual spectacle yet strong inferences for an audience. Likewise, most audience members have an intuitive "fashion literacy," and we infer personality from the way people dress onstage as well as in everyday life. Barry wore t-shirts and baggy pants to school almost every day, so these became the basic costume elements for the actor. The "look" suggested youth, informality, and unpretentiousness. Brad's "jungle boy" existence in the woods was reinforced through flannel shirts in natural colors, faded blue jeans, and hiking boots. The muscularity and sexuality of the participant was enhanced through tight-fitting clothing and strategic unbuttoning.

Collaboration (and Quality) in Ethnotheatre

Qualitative researchers and theatre artists serve each other through collaborative development and presentation of ethnodramas. Scholars in ethnography have much to contribute to those initially educated as artists, and artists well-versed in the creative process and products of theatre have much to offer ethnographers. Both disciplines, after all, share a common goal: to create a unique, insightful, and engaging text about the human condition. Theatre practitioners, through the nature of their training, possess several prerequisite skills for qualitative inquiry and thus ethnodrama and ethnotheatre, including: (a) the ability to analyze characters and dramatic texts, which transfers to analyzing interview transcripts and field notes for participant actions and relationships; (b) enhanced emotional sensibility, enabling empathic understanding of participants' perspectives; (c) scenographic literacy, which heightens the visual analysis of fieldwork settings, space, artifacts, participant dress, etc.; and (d) an aptitude for storytelling, in its broadest sense, which transfers to the development and writing of engaging narratives and their presentation in performance (Saldaña, 1999, p. 68).

The playwriting advice offered thus far has been for pre-scripted models of ethnodrama. But collaborative devising by a production company is another

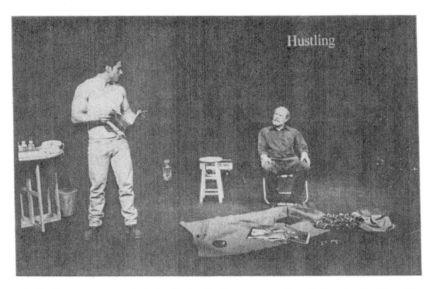

Hustling

Charles Banaszewski and David Vining in the turning point of *Finding My Place: The Brad Trilogy*

method of developing ethnographic performance work. Michael Rohd's Sojourn Theatre Company in Portland, Oregon, jointly explores and improvises during rehearsals how their interviews with community members can be represented through movement, poetic monologue, and reconstructed dialogue, similar to the Tectonic Theater Project's development of *The Laramie Project*. One researcher and two theatre artists (Chapman, Sykes, & Swedberg, 2003) came together with a set of interview transcripts to collectively select, shape, and arrange during rehearsals excerpts of the participant's stories on teaching and sexual identity. As a playwright, I transformed Vanover's (2002) narrative essay on his first years of teaching into a dramatic monologue as a first draft. Then, as a director, we revised the script jointly as I taught Vanover basic acting skills to enable this researcher—who came to the project without theatre experience—to perform his own story for peers in the most engaging manner I could bring him to during an intensive one-week rehearsal period (cf. Gray, 2003). In all cases, theatre artists, ranging from performers to dramaturgs (those who assist with script development and/or research for a production), were actively involved in the development of the ethnodramas. I claim, perhaps immodestly, that the aesthetic results were better as a result of collaborative effort than if the research had been adapted and presented by those without a theatre background.

Mary A. Preisinger, Celeste Schroeder, and Karen Scott-Hoy's interdisciplinary arts performance, *What Makes Me? Stories of Motivation, Morality and Me*, at the 2000 American Educational Research Association's arts-based research conference serves as one example of this principle. The three women explored Scott-Hoy's researcher struggles during her social work with the Aborigines through mounted paintings, monologue, and dance.[8] The event, scheduled as a breakout session in a space smaller than a standard school classroom, was one of the most aesthetically rich and emotionally evocative productions I've ever witnessed. When Mary and Celeste illustrated through dance the tensions between a participant and researcher during an interview, the meanings they suggested through elegant choreography were visually stunning. Karen's narrative on her emotional struggles with participants and herself was performed with riveting, confessional sincerity. This modest interdisciplinary arts production literally led me to tears. Truth and art, in all their magnitude, were captured that day for me without the bulky trappings of scenography or the contemporary dazzle of technology.

The critical factor that made the event so moving was the three women's background—they were not just researchers; they were artists. Their education in dance, visual art, music, and theatre gave them a performative edge over well-meaning researchers who attempt theatrical presentation, but who lack fundamental skills with play production including the actor's expressive tools: the body and voice. Just as no one wants to read mediocre research, no one wants to sit through mediocre theatre. (Professional courtesy stops me from "naming names" of the most atrocious ethnodramatic work I've read and seen at conferences.) Most playwrights don't enact their own scripts; they rely on collaborative efforts with directors, actors, and designers to realize their visions.[9] Each artist brings her own talents and gifts to the mix whose whole is greater than the sum of its parts. In other words, I'm advocating for artistic quality in arts-based qualitative work, and I recommend more collaborative efforts between theatre artists and researchers for ethnotheatrical production. There's no guarantee of success—not even when professional theatre personnel themselves collaborate. But odds are that qualitative researchers and theatre artists will find that they have much to gain if they are open to the spirit of cooperative development. Donald Blumenfeld-Jones, an arts-based educational researcher first trained as a professional dancer, proclaims that no one has the right to stop someone else from producing art. Yet he also advises that we have a responsibility, as audiences and cocreators of the performance event, to reflect on and critique the artistic quality of any venture in an honest and nurturing manner.

Closure

The "reality-based" mounting of human life onstage is a risky enterprise. Unlike the distancing one may experience when reading a journal article in private, the live performance (if well-produced) with live actors (if well-rehearsed) before a live audience (if well-engaged) intensifies the representation (Conquergood, 2003; Mienczakowski, Smith, & Morgan, 2002). The successful reenactment of nonfictional events exposes both the fieldwork experiences and the fieldworker himself to empathetic spectator involvement and value-laden public scrutiny, depending on the content (e.g., abortion, racism, suicide, sexual assault).[10] Both the researcher and audience gain understandings not possible through conventional qualitative data analysis, writing, and presentation from ethnotheatre's artistic rigor and representational power. At its best, a truthful text and believable acting in an ethnotheatrical performance create for its audiences a verisimilitude that can be labeled *ethnodramatic validity* or, in the broader context of arts-based research, *artistic integrity* (Meyer & Moran, 2004).

Debate continues, however, on the tension between an ethnodramatist's ethical obligation to re-create an authentic representation of reality (thus enhancing fidelity), and the license for artistic interpretation of that reality (thus enhancing the aesthetic possibilities; see Stucky, 1993). Scenes from *14* in Part I present a series of monologues with character-participants speaking in uhms, breaks in speech, and extended pauses. But the organizational flow of their stories has been recrafted and "tightened" for dramatic unity. *Wearing the Secret Out* in Part II includes verbatim participant interview excerpts—a condition required by the collaborators' university Human Subjects Review Board—while the stage directions suggest two performers creating highly symbolic and abstract movements throughout the piece. In one scene of *Baddies, Grubs & the Nitty-Gritty* in Part III, the police officers speak candidly and graphically about sexual assault, then segue into a satirical, cabaret-like revue with audience interaction. Several plays in this anthology illustrate departures from naturalism and experiment with mixed-methods genres and styles. They are not so much photographs of real life as they are impressionist portraits, multimedia collages, or three-dimensional mobiles. But do they "work"? Are they legitimate representations of a culture or fictive constructions—art for ethnography's sake? It depends on the playwright's goals and the participants' affirmation of their representation on the page and on the stage. Credibility and trustworthiness notwithstanding, the judgment of an ethnodrama's success as both art form and ethnography is ultimately for the reader or, in performance, each individual audience member to determine.

Many major subjects researched through ethnography have already been examined in a play or documentary for the stage, screen, or television. But there is still a need for more good scripts in both theatre and qualitative inquiry. I have been asked by several graduate students across the United States to review and comment on early drafts of their attempts at adapting their fieldwork into dramatic form. Though all of the plays have shown varying levels of promise as ethnodramatic scripts, I find myself offering each writer the same piece of advice: "Stop thinking like a social scientist and start thinking like an artist." This is not to suggest that artistry is less rigorous than scientific thought. Instead, it is intended as encouragement for writers to free themselves from the hegemony of traditional and stifling academic discourse, and to allow their creativity and dramatic intuition to imagine the aesthetic possibilities onstage. If all playwrights are ethnodramatists, then all ethnographers have the potential to become playwrights since the best lens for fieldwork views human action "dramatistically" (Goodall, 2000, p. 116; also see appendix). The contributors hope that this anthology of ethnodramas provides you with models and inspiration for future playwriting, and insight into their participants' unique lived experiences.

Part I—Ethnodramatic Monologue provides examples of the individual character-participant as solo storyteller. Part II—Ethnodramatic Dialogue with Monologue provides examples of how multiple character-participants interact onstage and, when necessary, speak in extended passages as monologue. Part III—Ethnodramatic Extensions provides examples of how playwrights and production artists can transcend realism to experiment with more presentational forms of ethnotheatre.

If you're not a theatre practitioner or if you're unaccustomed to reading contemporary dramatic literature, I advise you to pay comparable attention to the italicized stage directions as much as you would to the monologue and dialogue. Playwrights give careful thought to these traditionally italicized descriptive passages to (a) clarify character intention and action for the actor and audience; (b) specify particular and necessary theatrical effects such as lighting or sound; and (c) document how the play in production was originally staged. These stage directions are, in a sense, a dramatic text's field notes.

Finally, be advised that some of these ethnodramas contain—like reality itself—strong language and mature content.

Notes

1. This anthology includes plays that have not yet been published in book form. There are other outstanding ethnodramas that merit inclusion in this anthology, but those titles are already available in print for the reading public. Also, this discussion focuses on live theatrical production and does not examine ethnographic filmmaking.

2. Other terms found in the literature related to ethnotheatre include "scripted research," "research-based theatre," "research as performance," "ethnographic performance text," "ethnographic drama," "performance (auto)ethnography" (which can be radical, critical, and reflexive {Denzin, 2003, p. 33}), "generative autobiography," "performative inquiry," "public voice ethnography," "conversational dramatism," "theatre as representation," "reflexive anthropology," "narradrama," "docudrama," "metadrama," "documentary theatre," "interview theatre," "verbatim theatre," "presentational theatre," "living theatre" "ethno-mimesis," "natural performance," "everyday life performance," "conversational performance," "auto-performance," "informance," "mystory," "embodied methodological praxis," "dramatic commentary on interview data," and, as I have borrowed and labeled it for this anthology, "reality theatre." The Federal Theatre Project's "Living Newspaper" presentations from the 1930s are early forms of the mounting of real life onstage in the United States. A typology and analysis of the differences between these genres is a worthwhile exercise for a separate article, but in this book, for focus and clarity's sake, I will adhere to the terms "ethnotheatre" and "ethnodrama."

3. Theory is important and has its place, but critical, theoretical applications possess little utility during the stress-laden process of theatrical production, and may even suppress creative impulses for some. This introduction focuses primarily on practitioners', not theorists', contributions. See Gray, Ivonoffski, and Sinding (2002), Jackson (1993), Mienczakowski & Morgan (2001), Paget (1995), Rogers, Frellick, and Babinski (2002), and Stucky (2002) for excellent, pragmatic articles on writing ethnodramas. For the best theoretical discussions of performance ethnography, see Denzin (2003) and Pelias & Van Oosting (1987). For an outstanding discussion on and collection of feminist performance work, see Miller, Taylor, & Carver (2003).

4. The categories refer to the major content of the plays, since some titles could be placed under more than one category (e.g., under both Education and Vocation and Occupation). My criteria for ethnodrama were used to compose this list, though some of the playwrights cited may not label their works as such.

This is not a comprehensive list, but a series of titles I've read and performances I've attended at various conferences and events in North America. Also, some presentations, though labeled "performance" by their authors, did not conform to the definitions I outlined at the beginning of the introduction and are thus excluded from the list. Technically, the texts of some contemporary solo artists such as Kate Bornstein and Tim Miller can be considered autoethnographic since autobiography and the details of their gender, sexual, and cultural identities and interactions play pivotal roles in their writings and thus "autoethnotheatrical" presentations. But to include performance art pieces in the list starts muddying the waters and creates an unwieldy and lengthy typology. Also, I exclude one-person plays of historic figures from the list (e.g., Gertrude Stein, Mark Twain, Emily Dickinson) since different playwriting principles and biographical research criteria apply to these dramatic genres (see Miller, Taylor, & Carver, "Part I—Women's Historical Auto/biography," 2003).

5. McCall (2000) and Denzin (2003) profile earlier works and discuss contemporary ventures into performance art and guerrilla theatre (e.g., Gómez-Peña, 2000; Talen, 2003). In this introduction, I focus on the realistic, naturalistic, and presentational genres of drama for ethnotheatre since the examples in this anthology reflect these forms. One street artist I encountered called the capture of stark reality in art works "*for-realism*."

6. Playwright Cathy Plourde and Add Verb Productions of Portland, Maine, developed in 1998 a thirty-minute, one-woman touring show on eating disorders, *The Thin Line*, for schools and women's groups. Playwright/actor Ken Carnes tours a one-man show, *Last Words*, that re-creates actual testimony of condemned inmates through the story of one man facing his final appeal in court. The audience serves as a jury and renders a verdict.

7. See Glesne (1999, pp. 183–87) for a comparable method, "Poetic Transcription"; and Ollerenshaw and Creswell (2002) for "restorying." Extracting and composing ethnodrama from a data corpus, like qualitative data analysis, is a carefully considered yet highly creative cut-and-paste operation (Patton, 2002, p. 442).

8. Ventures into dance and visual art defy textual representation and necessitate technologically appropriate documentation such as CD-ROM, video, or website; see Bagley & Cancienne (2002) for an accompanying CD-ROM to their text on arts-based research.

9. Recent ventures into one-person, autobiographical performance are the exception.

10. The February 23, 2001, performance of *Finding My Place: The Brad Trilogy* at the Edmonton, Alberta, Advances in Qualitative Methods conference reinforced how powerfully theatre can provoke diverse and passionate reactions to a study's content and issues. It also reinforced how the playwright's vision and intentions, and selected audience members' responses, may be in total opposition (Ocklander &

Östlund, 2001; Schreiber, Rodney, Brown, & Varcoe, 2001; cf. Barone, 2002; Honeychurch, 1998, pp. 260–61; and Kulick, 2004). Wolcott tells us in the prologue to the ethnodrama, "No two individuals ever get exactly the same message"; and in scene two, "Some will hear only the story they want to hear." What some audience members interpreted as "unethical" behavior between an ethnographer and his case study, others perceived as "a love story" and "a caring relationship" between two consenting adults. When some audience members interpreted the researcher-participant dynamic as an "abuse of power," I sensed in them an inability (or, at worst, a homophobic unwillingness or unjustified transference of their own unresolved victimization from sexual abuse onto the character-participants) to understand the gay/bisexual character-participants' points of view. This feedback motivated post-production rewrites of the script to clarify and reinforce the playwright's perspectives for future productions.

Ethnodramatic
Monologue

This anthology of plays begins with three examples that showcase the individual character-participant as solo storyteller. The monologue is a basic form in dramatic literature that reflects the human need to tell an extended story from a personal perspective. The monologue in theatre training is also a self-contained exercise for beginning playwrights to compose and for beginning actors to perform.

One or more ethnographic interviews with a participant provide transcripts that serve as the foundation for reducing and transforming natural narrative into a more compact and aesthetic product. The goal is to capture both the essence and the essentials of a particular individual's worldview and culture. Scenes from Michael Keck's *Voices in the Rain* illustrate how a playwright can retell the stories of others based on interviews, participant observation, documents, and media reports. Scenes from José Casas's *14* also demonstrate the construction of monologues from interviews, and how multiple participants involved with the same issue each hold their own attitude, value, and

Michael Keck as Bug Eyes
in *Voices in the Rain*

belief systems that sometimes harmonize with and sometimes contradict each other. Charles Vanover and Johnny Saldaña's *Chalkboard Concerto: Growing Up as a Teacher in the Chicago Public Schools* illustrates how an autoethnographer (in collaboration with a theatre artist) can dramatize his or her own story for the stage. The play also demonstrates how the solo performer can portray not only himself but multiple character-participants, as needed, by assuming their personas.

Scenes from
Voices in the Rain

BY MICHAEL KECK

Editor's Introduction

Voices in the Rain was developed from stories collected through African American actor Michael Keck's drama workshops with prison inmates, interviews with inmates and their families, media reports, and letters. Though it may be perceived by some as stereotypical that the incarcerated participants in this selection are all African American males, consider that an August 2002 study by the Justice Policy Institute of Washington, DC, reported that more Black men were being held in prison than were enrolled in colleges and universities (Butterfield, 2002). The injustice of it all increases when the naïve and uninformed hastily deduce that the reason for a fivefold increase of African American men in prison over the past twenty years is because "they are committing more of the crime." To those with more socially conscious attunement, what has increased over the past twenty years has been an inequitable distribution of power and resources among the classes and races, a deteriorating education system that has failed many children of color, dysfunctional parenting across the generations, a mismatch between the cost of living and the minimum wage, an ineffective federal government with skewed priorities, and a biased criminal and justice system that unfairly targets the nonwhite.

Voices in the Rain, however, does not address these issues directly through overt political discourse. Instead, the play stays grounded in the poignant stories and evocative music of the individual men themselves—those incarcerated for decades and acquiescing to prison life, and those recently released and attempting to find their place in the community. Playwright Gus Edwards (1997), author of *Monologues on Black Life*, attests that a one-character dramatic text is a portrait in miniature that talks, moves, reaches, and cries out to us. He also acknowledges that the spectrum of experiences for Black Americans is "both universal and specific. Universal because we are all involved in the great human parade. Specific because of our history, cultural background, speech patterns, and attitudes" (p. ix). Though the majority of us will most likely never experience what it would be like to be imprisoned, the men of *Voices in the Rain* provide the specific details from *their* experiences to evoke the universal human emotions of frustration, fear, anger, dignity, and hope.

Keck is a New York–based actor, writer, and composer, and tours the nation with this one-man show in both a full-length and one-act version. The performance is a collage of poetry, monologue, and original music that not only dramatizes the culture of incarceration but also showcases Keck's extraordinary talents as an artist. He literally creates unique and distinctively different voices for each character-participant in *Voices in the Rain*, ranging from adolescents to an elder, from prisoners to a preacher, and from the emotionally enraged to the spiritually defeated. Keck's finely attuned ear for his participants' stories will only partially come across in the text below. One needs to *hear* Keck perform to appreciate the full impact of this work.

The full-length version of *Voices in the Rain* is over two hours in performance, but for this anthology only selected scenes from the ethnodrama are presented for readers. The excerpts feature the intermittent monologues of one particular character-participant—Bug Eyes—who gives the audience throughout the play a grand tour of prison culture and how he survives in it. Keck describes his fieldwork as "bearing witness" to the participants' stories. As audience members at his performances, we also bear witness to his masterful storytelling.

Scenes from *Voices in the Rain*

Character

BUG EYES: watch cap or doo rag, work shirt

bidness man

*(slide image: concertina wire. slide text: SURVIVAL. sound: cell door slam &
noisy cell block)*

I'm a bidness man . . . ain't frontin' you off. Though lyin' is an occupational necessity for a criminal. I'm a bidness man. I call upon a man of bidness during hours of bidness only to transact my bidness. Then I go about my bidness so he can tend to his bidness. I'm a bidness man. I'm down 15 for drug trafficking and involuntary manslaughter. They Test-a-LIED on me, 'cause I was innocent of starting the fire that killed that lady 'cause she stole my cocaine – never mind all that. I accept the punishment and I still be livin' lovely.

Me and my mellow-co-bidness man brotha "PEPE LUV" . . . we in complete control here. Ain't nothin' hap'n without our say so and approval. We got it goin' on . . . get you anything you need. Magazines, batteries, blankets, cigs . . . *zoo zoo's, wham wham's* . . . anything, as long as you willing to pay the "vig" . . . THE VIG! If I give you a cigarette you owe me a pack, if I give you a pack you owe me a carton, if I look out for you – you gonna be MY property. If the payment is late, the price goes up. We know you'll keep your word.

One inmate with plenty of drug money paid a officer 5 Gs to bring in live lobster. I brokered that deal. Got my client some prime 12 lb. BOSTON knuckle busters. You got the money, you can have anything, know what I'm sayin'?

danger zone

You think you can make it in here? You better have some heart if you want to survive. Which in here means, you may have to go crack somebody over the head with a rock in a sock or slash somebody's face from his ear down to his mouth, give him a souvenir he'll have for the rest of his life . . . and never give it a second thought. THE BIG HOUSE rules are simple, do worse unto others as they have done unto you, trust nobody, ride your own heat, and follow the code.

This *is* the danger zone . . . know what I'm sayin'? I seen a guy get 150 stitches over a pair of sneakers. Another *die* over a game of dominoes. Some of these guys take a razor, and stuff it right in their ass. Hey I ain't frontin' you off! You don't have closets at home that can hold as much as these guys can hold. We call it slammin', or packin'. The razor is wrapped in tissue paper, rubbed with Vaseline and then slammed. If the officers see an inmate with Vaseline on his lips or behind his ears, they know he's getting ready to slam something. It's against civil right to go in somebody's ass to get it out. Who'd want to do that anyway?

You gotta do something 'cause if a couple of fools jump on you the Cor-rect-ional Off-i-cers won't protect you. The C.O.s have to look out for themselves and their family. The bad asses intimidate the officers by droppin' a piece of paper with the officer's *home* address on it when he walks by their cell.

There ain't a C.O. anywhere lookin' forward to a riot. Some of these guys down for LIFE, "doing all day," and ain't got nothin' to look forward to, so conflict becomes everyday bidness. 'Specially over by the phone. The single greatest source of conflict is the telephone . . . next to old fashion racial hatred and that's mostly between Hispanics and Blacks. White guys are so outnumbered, they really not a problem. They're last for everything. The barbershop, commissary, recreation, whatever, the white guys are *last*. The occasional white guy who don't know how to keep a low profile, stake out a spot, gonna get stabbed.

getting high

(cell door slam, cell block)

They build walls 20 feet high, put people in cages, surrounded by concertina wire, 2, 3, and sometimes 4 layers deep and still can't stop people from gettin' high. It's everyday bidness! Easy as gum in a candy store. Lotta people, when confronted with a traumatic change in life *"medicate"* themselves to keep up, to keep going. People come up with some genius ways to bring drugs in because the demand is so great. Some of our bone-head-uniformed-baby-sitters value an En-tre-PREY-neurial relationship with us. Like they say, money ain't everything as long as you have enough.

Someone might come to prison clean . . . drug free. But because drugs are so easy to get, and sentences getting so long, they'll catch a serious jones in *here* if they start messin' around.

I know you never heard about the guy on death row who got hold of a set of works and almost overdosed the night before his execution. They had to revive him before they could strap him down to kill him. You didn't see that in the newspapers . . . bad public relations for the *war* on drugs . . . which is mostly a war on people, 'cause if America was hell bent to win the war on drugs, wouldn't prisons be the most drug-free places of all?

first time down

(cell door slam, cell block)

Goin' to prison was like walkin' around the corner. Most of the people I know here, I knew growin' up, kickin' it, talking all kinds of shit . . . *Yeah man . . . We do a 6 month "bit". . . we the man . . . we got some juice . . . we be cool and shit.* Like going to prison was a badge of honor. But the first time I heard that big gate slam, I was scared mad. Nobody ever told me how it really was. First day I stepped out in the yard it was like:

(as one inmate)

Zzzssst! Yo . . . Cope! What's up Cope! I know who dropped the dime on you Cope!

(as another inmate)

Yo! Cope Mutherfukah it's payback time that's what time it be!

(as himself)

Yeah! Going to prison was like walking around the corner.

temporary insanity

(cell door slam, cell block)

Tem-po-ra-ry insanity? That's a bullshit defense. I been tem-po-ra-ri-ly insane. I put some toilet paper up to a bare lightbulb in my cell and held it there 'til it caught and then I set the mattress on fire. I told 'em *Go 'head write the ticket. I don't give a fuck 'bout no infraction. I told you I have a court date tomorrow. Why can't I get a haircut and shower? Hey . . . Yo! Yo, can I get some attention here? Hey bitch, what do you use for birth control? Your personality? YO! If you ever become a mother, can I have one of the puppies?* I told 'em. Got my haircut. Temporary insanity . . . That's bullshit for a murder defense. People do kill people, that's an animal instinct. That makes sense. But breaking into somebody's house and ironing all their clothes, now that's temporary insanity.

badge of honor

Didn't you pass the iron pile on your way in? Did you see all the self-made men? Living proof of the horrors of unskilled labor! The Superintendent is foldin' under pressure from the conservatives who wanna ditch the iron, but that's a bad idea. Pumping iron keeps the frustration down. The same die-hard prisoncrats even wanna dump the education programs. I see them on TV talkin' about . . . *"Life is too good for them. They supposed to be locked up for punishment! They gettin' three hots and a cot, they gettin' free cable TV, they gettin' free newspapers in various languages, free health care and psychological counseling and blah . . . blah . . . blah . . ."*

None of *them* ever drop by to take a real look, unless they get *caught* with they fingers in the cookie jar and become one of us. If prisons are such resorts, why don't they just throw open the gates and see how many run out . . . and how many run in. They don't want us to exercise our bodies or our minds. But never mind all that. We do our own *ed-u-ma-catin'*. See . . . I wasn't a crimin- . . . uh, bidness man the first time I got popped for small-time drug possession. But since then I'm improvin' my skills and expanding my knowledge every day. Like I told you, I accept my punishment.

Not everybody in prison is a loser. But one look around the yard is all it takes to figure out why you need a place like this. However, if you lock a bunch of problems . . . you gonna have a bunch of problems in one place and the neighborhood still not gonna be a Shangri-la. The neighborhood's ready for change, but the upper class hasn't felt the pain . . . yet.

I wish you could take a few snapshots of me out in the yard. Or better still in front of my estate. A picture to go along with my story. Look here now — *make sure you remember my name*. Copeland . . . Naaaa naaaa, Bug Eyes. That's my name now. I like it better. Remember. I'm surviving this. That's my badge of honor. I'm a bidness man. I'm just an average guy with predatory instincts without sufficient funds to form a corporation.

(cell door slam)

Scenes from *14*

BY JOSÉ CASAS

Editor's Introduction

In the southwestern United States, borderlands issues with Mexico are contentious. Social and political debate often verge into nationalist, xenophobic, and racist ideology and policy on the part of non-Hispanic Americans. Investigative journalist and anthropologist Ted Conover's (1987) *Coyotes* gave the field an insider's view of the life of Mexican migrant workers and their harsh journeys on both sides of the border, while Mary Gallagher's (1991) play, *¿De Dónde?*, dramatized the multiple, conflicting, and complex perspectives of constituencies involved with immigration. The conditions for crossing covertly into America from Mexico in search of a better life are dangerous and sometimes deadly. Frequent regional news items report on Mexicans suffocating in railway boxcars, getting shot by rural Arizona landowners as they trespass, and dying of dehydration as they attempt to cross the desert. "14" is the symbolic number of a recent case in which that many migrants died in one tragic attempt, and it became the provocative title for this ethnodrama by a Latino artist.

14 is the result of grant awarded to playwright José Casas by the Arizona State University Department of Chicano and Chicana Studies. Casas interviewed a number of people in Arizona—Latino/a and non-Latino/a—with both tangential and significant connections in one way or another to border crossings, using the fourteen deaths as a starting point for inquiry. These interviews, along with newspaper stories and media reports, were then adapted and recrafted with a playwright's artistry into a series of monologues and scenes in English and Spanish. The production was mounted in September 2003 by Phoenix's bilingual theatre company, Teatro Bravo. Christina Marín, director, stated that "each character in this play brings to the table their own cultural constructs which inform and define their words and actions. The beauty of *14* is that they are all sitting at *the same table*. This, I believe, is the first step in starting the dialogue" to transcend the physical and psychological borders existing in our lives.

Casas, one of the nation's most exciting new Latino voices in theatre, brings to his work superior craftsmanship, insight, and passion. He also brings a strong sense of cultural identity and the ability to portray that identity with astute perception onstage. Since the participants for Casas's fieldwork resided in Arizona, the production of *14* resonated with many Arizonans in the audience. We chuckled knowingly at the character-participants from the cities of Sedona and Scottsdale who seemed to embody and represent the general lifestyles of those particular townships. Latinos in the audience also voiced affirmative responses out loud to their *hermanos y hermanas* onstage when their monologues cut to the "truth" of borderlands issues from their perspectives. *14* is a consummate example of a commissioned work for a particular locality and its issues, yet one that still maintains relevance for the entire United States since its Hispanic population is the fastest-growing ethnic group in the country. The play is also a fine example of how complex sociopolitical matters can be addressed dramatically without intellectual dogma or an "ivory tower" mentality. *14* portrays ordinary people making sometimes extraordinary insights about the human condition. They speak honestly about what's in their minds and hearts—all we have to do as an audience is *listen*. Ironically, Casas unknowingly developed an ethnodrama; he had never heard of the genre when he wrote *14*. He simply created the best play he could about a subject for which he cared deeply. And perhaps that is why the work is so outstanding as a form of arts-based research.

14 is a full-length play script over two hours in length during performance, but for this anthology only selected scenes from the ethnodrama are presented for readers. Casas also abandons capitalization in his printed texts and the format is followed in the excerpts below. The original cast featured Barbara Acker, Christina Marín, Christopher Miller, and Adrian Villalpando. Production team members were Eunice Bravo, Robbie Daniels, Erin Looney, Fernando Pezzino, Mauricio Duarte-Medina, Brian Morphew, and Guillermo Reyes.

Scenes from *14*

production notes

a slide/video projection should be shown at the beginning of each monologue (interview) giving the name of the piece, the name of the character, their occupation and their hometowns (as is shown in the script). . . . also, slides can be used to suggest setting if setting requirements for specific pieces are too cumbersome.

throughout the play, there is extensive use of the *(extended beat)*. these are meant to give the characters unspoken dialogue. they can range from an extended pause to a character action depending on the context in which they are inserted. actors are encouraged to experiment with these extended beats . . . to explore their "true" meanings. . . .

translations of the pieces "virgencita linda" and "muñequita" are included with the script as a courtesy, but those pieces *must* be performed in spanish.

prologue

(in the darkness a spotlight shines on the back wall/video screen . . . the slide reads:
may 19, 2001
a smuggling guide abandons more
than 30 mexicans crossing
east of yuma.
dehydration kills 14.
their deaths trigger renewed
binational debate over immigration.
the dead are:
{the next series of projections are individual slides
showing the names of each victim:}
lorenzo hernandez ortiz,
raymundo barreda landa,
reyndo bartolo,
mario castillo fernandez,
enrique landero,
raymundo barreda maruri,
julian mabros malaga
claudio marin alejandro,

arnulfo flores badilla,
edgar adrian martinez colorado,
efrain gonzalez manzano,
heriberto tapia baldillo.
{final slide of prologue:}
two others have yet
to be identified.

{extended beat}
as the projection on the screen slowly fades into darkness, guns-n-roses' "wel-
come to the jungle" begins blaring)

"virgencita linda"
luz ortiz – maid – guadalupe, az

(the interview is taking place in the backyard of luz ortiz, a mejicana who is
sixty years of age; she sits near a makeshift altar that her family has created;
the virgen de guadalupe being prominently displayed; the time is early evening;
she has just returned from the hotel where she works as a maid)

forgive me for being late. mija needed to put gas in the car. i usually walk
to work. it's just down the street, the holiday inn hotel. el express . . . right down
the street, across from that big market. *(luz responds to her daughter's comment;*
amused) oh, forgive me. i meant to say "el mall." my daughter loves to spend
hours walking around that thing. me? i don't have much money so i don't
bother. i don't see the point in it. *(beat)* but, it's only fifteen minutes to walk
to work. short walk. at night, my viejo or one of my kids will come and walk
home with me. i tell them it's not necessary, but they worry for me . . . i wanted,
i didn't want to be late tonight. when mija told me about the gas . . . aagh. i just
want to thank you for being patient and to apologize about my appearance.
i didn't get a chance to change out of my work clothes. you sure it's alright?

(beat) i'm so excited to have you in my home. my daughter goes on and
on about you. she says you're a very good writer. *(responding)* thank you so
much. yes, i am proud of her. she was my youngest and i had her so much later
than my other child. i was almost forty when i had her. she says she wants to
be a teacher. i ask her if she would rather be a doctor or a lawyer like her
brother. something that pays better, but she just wants to help kids. she's always
thinking of others before herself.

(beat) tell me something about yourself. were you born here in arizona?
los angeles? hmm . . . i've been there once. i thought it was nice. i very much
liked the beach, but i wouldn't want to live there. no offense. i just think it's so
big and there are so many people there. i'm happy where i'm at.

(beat; amused) don't worry about your spanish. no eres pocho . . . i understand you just fine. it's nothing to be embarrassed about. i know how difficult it is to juggle two languages. i'm always running around in circles with my oldest son. i'll talk to him in spanish, but he usually answers me in english. i constantly have to remind him, "en español, mijo" but he jokes it off like it doesn't matter. i know it does, but he's getting better at it. he's a good boy, though . . .

and, your parents? were they born here? ah, zacatecas . . . and, your mother? monterrey. i knew it. there was something familiar about you. i couldn't pin it down, but now i can. i grew up in monterrey. most of my familia still lives there throughout the area: colonia metalurgica, colonia nueva aurora, colonia torreon jardin. do you know which one your family lives in? colonia vencedora? ay, yes . . . two of my uncles live in the exact place. next time you talk to your mother ask her if they know anyone from the gallegos familia . . . ask her if that name sounds familiar. juan carlos and edwardo gallegos . . . ask her.

(beat) i try to visit mejico every few years, but it gets more difficult as i get older. do you still have familia there? how long has it been since you've seen them? aye, mijo, that's much too long. you need to go and see them. they are your blood. *(responding)* yes, things cost money. it's an expensive world, but if you get the chance, start saving your pennies because your familia won't be around forever. none of us will. plus, you shouldn't forget that mejico is as much your home as it is your parents'. please don't ever forget that . . .

i know that i miss mejico so much, sometimes, but i love guadalupe. it's the closest thing to mejico that you can find around here. it's not as nice as the other places, but it's home. the white people, they don't much care about what happens here. at least, that's what i think. i don't have to tell you. i know you know that. you can see it yourself. look at baseline street. look at the other side and look at the guadalupe side. it's like crossing from san diego into tijuana. el mall y todo. all nice and new. lots of places to spend. down the street there is this beautiful park that is so green. but, they don't care if guadalupe isn't green. they don't care if the schools are bad.

(beat; annoyed) around the corner they just made a place for the little ones to play baseball. it's pretty. i am happy for the kids. it's green like the big park, but one little piece of land still isn't enough . . . guadalupe is still nothing but dirt and rocks. next to the church where the older men play sports, that's all it is. dirt and rocks. sometimes broken pieces of glass and trash. there are many open areas like that. it's almost like they are laughing in our faces . . . as if to say to us, you want to play somewhere nice, then cross the street to do so. we don't care . . . you eventually have to cross back anyway.

(beat; apologetic) forgive me. i am angry, yes, but i don't want to come off hateful. i am a good catholic. i believe in god and jesus and la virgen linda, but i am not blind . . . but, with that said, i am thankful. thankful that i have my small little house and food on the table. a television to watch my novellas on. my viejo treats me good and my children are good people . . . guadalupe has been good to us. to most people here. i mean, there isn't a lot of money, but we go on because we must. even with all the bad around us, we still find the time to share our stories and cafecitos. in guadalupe familia means familia. believe me, what little we have is a world's more than what most people in mejico have. we appreciate the little things like soap and toilet paper. those are the things i bring to mejico to give to my familia . . . the little things other people don't think twice about.

(beat) it's because la virgencita protects us. she looks over us. we are lucky to have her in our lives. that is why almost every house in this neighborhood has la virgencita standing guard over them. we must always remember that she was the one who watched over us as we crossed the border. she protected us. she held us when nobody else would.

(beat) i was only sixteen when i crossed . . . alone with people i didn't know. *(responding)* no . . . my mother didn't want me to go, but in mejico you can't tell anyone not to cross, you can only tell them that you will say a prayer for them. that is all. *(closing her eyes)* that first night with the coyotes howling and the heat unbearable i can still remember how tightly i was holding onto my tiny little statue of la virgencita; nearly crushing her. it was the longest night of my life.

(beat; emotional) a few days later when i snuck across, a coyote was herding us into the back of this big truck like cattle and i slipped as i got on . . . i dropped my little virgen onto the ground by accident, but i didn't see her until i was all the way inside. i sat down with the others when i noticed. i yelled for the coyote to please pick it up. please give her to me i said . . . but he just yelled for me to shut up and with those words he slammed the door in our faces . . . five hours later i found myself in the back of a garage in tucson. two days later i found myself in a watermelon field west of phoenix . . . when i found a few minutes, for myself, to get a drink of water i would think of mi virgen linda . . . being stepped on . . . forgotten in the desert . . . like so many of the pobrecitos who prayed to her during their journeys.

(extended beat)

i still pray to her because she has never left me . . . even when i look out across the street at el mall and the new cars and nice houses . . . even now.

(beat) she is with me.

"a man's home"
charlie clarkson – rancher – douglas, az

(this interview is taking place in the early morning hours, outdoors on the ranch of a mr. charlie clarkson, a white man in his early seventies; he is the leader of "voices for a free arizona," a group of ranchers united together to combat immigration on the border; he holds a remote control and in the distance {offstage}, on the desert floor, is a drone, a large model airplane; atop of it lies a tiny camera)

this is the next wave of technology. (responding to a question) the fancy name for them is drones, but it's plain to see that they're model airplanes . . . but, these are amazing little things. they got these little cameras on top of them. complicated, though. they work off these sensors that have been placed in strategic areas and— (beat; annoyed) i know this isn't a toy!

(extended beat)

we need all the help we can get. times are changing. america is under siege. the world isn't a safe place anymore . . . or haven't you liberals been watching the news lately?

(extended beat)

i started voices for a free arizona about five years ago. a couple of friends and i got to the point where we were sick and tired of seeing our land destroyed. empty water jugs. food and candy wrappers. dirty clothes. human waste. you name it. there was trash as far as the eye could see. i spent half my time picking up after them . . . one day i said, "enough is enough!" this is my land and i'm going to see that it stays that way. (beat) we're just a bunch of old ranchers sticking together to maintain our way of life. i don't see what all the commotion is about. this is my home, i paid for it. (beat) let me ask you something. if someone was breaking into your house, what would you do? exactly . . . no one would give you any gruff over it. you got to understand something. the need to protect ourselves is even greater now. (beat) my wife and i aren't getting any younger.

(extended beat)

if we don't protect ourselves, no one else will.

(a noise in the brush can be heard; charlie and the interviewer notice an animal running across the way from them; beat; charlie takes a bag of chewing tobacco out of his pocket and places some in his mouth; he offers some to the reporter, but is rebuked; charlie shrugs it off; he places the bag back into his pocket; beat; looks out again; he begins chewing his tobacco which he spits out throughout the rest of the interview)

just a jackrabbit . . . you hunt? shoot, next time you come for a talk give me more of a warning. i'll take you hunting. there's some good hunting in these parts. *(beat)* it's a shame what happened to those people. but, those are the chances you take, you know? you have to be brave to challenge mother nature. *(beat)* the desert sun can do some vicious things to a man. destroys both his body and his mind. poor saps didn't know what hit them. that's for sure. ain't much i can do about it. i don't make the laws. if someone wants to test fate, let them. who am i to say otherwise? as long as they take it someplace else . . . you enter my land, you're trespassing. you trespass, you get shot. no ifs, ands or buts . . . i won't like it, but i'll shoot you down without thinking twice about it . . . nothing personal.

   (charlie reacts to a comment; beat)

   (annoyed) of course. i know why they come! i know they got families like me . . . that they want to make a living. feed their children, but who's to say that one of the people crossing isn't one of those drug dealer or terrorist fellas. how am i supposed to know, huh? i can't assume they aren't. one of them shot at an agent a couple of weeks ago. logic tells me i got to protect what's mine. *(beat)* people crossing the border got to know these things. it's only common sense. you walk into a man's home you don't— *(beat)* you don't litter. you don't treat another man's home like it's your own personal toilet. you respect a man's home as if it were your own!

   (extended beat)

   (defensive) my friends and i are not vigilantes!

   (extended beat)

   (charlie turns on the remote control and turns on the drone; the sounds of it flying can be heard; charlie looks up at the sky)

   listen, i won't shoot at anything during the day. if i catch them on my property i call border patrol and they come and pick them up. shoot, other ranchers aren't as generous as me. but, like i was saying . . . during the day, i'm cool as a cucumber . . . at night . . . that's a totally different story. *(fidgets with the remote control again; beat)*

   watching those things soar through the air brings me a sense of calmness.

   (extended beat)

   i'd probably do the same thing. a man has to be strong for his family . . . needs to be able to provide for them . . . if a man can't do that then he ain't a man. *(beat)* can't say that i blame them. *(defiantly)* just not on my property.

"our song"

monica flores – kindergarten teacher – chandler, az

   (the heatwaves' "always and forever" is playing; monica flores is a chicana in her mid-twenties; located upstage is an altar; it contains candles and pictures

of monica's deceased husband, pedro; she is lighting a candle; monica crosses back to her chair; beat; the song plays for a while and as it slowly starts to fade away, monica begins to talk)

he dedicated that song to me during our senior prom . . . always and forever by the heatwaves. *(beat)* I knew right then, that he would be the man i would marry.

(extended beat)

he was the nicest guy you would ever want to meet. he was smart . . . funny . . . polite. *(beat; fondly)* and, he had this smile that, i don't know, there was something about his smile that was just so perfect.

(extended beat)

(monica responds to a question)

he wanted to make sure he did something positive with his life. you see, for him, it was more than just about getting a job. to him, anyone could do that. that's not what he wanted. *(beat)* he had gone to community college for a couple of years to sort things out in his mind, you know, try to find himself. but, all along, i knew he'd do something i didn't want him to do . . . i figured he'd be a fireman or a policeman; something of that nature. i think he just went to school to make me feel better. to show me that he was making an effort to explore his options . . . but it wasn't in his nature to sit behind a desk shuffling papers and crunching numbers.

(extended beat)

from the first moment they met, pedro and my father had had a great relationship. since my two sisters and i were the only children my parents had, my father took to him as if pedro was his own son. *(beat)* overnight, things changed.

(extended beat)

my father couldn't even look pedro in the eyes. it was as if my father had had his heart ripped out . . . to make matters worse, it felt like the rest of my family was following his lead and i was caught in the middle. *(beat)* i didn't agree with pedro's decision and he knew i wouldn't, but it didn't stop him from going through with it and that caused problems between us because i knew there was no way i was going to be able to change his mind.

(extended beat)

(near tears) and . . . and, uhm . . . the thing is . . . a few years ago during the i.n.s. raids in chandler . . . uhm, my father had been one of those taken into custody. when they stopped him he had been on his morning run and didn't have his i.d. on him. *(beat)* i remember that day like it was yesterday . . . for pedro to stand there in front of my father and tell him he had applied for work for the department of immigrat-

(extended beat)

(quietly) i had to stand behind pedro . . . he was my husband.

(extended beat)

i remember when he began his training and how it would affect him. i can't tell you how many times we would have conversations where he was on the verge of quitting. i could hear it in his voice and everytime it killed me but, at the same time, it gave me hope that he would go onto something else. *(beat)* i remember this one night, he told me about this thing called tonking . . . he was instructed that tonking was the sound one of those heavy metal flashlights makes when it's smacking someone's head, but it wasn't necessarily seen as a bad thing . . . only part of the job. this was the type of thing my husband was learning!

(extended beat)

growing up, my father used to say that the only good border patrol agent was a dead one. *(beat)* so, i asked him if he still felt that way knowing that pedro was working for them . . . without the slightest hesitation, he said, "yes." that was my husband he was talking about! the future father of my children . . . of his future grandchildren.

(extended beat)

i haven't spoken to my father since.

(extended beat)

i'd yell at pedro. "why is this job so damn important to you? don't you see what you're doing to this family! don't you care about your people!?" he'd yell back, "don't you ever tell me what i'm thinking! i've told you the stories of my father crossing the border. the shit he had to go through to get here. what? you think this is just one big fucking game i'm playing!?" *(beat)* and, he stopped for a moment . . . because he had realized he had been yelling at me, then, he pulled me towards him. he kissed me on my cheek and held me for what seemed forever. like he didn't want to let it go . . . and . . . he, uh, whispers to me, "would you rather have some racist white dude dealing with our people. *(beat)* or . . . me . . . someone who's going to make sure they're treated like human beings."

(extended beat)

you hear stories all the time about latino border patrol agents who are worse than the white officers . . . they're so afraid of appearing weak that they go to the extremes to build a reputation . . . in the process, not only do they lose their souls, but they lose their dignity. *(beat)* pedro wasn't like that. he treated every single person he stopped with respect. didn't matter what color they were . . . because of that, he was respected by most, resented by others.

(extended beat)

it almost never failed. pedro would catch someone and a few days later he would catch them again. the funny thing is, believe it or not, some of them didn't mind being caught . . . as long as it was pedro, that is. they would even greet him with a friendly "hello." it wasn't like they didn't know the routine. they get caught. processed . . . and, given a happy meal from mcdonalds . . . then, tomorrow would roll around.

(extended beat)

after a few years, i came to understand that pedro wasn't there to hunt down people crossing the border. he was there making sure they would have another chance to try again. *(beat)* i once remember him joking around one day . . . he said, "if they get past me, the more power to them." i didn't think much of it at the time, but now that i look back at those words, i realize that he meant them. he knew people living in this neighborhood who were here illegally. didn't matter. he'd strike up a conversation with them. maybe, share a story or two. but, he didn't turn them in . . . you see, the borderline was his workplace . . . anyplace other than that . . . wasn't.

(extended beat)

he was having some drinks with some of his softball buddies at this bar. nothing unusual about that . . . he was just relaxing. after his friends had left, he had struck up a conversation with some other guys at the bar and, from what i was told, they seemed to be nice guys. apparently, during their conversation, pedro had mentioned to them that he was an agent for the border patrol. *(beat)* they found his body a few feet away from the border. he was murdered execution-style. authorities told us that they think those guys might've been drug dealers or coyotes and, that, uhm, when they found out that my husband was an agent. *(beat)* they didn't take anything from him. he had all his money and his keys.

(extended beat)

(near tears) they found his badge laying on top of his chest . . . for everyone to see.

(extended beat)

(angrily) i don't care what any goddamn person has to say . . . even my father!

(extended beat)

my husband was a good man.

"muñequita"
oscar garcia – day laborer – mesa, az

(it is the middle of the day; the interview is taking place on a busy mesa inter-section where day laborers gather around, searching for employment; oscar gar-cia, thirty, is a mejicano; he is slight of build and the effects of the arizona heat has his skin looking darker than it usually would be; his clothes are worn and he carries a weathered tool belt {with a few basic tools}; his mini-icebox/lunch pail lays next to him; in the background an out-of-focus but definitely recog-nizable "home depot" sign can be seen and the sounds of men talking in span-ish can also be heard)

that's right. i knew enrique. he was a good guy . . . very friendly. you see, he was my primo's friend so whenever i'd visit my primo he was usually there talking shit, making jokes, sharing his beers. like i said, he was a stand-up guy. *(extended beat)*

no. i didn't know . . . no. even when i saw the news on t.v. same story dif-ferent day, that's the way it is. we all know that. there's always a chance we won't make it. the shit is fucked-up, but there is no other way. mejico is a poor coun-try, like its people . . . i quit school when i was like, uhm, seven. my familia needed me to help. everybody's story is the same, you know? *(beat)* a few pesos isn't enough, not even close.

(looking down at the floor) we may be poor, but we're not stupid. we know that death is following us . . . ni modo. i can still feel bad for them. *(looking back at the interviewer)* the thing is to see, uhm . . . all at the same time. i had never seen that before. so many people dead at one time. in one place . . . yes, i was especially sad that day . . . and, the fact that they were from sinaloa. damn, man!

sinaloa is my land. those were my brothers, my compadres. *(beat)* i didn't know about enrique until a few weeks later. sure, i knew he was going to make the crossing. we all had talked about it. i knew that, but he said he would wait awhile. his wife was pregnant and he wanted to see his child be born. he didn't want his wife to be alone. he was that kind of guy. when i finally got my primo's letter, he told me that enrique was one of the fourteen—*(beat; sadly)* i guess he couldn't wait long enough. *(beat)* his wife had her baby last week. a son . . . she named him enrique. *(beat, changing the subject)* fucking hot! you know? want a soda or something. i have an extra one if you'd like. *(oscar bends down and grabs a soda for himself; to the interviewer)* you sure? alright, then, but don't be afraid to ask. what's mine is yours.

(oscar stands back up; he opens the soda can and practically drinks the whole can in one motion; a little bit of the soda runs down his chin; he wipes it off)

me? a few months . . . ever since august. *(responding to a question)* august is the best month because it's the most difficult month, my friend. the weather is better in the winter. more migra patrol then. they know more of us will try when the weather is cooler. not me, though. i wanted to make it as hard for them to catch me as it was for me to get here. i know that sounds crazy, but that's just me . . . isn't that right, fellas!?

(the sound of men agreeing can be heard; oscar begins talking in a louder voice to communicate his thoughts to the whole group as well as the interviewer)

shit. la migra hates the heat as much as we do . . . only difference is that for us it's a matter of life and death. for them, it's a pinche inconvenience. they get a sunburn. it's those damn mojados. they get pricked on a cactus. it's those damn mojados. *(chuckling)* they can't find a woman to marry them. it's those damn mojados.

(laughter erupts from the group of day laborers; as the laughter dies down, oscar becomes a bit pensive; beat; to interviewer)

hear that? the laughter. that's the only thing we own out here. when you struggle so much to try and survive you're already dead . . . in a way, that is, but a good laugh . . . well, a good laugh . . . well, you know.

(oscar finishes his soda; he stands the can on the floor and crushes it; he then places the smashed soda can in his lunch box)

(extended beat)

i miss my daughter's laugh. my little baby girl. estrella. she was a christmas baby. she's blessed . . . would you like to see a picture of her?

(the interviewer agrees to see the picture; oscar pulls out the picture and shows it to the interviewer; pointing)

this was her when she was born. i remember it like it was yesterday . . . she's so much like her mother. look at her. isn't she the most beautiful baby you've ever seen? yeah, i know. every father talks like that but, in this case, it's true.

(oscar puts the picture back in his wallet into his pocket)

she just started school last week. six years old. *(smiling)* already, she's smarter than her father. i want her to go to school. i don't want her to—

(a truck horn can be heard; the sound of men responding can be heard; oscar, instantly, forgets that he is being interviewed and begins jumping up and down, hand waving in the air, trying to get the truck driver's attention; after a few moments, oscar stops his actions; he watches as the truck drives away; beat)

(embarrassed) sorry. i didn't mean to be rude. *(beat)* sure you don't want anything to drink?

(extended beat)

(to the interviewer) i've saved a little bit . . . a few dollars. this christmas i'll be able to send a little something to my familia. i have enough to get a simple mattress for my wife and child to share. money for food and other things. there might even be a little cash left over for a small radio. our old one is no good anymore. *(beat)* they like to listen to the songs on the radio together.

(extended beat)

next year, though . . . even if it kills me . . . i am going to get estrella a real christmas present. a real birthday present. *(beat)* she carries around this ugly little doll. cheap plastic. practically naked and missing an arm. my little girl deserves better. i'm going to get her one of those american barbie dolls. but, not just that. i'm getting her the whole setup. the girl barbie. the boy barbie. the big dollhouse. the car. the whole thing. i already did the math. fifteen dollars for each barbie doll. the boy and the girl. twenty for the car and the house is eighty dollars. can you believe that!? so much money for a doll's house? *(tabulating in his head)* another, i guess, i mean, i think, it should be another, i don't know, fifty maybe . . . to mail it. that's almost two hundred dollars. *(to himself; worried)* two hundred. *(beat; to the interviewer)* i don't like the doll she has now. it's dirty. it's broken. girl dolls are supposed to be pretty.

(extended beat)

(oscar looks around for a few moments, hoping to see a prospective employer; beat; proudly)

i work hard. these are my tools. tools that i use to build and fix things. i don't steal or nothing like that. i am an honest man. it's not fair what people say about me and my friends. they treat us like we're animals. that's not true. they do not know how we feel. how much we miss our familias. i love mejico. soy mejicano . . . but, there are no jobs in mejico. i am only doing what i need to do. i'm not hurting anybody. you make sure to tell people that. we are not criminals.

(extended beat)

(solemnly) criminals don't buy american barbie dolls.

"agua/water"
reverend clay nash – pastor – tucson, az

(in the darkness, america's "a horse with no name" is playing; after a few moments, the lights go up; the interview is being held outside in the desert outside of tucson; reverend clay nash, a white man in his early fifties, has a texas drawl and a cross hangs from his neck; he is putting up a water station; the water station consists of a large plastic barrel painted light blue which is placed atop a makeshift stand; a water valve is located at the end of the barrel and above it are stickers spelling out the word "agua"; next to the water barrel/sta-

tion is a tall pole that stands anywhere from ten to twenty feet; atop the pole sits a blue flag—an indicator to immigrants that a water station is present; it is the middle of the afternoon and the temperature is easily over 110 degrees; reverend nash wipes his brow with a handkerchief; the song slowly fades away as reverend nash begins to talk)

oohee . . . i'd say is about one-fifteen maybe, but the day is still young.

(extended beat)

the day those fourteen people died, the temperature was well over a fucking 117 degrees.

(clay places his handkerchief back in his pocket)

this area is classified as a "high risk zone" by authorities . . . no surprise there. right at this second, there's some agent wandering around "the devil's road" looking for some poor souls. *(beat)* now these poor folks are being forced to travel to god knows where . . . only to die . . . not to be apprehended. the powers that be know that all too well. *(looking at the water spigot)* you don't mind if i check this right quickly, do you?

(clay checks a water spigot)

(angrily) damn coyote left them out there to die.

(extended beat)

there were over thirty people in that group. did you know that? the youngest survivor was sixteen. *(beat)* think about that for a second. a sixteen-year old.

(extended beat)

think about this even more . . . two weeks earlier, agents found the body of a ten-year old girl . . . a ten-year old . . . still just a baby.

(extended beat)

(clay kicks a rock out of the way)

when the survivors reached the hospital they were burned black and were covered in cactus spines from the cacti they were trying to eat for food . . . one doctor at the hospital described the survivors as looking like mummies . . . you spend enough time under these conditions and your kidneys are liable to explode . . . and, i definitely mean that in the literal sense.

(clay walks around, looking for immigrants)

(to himself) pretty quiet on the war front.

(extended beat)

these people really have no idea what it's like. no one can really. you hope for the best and you hope god is carrying you. but unless god is carrying jugs of water you're shit out of luck . . . there's no habitation, no ranches, no roads, no water. *(beat)* they start off their journey, if they're lucky, with one, maybe two gallons of water. they think it's going to be all they need, but it gets real clear real soon that the shit isn't going to last.

(extended beat)

most people don't think about water . . . even when there's a drought going on, they don't think about it. how many times have you left the sink on when the phone rings? and . . . what about when you shower? ten . . . fifteen minutes. do you realize how much water that is? that's more water than some families in this world have in a week . . . probably, even longer in most cases. water is life.

without it . . . you ain't nothing but a heap of fucking ashes . . . that's why i decided to put up these water stations. too many brown faces dying . . . if they're lucky, they'll be sent home in a wooden box. for the ones that are never found, well . . . a man should die amongst the living . . . not the dead.

(extended beat)

i can go on and on about the policies and, trust me, there isn't one politician in arizona who doesn't know me.

(extended beat)

it's not like i have much of a choice. hear what i'm saying? i don't do this for publicity . . . i'd prefer y'all just leave me the hell alone.

(extended beat)

(responding to a question) hmm . . . let me see. the first two that we built were in the organ pipe cactus national monument. the others were placed on some private land south of tucson and just north of rio rico, but that was just the first of many to come . . . there are going to be plenty more. believe you me. *(beat)* there's no way of knowing exactly how many people are being saved, but it's helping. that i know for sure . . . providing this water is nothing more than an act of faith and conviction.

(extended beat)

what irritates me are those people who criticize what we're doing . . . saying that we are not only contributing, but encouraging illegal immigration . . . and, i use the word, illegal, loosely. that word should be reserved for those who are truly breaking the law . . . rapists . . . murderers. *(beat)* that isn't the case here. the only thing these people are about is survival.

(extended beat)

it boggles my mind to see how desensitized civilization has become . . . the sight of fourteen deceased bodies on a dried up riverbed and the only thoughts that pass through their hollow minds is "we got to do something about illegal immigration. it's getting out of hand."

(extended beat)

(angrily) regardless of which argument you side with, when you see a person dead in front of your eyes your thoughts should be on him or her. honoring that person while, at the same time, being grateful that you get the chance to see another day!

(extended beat)

i doubt that people are risking their lives for a sip of hot water in the middle of the desert! nothing you or i—

(extended beat)

(composing himself) we can't forget that these people are our brothers and sisters . . . children of god . . . they're human beings, people with dignity, dreams and desires who have enriched this country with their work and talent. for every penny they've taken out of this country, i believe they've put two pennies back in . . . and, there are some realities, that as a people, we are going to have to face. we can no longer look at ourselves as two nations divided by a river or some fence. we have to look at ourselves as a region that's going to live together, that's going to work together, that's going to make some damn progress together.

(extended beat)

(clay sees a person in the distance and waves him down)

(yelling) aqui, señor . . . agua . . . aqui!!!

(clay looks off into the opposite direction)

john . . . over there! see him. bring him on over to the station!

(extended beat)

(clay stands silent for a moment, then begins to quietly say a prayer, ends it with a sign of the cross)

(extended beat)

(clay looks back toward the interviewer)

(solemnly) looks like today's your lucky day . . . care for a cup of water?

(lights go to dark as a spotlight hits a screen that is either located upstage center or on a back wall; the final slide appears; it is a quote that reads:

> *"a man's dying*
> *is more*
> *the survivor's affair*
> *than his own."*
> *—thomas mann*

{extended beat}

lights fade to black)

Chalkboard Concerto: Growing Up as a Teacher in the Chicago Public Schools

BY CHARLES VANOVER
AND JOHNNY SALDAÑA

Editor's Introduction

Chalkboard Concerto: Growing Up as a Teacher in the Chicago Public Schools, as an ethnodrama, originated from educational researcher Charles Vanover's (2002) autoethnographic report, *Attunement,* which he presented at an American Educational Research Association (AERA) conference session. Charles read his article while seated behind a table, as many will do at professional presentations. Saldaña, in attendance that day, was captivated by Charles' personal story of the difficulties of an unprepared and novice teacher in an inner-city elementary school. It was a tale told directly, truthfully, and vividly about the details and emotional struggles of daily classroom life. As *Attunement* was read, Johnny visualized the story being performed on a platform with an old teacher's desk, a chalkboard, an attendance book, and other props and set pieces reminiscent of an elementary school. He imagined the audience seated in traditional rows of classroom chairs with folding desktops.

After the reading, Johnny initiated discussions with Charles to negotiate the transformation of the article into a staged performance piece for a broader and larger audience. Charles agreed to the venture, but only under the condition that he, not a university actor, portray himself. Collaboration between educational researchers and theatre artists was advocated by Saldaña (2003, pp. 228–30) to potentially enhance the quality of ethnotheatrical productions and to demonstrate and promote the rigor of arts-based educational research. Thus, *Chalkboard Concerto* previewed as a workshop production (with Caitlein Ryan-Whitehead as assistant director) at Arizona State University in February 2003 for an audience composed primarily of theatre practitioners, and was next performed at the Chicago AERA conference for the Arts-Based Educational Research Special Interest Group in April 2003. Due to its success, Charles has subsequently performed this piece at other professional conferences as a form of "touring research."

Charles wrote in the original program, "This performance is a work of memory. The world our play describes—Chicago in the early 1990s—is no longer the world where the city's teachers work. Chicago has changed for the better and this performance is dedicated to all those whose labor has helped create a more humane city. The road that connects Erickssen Elementary School (pseudonym) to the Eisenhower Expressway is no longer covered with potholes. Businesses have opened on the neighborhood's streets and new low-rise public housing units have been built near the school. Erickssen's playground is now covered with asphalt and the community's children play on an elaborate set of recreational equipment. The school building has been renovated and its classrooms have a fresh coat of paint."

"The events in *Chalkboard Concerto* take place during a very difficult moment for that community and for those teachers. Times are still hard for all who live in Chicago's poorest neighborhoods and for all who teach the city's most deserving students, but they are not as difficult as they once were. This performance and all subsequent performances are dedicated to the many people whose work has helped make our world a better place. Let their struggles continue to bear fruit."

As you read *Chalkboard Concerto*, take note of how the performer shifts between stories of classroom life and memories of the concerts he attended. We believe that the music indicated in the stage directions plays a critical role in communicating the emotional and spiritual meaning of the piece. The style changes from classical to jazz to help transform Charles' journey from one man's personal story into a communal experience that, as subsequent performances have shown, can be shared by many members of the audience.

Chalkboard Concerto:
Growing Up as a Teacher
in the Chicago Public Schools

DEDICATED TO THE MEMORY OF THE ANGELS

Character

MR. CHARLES VANOVER: a librarian, White, mid-20s, clean-cut; casual slacks, slightly beaten up walking shoes, oxford dress shirt with tie, and a slightly worn but once expensive thrift-shop jacket.

Setting

Chicago, the early 1990s; a traditional teacher's desk center stage with a chair and a freestanding chalkboard behind it.

Production Notes

Hand props and costume pieces are pre-set on or behind the desk, in desk drawers, and in CHARLES' pockets. Tape-recorded music should be played on a good sound system. A wireless microphone is recommended for the actor.

(as the audience gathers, Bach Violin Sonatas play as pre-show music; house lights fade to black, leaving a dimly lit stage area; Verdi's Requiem & Kyrie *play softly under as CHARLES enters from stage left; he crosses to the chalkboard, picks up a piece of chalk and writes "Mr. Vanover" on the board; stage lights up as he uses the chair to rise and stand on top of the desk; music continues softly under)*
The first time I heard the Chicago Symphony, Barenboim conducted Verdi's *Requiem*. I can recall how softly the orchestra played at the beginning of the

mass, and how tender the violins and chorus sounded. I sat in the Orchestra Hall gallery and I could see the soloists and all the players. The music took me to another place. I felt I was in another world.

(CHARLES sits on the desktop)

Going to the symphony series was an interesting idea that I at first thought might not come to much. It was a treat I gave myself for getting my first full-time job as a teacher in the Chicago Public Schools. I didn't understand what the orchestra would mean to me as I continued my career. That first evening, I liked what I heard, but I wasn't used to classical music, and sometimes I lost focus and just thought about my day. Then a solo or a chorus would bring me back and I would feel part of the orchestra.

(music fades out gradually)

I knew that I would never become famous. I knew that I would never make a million dollars. I also knew that when my students were gone I would be completely forgotten and no one would remember my name. The orchestra made it OK, somehow. I was part of something larger than the particular moments of my life. Teaching was hard work but it was a really good feeling. I was doing something that mattered. I was making the world a better place. I wasn't the greatest teacher, but I had my moments of grace.

(music up softly and builds: Verdi's Tuba Mirum *from the* Requiem; *CHARLES stands on the desk)*

It was amazing to hear the symphony brass shake the hall during the first part of the *Tuba Mirum*. The Italians understood death. They understood how to live and they knew how to die. When the chorus sang I mourned for my students. When the baritone sang I grieved for the teachers I had met.

(music plays loudly as CHARLES immerses himself in the piece and sings with the chorus; music then fades softly under)

There was a lot of joy in the system, but there was also a lot of heartbreak.

(CHARLES sits on the desktop)

I listened to the violins and the cellos and the drums. I'm sure there were many other people in the audience and on that stage who were also grieving. It was 1993 and people were dying everywhere. That's just the way things were. During those years there were a lot of people dying in a lot of different places.

(music fades out)

When I heard the *Requiem*, the orchestra wasn't mine in the way that it became part of me during my last years in the public schools, but I felt something change inside me as it played. The chorus took me into another world.

Before I became a teacher, I would try to find love, but it would never work and, besides, I had other things to do. I had other things to live for. Love wasn't something that came naturally to me. It wasn't something I was good at. It wasn't something that I lived with every day. The Chicago Public Schools taught me how to love. As difficult as my first years were, those days taught me how to open up. I broke through some of the emptiness that had hollowed out my life and became a better man.

(music up: Mozart's Piano Sonata K330, 2nd Movement; *CHARLES rises, gets the chair from behind the desk, places it in front of the desk and sits)*

It was 1991. I couldn't find a job. The Board of Education offered 55 dollars a day for subs with a college degree but no other credentials, and I decided I would rather substitute in the public schools than wait tables. Every day the Substitute Center sent me somewhere different. Every day I went to a stranger and crazier place. Every day I was exploring and learning and making stupid mistakes.

(music fades out)

I moved from class to class. I traveled from school to school. I started as a high school substitute and the work wasn't extremely difficult. After the first period, word would get out that there was a sub and most of the students would cut the class. There would rarely be anyone left in my room at the end of the day.

(rises and crosses to chalkboard)

But in those mornings, I had no choice but to stand in front of a chalkboard and talk to a group of strangers for 50 minutes.

(he rushes downstage toward the audience, walks back and forth as if inter- acting with a class)

I kept the class in order. I bantered with the boys in the back. I helped those who did the assignment. Sometimes the kids challenged me. Sometimes I yelled at them. Whatever I did in those classrooms I had to do right then at that moment. There was no margin for error, there was no time to think it through. I had to do something, even if the things I did, did not work.

(Mozart music up again, plays softly under; CHARLES sits on the chair)

Despite everything, my travels suited me. I wasn't sitting at a desk or going to a meeting. I didn't have a boss. I didn't have to suck up to people I didn't like. I didn't spend my free-time sending breezy cover letters with my resume attached. I taught in the Chicago Public Schools.

(music fades out)

Love was part of the compensation package the Board of Education offered me when I started substitute teaching. I didn't know it then. I thought I was just passing through when I filled out the paperwork. I thought I was just there for a little while until I found another job downtown. I thought a lot of things— until I start working at Erickssen.

(music up softly: Coltrane's Tipin')
Erickssen was a huge elementary school in the heart of the West Side. The Substitute Center sent me there on a Wednesday when all the high school teachers had decided to come to work. The streets that connected Erickssen to the highway were covered with potholes. The building was surrounded by vacant lots. The children the school served were very poor and they lived hard lives. All of them were African American or Hispanic.

(CHARLES rises, crosses behind the desk)
Erickssen was the first place I subbed where someone helped me. I think the teacher whose room they sent me to was really good. I stood in front of the chalkboard and I taught. It was a very strange feeling. The students were Black. I was White.

(picks up a lesson plan on top of the desk)
The teacher had left a plan. We followed it. I did nothing special, just gave them their teacher's math assignments and social studies dittos,

(picks up some word-searches on top of the desk and distributes a few to audience members, returns to desk)
as well as the word-searches and crossword-puzzles I pulled from the papers in my sub-pack. In the afternoon, when things got difficult, another teacher came in and took out some of the boys who were troubling me. It was an amazing experience. I can't describe what it meant to stand in a school on the West Side of Chicago and look out those windows and teach.

(music fades out; CHARLES sits on the chair)
When I went to check out at the end of the day I told the clerks that I would be happy to come back. At Erickssen, I learned that love is not a relationship you have with a person. It's a stance. It's a way of life. It's a power that you invoke if you're worthy of it. Many of the teachers who worked at Erickssen were worthy. Most of them were African American women who were fiercely organized and very proud. I was none of those things, and not worthy in the slightest, but I kept coming back to that school because I wanted to learn to do what they did. Every day I would get in my car and drive to Erickssen and the clerks would give me more work to do. I went from room to room for three long months. I didn't know the children. I didn't know how to teach. I didn't understand that one of the main reasons that everyone put up with me was that Erickssen never, ever, had enough subs. Teaching in that place was the hardest thing I ever did in my life, and that's why I did it. I couldn't leave it alone.

(sound effect: noisy children in a classroom; CHARLES rises and paces back and forth quickly)

Children create an emotional energy. They change the way that you move and the way that you feel. Thirty poor kids, sixty eyes looking up at you, sixty hands, three hundred fingers, there's so much going on, there's so much happening, it never stops, the classroom never slows down!

(sound effect out)

If you can ride with it, if you can move with it, if you can figure out that

(in a gentle voice)

this kid needs to be talked to in this way

(in a harsh voice)

and that kid needs to be talked to in that way,

(in his regular voice)

if you can communicate, if you can join together, there's no better feeling. You become part of a whole, you create a dance, the classroom has a life of its own. You're not in control, but you're conducting. You fly!

(crosses to chalkboard)

You stand there in front of the chalkboard and look at each of those faces. You glance into each of those eyes.

(he picks up a copy of Dr. Seuss' One Fish, Two Fish, Red Fish, Blue Fish
from the desk, stands in front of audience to show them the book cover)

Energy travels from them into you and then out and back again:

One fish, two fish,

Red fish, blue fish.

(he looks at the book admiringly and turns to another page)

Just holding the yellow book in my hand and showing the pictures to the Head Start kids and reading those words:

(holds the book to show the illustrations to the audience)

This one has a little star,

This one has a little car.

(he closes the book, looks at the audience)

They were poor children. They were very poor children.

(he sets the book on the desk, sits in the chair; music up softly: Tipin'*)*

After ten years of pro-business policies designed to stimulate the economy, nobody in their neighborhood had a job. Most of the local stores had been burned in the '68 riots. The factories that employed their parents had moved offshore. There was no work anywhere. Every morning as I drove to Erickssen I listened to stories about the Gulf War. Troops moved from place to place. Missiles were fired. When I turned off the Eisenhower Expressway I traveled past vacant lots and boarded-up buildings. Some of the residential streets looked pretty good. Block club signs had been posted at many corners, and some of the homes were surrounded by patios and gardens. But the street I drove down to Erickssen was a war zone. There were abandoned factories and vacant lots filled with trash and abandoned cars.

(CHARLES rises, takes the chair behind the desk, stands; music fades out)
I parked my car on the street outside the school and walked through the metal front doors to the office. On good days, the clerks would send me to Head Start and I would dance and sing until 2:30.

(he sits at the desk, picks up a pencil and writes on a notepad as he looks at a wall clock)
On bad days they would send me to a fourth or fifth grade room and I would prepare my lessons in silence as the hands on the clock turned slowly towards 9:00.

(sound effect: school bell; CHARLES rises, rushes to the front of the audience)
When the bell rang, I picked up my class in the playground, marched them to their room, and walked from desk to desk for the rest of the day and was flooded with emotion. I stood in those rooms and walked those endless corridors and looked at those faces. I thought I could feel all of my students' anger and all of their love and all of their sadness and all of their joy. I didn't know if I was right to feel this way, but I was new and that was how I felt. There was so much life. Even when my classes went out of control, and some of them went completely out of control, there was so much *life* in those rooms. Teaching was a better way to live. I was telling stories. I was singing songs. I was shouting at my class to stay in line when we walked to the cafeteria.

(crosses behind desk)
I was laughing in the break room. I was smoking outside with the other substitutes.

(music up softly: Coltrane's The Kiss of No Return; *CHARLES picks up a small orange chair, sets it on top of the desk, climbs up and sits on the small chair, mimes working with a child)*
I was working with the kindergarten teacher helping the boys write their names. She showed me how to hold the children's hands in mine and move the thick pencil across the page. I sat on a tiny, orange seat and worked at a round table that was only two feet off the floor. I remember the way my arm wrapped around the boys' shoulders while I held their hands in mine. I remember listening to them talk about their mothers and their cousins and their brothers and their grandmothers. I remember the smell of their bodies and the sound of each voice.

(rises, take the small chair and himself off the desk; stands behind the desk; music fades out)

The kindergarten teacher was old and White, and the office sent me to her room when they didn't have anything else for me to do. She was supposed to have two aides because of a grant, but I think one of them was always sick. She looked *exactly* like a teacher.

(picks up a pair of thick eyeglasses from the desk, crosses to the audience)
She had thick glasses and wrinkles on her face and wore dresses from Sears and Fields. She helped me and she told me stories. Once, she saw me walking back from the office after I subbed in another classroom and had a terrible day. She told me:

(puts on eyeglasses; in the voice and posture of the kindergarten teacher)
"Your problem is you are a young man and these older ones are going to challenge you. That's the way they are. It's difficult for every teacher that comes here, White or Black. It's especially difficult for young men. I think you are very brave and I want you to know that it is really worth it. If you can earn their respect; if you can prove yourself to these people, there's no better job in the world. I've worked here thirty years and I have the best life of anyone I know. It's hard, but I wouldn't do anything else. If you can gain your students' trust and earn their confidence, they'll care for you here in a way that they don't other places."

(music, The Kiss of No Return, *rises softly in the background; CHARLES takes off and returns the eyeglasses to the desk, gets the chair from behind the desk, crosses with it to the front of the audience, sits)*
I signed out at the office that afternoon and walked back down the hall and into the parking lot. I pulled my keys out of my pocket and I opened the front door and I sat down in my car and locked my doors. I was exhausted. The class had been really out of control. Two of the boys had spent the last fifteen minutes running around the room. A girl had started to cry.

(CHARLES takes a tissue from the Kleenex box in the desk, wipes his forehead)
I was shocked and angry and worn out and sad. I was covered with sweat.

(throws the Kleenex into a gray metal trash can)
I had started going to night school, and I was always tired.

Every afternoon when I pulled out of the parking lot and drove to night school or downtown to my second job, I wept. Tears never came. I had cried so much when I was a child that I couldn't do it anymore. But I wept, anyway. I drove past abandoned factories and boarded-up shops and I tried to sob. I cried for the children I served. They were so beautiful. Their eyes were so bright. There was no sense to it. They deserved so much and the world had given them so little, and there wasn't much that I could do to make their lives any better.

(music fades out)

I cried for the cracks on the playground and the building's peeling paint. I sat in my car waiting for the light to turn at an intersection where all the shops were boarded up and I cried for myself because

(beat)

I wasn't a good sub. The other teachers were better than me. They could get their kids to line up. They could lead them from their rooms, through hallways, down the stairs and into the cafeteria and then back again without raising their voice. I couldn't do that. I didn't know how. I cried because many of those kids were sick. All of the boys seemed to have asthma or bronchitis. I cried because I had always thought there was some fairness in the world. But as I drove down Crystal Avenue to the Eisenhower Expressway and flew down the ramp that took me downtown, I knew there was none of that. Nothing like that at all.

(rises, crosses behind the desk; music up softly: Mozart's Serenade, *5th Movement)*

But there were also moments of grace. It's important that I mention that. It's important that I emphasize that part of the experience.

(CHARLES crosses to the front of the audience, paces quickly back and forth)

There were moments when the lesson *worked*, and the class came together and energy rushed and the whole room began to move. Hands were raised, pencils hit paper, work got done, progress was made. I was alive. I was doing something! I was conscious of my entire body. I could feel my voice hum in my chest and the sweat drip underneath my arms. My back was always tense and I was always moving from seat to seat and from desk to desk. My heart opened up to the children I served. It was just one moment, it was just a day or sometimes just an hour in their lives, but I wanted to give them what I could.

(sits on the chair)

All the other subs were Black, and even though they didn't have as many problems as I did, it wasn't easy for any of us. We all had days that lasted for years, and hours that lasted for weeks, and minutes when the clock stopped and the kids refused to mind us, and it was all we could do to survive until 2:30.

(rises, takes the chair behind the desk, steps on the chair and stands on the desktop)

The best program I ever saw was performed by a Black conductor. It was just one of the performances on my series and I went without thinking much about it. I didn't know who the conductor was. I think he worked with the Seattle symphony, but I'm not sure. The orchestra came alive for him the way it did for some of the young conductors. It was clear that there was nothing he wanted to do more in the world than to conduct the Chicago Symphony. He made no flourishes or big gestures, but he was able to communicate. During the second half of that program, the Chicago Winds played Mozart's *Serenade*. The conductor barely moved. He kept time gently. His body seemed loose. The players made the music seem effortless. The sound was lush and smooth and I never wanted it to stop. There was nowhere else I wanted to be. I was in heaven for a moment. I had sung in the church choir until I left home for college, and I felt I had gained something I had lost a long time before.

(music fades out; CHARLES takes a tissue from the Kleenex box, wipes his forehead)

Teaching is very hard work.

(tosses Kleenex in the trash can; gets off the desk, crosses to the front of the audience; music up: Coltrane's El Toro Valiente)

Mr. Johnson.

(walks toward the audience)

Mr. Johnson!

(stands in front)

Mr. Johnson taught me how to be a teacher. He was my role model, my exemplar. He could substitute in any room in Erickssen School and make it work. He could walk the tightrope and never fall off. He was always part of the moment, always riding the wave, always moving with the beat. He could make the eighth graders mind him and the little kids jump for joy. He could reach almost every student in that building

(beat)

and I could not.

(CHARLES crosses behind the desk, gets a winter jacket and puts it on as he returns to the front of the audience; music fades out)

Mr. Johnson was Black, as tall as I was, but much more heavyset. He had a broad chest, thick shoulders and legs, and he spoke with a deep gravelly voice. What I remember most is standing outside the cafeteria where no one could see us, and looking out at Erickssen's concrete playground and the cars in the teachers' parking lot and lighting a cigarette and listening to him speak. His voice changed my life. I can still hear it today. The timbre was deep and rich. His voice was more than a set of words. It was a song, it was a melody. Mr. Johnson spoke with his entire body. We would stand there looking at the grass that grew up through the cracks in the parking lot and we would just laugh about whatever had happened that day.

(in a deep gravelly voice as Mr. Johnson)

"Mr. Vanover."

(in his own voice)

He said it differently than anyone else. He put stress on the *ov* and not on the *Van*.

(as Mr. Johnson)

"Mr. Vanover."

(in his own voice)

We stood there in the back of the cafeteria looking at the teachers' Cadillacs and Saabs. Sometimes I would sip a styrofoam cup of sugared cafeteria coffee. It was January and it was always cloudy, and as we smoked our cigarettes he would tell me stories.

(as Mr. Johnson)

"Mr. Vanover, it's crazy there today. The aides don't want to come to my class-room. No one wants to volunteer to give me my breaks. They tell me, 'Mr. Johnson, your kids are wild. They are ready to fly away. You had better calm them down.' I can't do that. No, Mr. Vanover. I can't do it. It's every man for himself at this school. What I do is I come in there with a bag of Chips Ahoy, or something really nutritious like hard candy.

(reaches into his jacket, pulls out a small bag of Chips Ahoy)

When the kids walk in after they have hung up their coats, I flash the bag. They know what that means, Mr. Vanover.

(puts the bag of cookies back in his jacket)

I tell them, 'If you're good, you might get a cookie.' And you know what happens when you give those kids chocolate, Mr. Vanover. You know what happens when you give them caffeine! Even a little sugar is enough to make them crazy. But it's every man for himself in this school. I have to do what I need to do to survive. There's not much of a lesson plan in my classroom, Mr. Vanover. I look at what the teacher leaves,

(frowns and rolls his eyes)

but most days that's not going to happen. I tell the kids, 'If you are really good, we might just skip the spelling dittos and act out one of the stories from your reader. But only if you are really good,'

(turns toward Mr. Vanover)

Mr. Vanover. 'Only if you sit at your desk with your hands folded and your back high and then do every single problem in your mathematics assignment without talking.' Oh, those kids, those kids, Mr. Vanover. They know nothing. They know nothing at all."

(music up softly: Coltrane's Midriff; CHARLES takes off the jacket, puts it away behind the desk, returns to the front of the audience; in his own voice)

Mr. Johnson had been a dancer in college and had taken a lot of improvisa-tion classes. His body was beautiful. His muscles were all organized. Just to see him march down the hallway with the kids flying behind him was an edu-cation. I watched his legs and shoulders, his neck and chest. I watched him project himself into every challenge he met and leap into every problem he faced. I watched him set a tone and create a mood.

(sits on the desk)

The kids loved Mr. Johnson. They ran up to him in the playground and hugged him. They cheered when he walked into their room. Love was in his arms, it was in his eyes, it was in the sound of his voice. Mr. Johnson could take all of his students' love and all of their kindness and all of their hopes and all of their fears and give the best parts back to them. He could walk into any room in the school and make it his own. Nobody else could.

(beat, he looks downward; music fades out)

Nobody else could. I know that I put Mr. Johnson up on a pedestal, but everyone did. He was what it was all about. He was the real thing, the very best thing. He represented the best of the world that had been lost. Mr. Johnson was church socials and mass choir rehearsals and huge Sunday dinners and house parties and juke-joints and lots and lots of little kids who were impossible not to love. He was all the good things people can't be anymore because the world's no longer that way. One can't be that open. One can't be that free.

(music up: Berg's Violin Concerto)

But it was possible for Mr. Johnson to be that way at Erickssen Elementary School.

(CHARLES rises, crosses behind the desk, climbs up the chair to stand on the desk)

On the same program where the winds played Mozart's *Serenade*, the orchestra performed Berg's *Violin Concerto*. I've heard that piece other times and it didn't touch me the way it did that evening. Maybe it was the playing. Maybe I was just ready for it. Maybe it was just one of those nights.

(CHARLES sits on the desk in a fetal-like position)

When I was a child, my best friend was Jewish. We would walk home together and I would sit with him in his house. I practically lived in his kitchen. His mother fed us bagels and corned beef and bialys. They had a drawer in their kitchen that was filled with candy and you could take as much as you liked anytime you wanted. We ate and drank pop and watched TV. I liked it so much there I didn't want to go home. It's a strange thing to say. I was White and I lived in the suburbs and I was only in the 3rd grade and already there were days I didn't want to go home. That's the feeling the music made that night when I sat in the gallery and watched the orchestra play Berg and Mozart. That's the song I heard as the soloist played.

(CHARLES begins to conduct with his hands)

The Black conductor kept time slowly. He was very calm. The violin grew loud and soft and bitter and sweet. I didn't want to go home.

(CHARLES moves to sit on the desk in a more comfortable position)

Teaching was never easy for me. I was always running. I was always out of place. I hadn't grown up in the city, and I didn't know how to act. I didn't understand what was going on around me. I had to change the way I spoke and the way I moved. Working at Erickssen was the hardest thing I ever did and I wasn't the only one who felt that way. Sometimes the other teachers looked more tired than I did at the end of the day. And maybe it was easier for me to work that job because I didn't know those students. I didn't know that neighborhood. I didn't have an older brother who'd gotten shot, or a cousin who was beaten up by the cops, or parents who were prisoners in the home they had worked for all their lives because the neighborhood had changed. Ignorance can be very underrated.

(music continues in the background)

Even though the schools I grew up in were better places for children than the schools where I worked, I never saw teachers when I was a child who were as good as Mr. Johnson, or who cared for their students in the way that the best people in the system cared for them. The teachers that I grew up with were kind and dedicated, hard-working, smart and skilled, but they didn't matter as much as the best people in Chicago mattered. They didn't spend their careers sailing though stormy seas. They weren't light in a bushel. They weren't comfort for the forsaken, nor rest for the weary. None of them were called to give their lives. Mr. Johnson stayed at Erickssen Elementary School the rest of his career. He told me the first day that Substitute Center sent him to Erickssen he thought that he recognized the place. But it wasn't until he marched his class to the primary building's cafeteria and saw all the small tables and chairs, that he remembered where he was. He told me that one year when he was little his parents had moved a few blocks off Crystal Avenue. Mr. Johnson said he had gone to Erickssen for kindergarten or maybe first grade. He couldn't leave.

(beat; he rises off the desk and stands in front of the audience; music fades out)

I left. Erickssen was too far away. The commute was too hard. I made too many mistakes. There were other schools. There were other classrooms. I became a teacher, but I never taught at Erickssen after those first few months.

I saw Mr. Johnson once more after that time. I stood in one of the hallways in the old warehouse on Pershing Road where the Board of Education put its offices. Both of us were tired. I saw the circles under Mr. Johnson's eyes and I know he saw the circles under mine. But we laughed. We smiled. It was a good moment. He was there to fill out some paperwork because the Board had forgot to pay him that Friday. I was there because I was looking for another job.

(crosses behind the desk to suggest a transition, returns to the front of the audience)

I found what I was looking for in February of that school year. I left the elementary schools that had given me my first full-time job in the system and started teaching high school.

(music up: Mahler's Symphony No. 7, 5th Movement*)*

From the moment I walked in the door everything was easier. Everything was simpler. I was suddenly the man I wished to be. There was another librarian there and the two of us had the time of our lives. We shelved books. We fixed computers. We wrote reports and worked on the budget. We taught the history fair for the social studies classes and the research paper for the English classes and the science fair for science classes and sometimes we didn't sit down until the last bell rang. My partner taught in the morning. I taught in the afternoon. She came in early and got things organized. I stayed late and put the library back together. I didn't want to go home.

(CHARLES crosses behind the desk as a transition movement, returns to the front of the audience; music switches to Mahler's Symphony No. 7, *1st Movement)*

In the evenings, as I walked to my apartment, I saw busses rush down Salmon Avenue towards sunset on the first week of school. I saw leaves fly off trees and rush under streetlights. I saw the moon shine deep into January skies. I jumped over mud and puddles. Sometimes, instead of going home I walked along the lake. There were afternoons I saw sailboats and evenings I saw thunderstorms and nights I saw snow. I bought my stereo. I went to the symphony.

(music fades out)

I had long conversations with my students about the most important things in the world and—unfortunately for me as it turned out—I argued with my principal.

(CHARLES crosses behind the desk, gets the chair and moves it to the side of the desk, music up softly: piano solo from Coltrane's Tipin'*; CHARLES sits, gets a can of pop from a desk drawer, opens it)*

One May evening, after I had been elected the associate union rep for my high school, I went to the Chicago Teachers Union's Legislative Dinner. I sat at a table with five female teachers, and after about five minutes we recognized each other. They were from Erickssen. I really *was* "Mr. Vanover." I couldn't stop laughing! I could only imagine the stories Mr. Johnson had told them about me, but I was really glad to see them. The dinner was really fun. We had corned beef and cabbage. The teachers told great stories about the principal and some of Erickssen's more famous lost souls. We drank pop and ate apple pie. We laughed and laughed. It was one of those moments that I just wanted to hold forever.

(music fades out)

Then they told me about Mr. Johnson.

(beat)

He had worked himself to death.

(CHARLES rises, gets a Kleenex to wipe his forehead, throws it away, crosses behind the desk, addresses the audience)

I won't say what happened to him. Whatever you *think* happened, I promise you that it was worse than that, and I don't want him to be remembered that way. I can tell you the story of how he lived. I cannot tell you the story of how he died. I wasn't there. I was somewhere else. Mr. Johnson was HIV positive. He was not as careful as he should have been. So, let me just say that: he worked himself to death.

(crosses to the front of the desk, sits on it)

When I came home from the dinner I figured out that Mr. Johnson died a few months before they started to prescribe protease inhibitors in the 1990s. A few months. If he had taught anywhere else but Erickssen, he would be alive today.

(beat)

Mr. Johnson and the rest of the teachers at Erickssen Elementary gave me a start and, as I discovered, the Chicago Public Schools were happy to provide me with as many lessons as I needed to get it right. But that was the end of my time teaching at Erickssen. One spring afternoon I drove out of the parking lot and I knew I would never come back. There was nothing left for me at that place. It was time for me to cut my hair short, get my resume out, and make some calls. It was time for me to end one story and begin another. It was time for me to . . . let it go.

(he picks up a conductor's baton from the desk and looks at it; he climbs to the top of the desk and stands; lights focus intensely on CHARLES)

The last year I worked in the Chicago Public Schools, I went to the symphony twenty-five times.

(music up: Mozart Piano Concerto No. 24, end of the 1st Movement)

I went during the weekdays and I went during the weekends. I went when I was tired and I went when I was sick. There was music that made my soul leave my body. I heard Barenboim play a Mozart piano concerto with the first chairs as backup, and I was in the center of the world. There was no other life I wanted to live. No other place I wanted to be. Every moment was . . . perfect.

(as CHARLES conducts with the baton, stage lights fade to black as the music continues then fades out)

(post-show music: Coltrane's Not So Sleepy)

Ethnodramatic Dialogue with Monologue

he anthology now proceeds to ethnodramas with two or more character-participants in naturalistic and realistic exchanges. "Acting is *re*acting" is a common adage in the culture of theatre. During onstage scripted work and improvisational exercises, the actor is taught to *listen* to fellow actor-characters for what immediately precedes her own lines so she can deliver the most appropriate reaction when it becomes her turn to speak. An actor is also trained to discern the specific attitudes her character holds toward others in the play. This enables her to interact in appropriately different ways with each individual character. For example, an actor's characterization may demonstrate impatience with and underlying hatred toward her husband, while demonstrating compassion and love toward her child. In ethnodrama—and life itself—social action is interaction; interaction is reaction.

Like *Chalkboard Concerto* in Part I, Elissa Foster's *Storm Tracking: Scenes of Marital Disintegration* in Part II is also an autoethnographic play. But instead

Jennifer Chapman and Anne Swedberg in *Wearing the Secret Out* (cowritten with Heather Sykes)

of merely speaking about or portraying all character-participants herself, she includes a key figure in her ethnodrama by physically representing him onstage. Thus, the impetus for dialogue—at times conversational, at times conflict-laden—is present, accompanied by the necessary supplemental monologues for telling a more complete story. Matthew J. Meyer's *The Practice* illustrates how a fieldworker can reconstruct and re-create multiple participants engaging in social interaction into stage action. Jennifer Chapman, Anne Swedberg, and Heather Sykes's *Wearing the Secret Out* includes verbatim interview transcript excerpts for their ethnodrama. The text is firmly grounded in the data, but also illustrates how just two performers can portray a variety of character-participants delivering monologue, exchanging dialogue, and speaking in choral forms.

Storm Tracking: Scenes of Marital Disintegration

BY ELISSA FOSTER

Editor's Introduction

Foster (2002) notes that *Storm Tracking*

> was developed from research notes, contemporaneously recorded during the weeks leading to [my] separation from [my] husband, using autoethnographic processes of systematic introspection. The play script form was adopted to reflect the constructed, embodied, and embedded nature of relational cycles. A story in and of itself can "call" us into the heart and mind of another person, and a script shared publicly in performance can extend the process of relationship inquiry into another experiential domain. (p. 804)

The battle between the sexes is one of the most common themes in dramatic literature, ranging from Euripides' *Medea* to Shakespeare's *The Taming of the Shrew* to Ibsen's *A Doll's House* to Albee's *Who's Afraid of Virginia Woolf?* This universal topic for adult (heterosexual) audiences engages us by letting us

81

watch conflicting perspectives on the historic, socialized roles of men and women enacted onstage as we take sides—but ideally, we sympathize and empathize with both characters, regardless of how a playwright portrays the protagonist and antagonist. Nevertheless, most plays are told from a central character's point-of-view, and Foster makes no apologies for telling her side of the story. A personal work can sometimes evolve into a self-indulgent, boring, and embarrassingly cathartic text, as sometimes happens with autoethnography. Fortunately, *Storm Tracking* is instead an intimate play, layered with the irony that a husband cannot communicate with his wife—an interpersonal communication instructor.

Though I have never seen *Storm Tracking* in performance, and the play has not been staged formally elsewhere aside from an informal reading at a research conference, when I first encountered the script it excited me as a director of ethnotheatre. Foster's monologues and dialogue reveal vulnerability and painful honesty, laced with wry, humorous asides. The play is structurally elegant with a focused through-line. The protagonist's struggles and her unsuccessful search for solutions are those that many of us have encountered in adult relationships. By unabashedly revealing the truths from her life, Foster gives her audiences a truthful experience through drama. Unlike other ethnodramas in this anthology, there is no overt pedagogical purpose for this play. There is, instead, the need for an author to tell a personal story through her writing—similar to the artistic impulse that drives a playwright to generate a script.

When *Storm Tracking* first appeared in print in the journal *Qualitative Inquiry*, the play script included nineteen footnotes and thirty-nine references to related books and articles. They are excluded from the script in this anthology so as not to distract from the flow of the drama. Unfortunately, some scholars in the social sciences feel that arts-based work is not "academic" or "rigorous" enough without some citation of the research literature and a necessary discussion of the theoretical background informing the work. Some will say that without these references, arts-based research loses its credibility and trustworthiness as a mode of presenting and representing the study of social life. I say that without these references, ethnodrama breaks free from the shackles of traditional, hegemonic academia and transcends into a more aesthetic and evocative form, one that is no less credible or trustworthy than the juried journal article.

Storm Tracking:
Scenes of Marital Disintegration

Characters

DEBORAH: twenty-eight, a graduate student and teaching assistant
BRETT: twenty-nine, a videographer
WEATHER ANNOUNCER: male, maybe played on or offstage, with the
    smug tone of a network television announcer

Staging Notes

The following dialogue represents Deborah's psychological reality rather
than a conventional drama between two characters. The action represented is
Deborah's perception of events. Staging should include only minimal set pieces
to support the settings implied in the script. At various points, sound effects
are suggested to support the psychological metaphor of a hurricane. Only minimal stage directions have been provided for the performers so that the action
remains embedded in the characters' interaction. Performers should be prepared for laughter from the audience but resist the urge to "play for laughs."
The performer playing Deborah should enact clear distinctions between the
private thoughts she shares with the audience and the self she presents to Brett.

Scene 1

*(BRETT and DEBORAH's apartment, signified by two wooden chairs, placed
back-to-back in the center of the stage about two feet apart; upstage right is a
hat rack holding one of DEBORAH's jackets; downstage right is a lectern to
represent DEBORAH's classroom; DEBORAH walks downstage at the end of
the announcer's spiel; BRETT stands on one side, waiting to enter the scene)*
WEATHER ANNOUNCER: Well, folks, we're entering the busiest period of
    hurricane season and—just to prove it—that tropical depression has just been
    upgraded to a storm directly north of the Dominican Republic. Get your
    tracking maps out and get ready for the coordinates, this one's called Tropical
    Storm Fred. It may seem a long way from Houston now but remember that
    we've got to look out for these early signs. That former depression could
    intensify to a hurricane in our neighborhood in a matter of days.
DEBORAH: *(to audience)* I should have seen it coming.

BRETT: *(walks briskly to join DEBORAH)* I hate my job. I want to go back to Savannah. I'm going to ask for my old job back.

DEBORAH: You won't even consider looking for another job here in Houston?

BRETT: Maybe. Maybe I could do that.

(BRETT turns away as DEBORAH turns to address the audience)

DEBORAH: How many times have we had this conversation? Still, I feel like the world's been washed out from underneath me. How typical of him to do this on my second day in the doctoral program. Listen to this. Two years ago, I postponed grad school to live with Brett in Savannah. One year ago, he asked me to marry him and stay for another year. At the end of that year, after resisting the move for so long, Brett immediately found a job here in Houston, and he ended up leaving before I did. Then, three weeks ago, the phone rang as I was packing for the move.

(flashback to three weeks ago; BRETT and DEBORAH walk to the chairs at center stage and sit back-to-back to "talk on the telephone")

BRETT: I hate my job. I made a terrible mistake coming down here. I want to ask for my old job back, in Savannah, but it's too late. I'm in a job I hate and I have no options.

DEBORAH: Of course you have options! *(to audience)* Fuck him! I've had enough. I will *not* beg him to stay with me. *(back to BRETT)* You could call Karen up tonight and ask her for your job back. You're not stuck. You've deliberately painted yourself into a corner. If you want to move back, MOVE BACK. *(to audience)* I don't care. I haven't signed the contract for the movers yet. Maybe I could live on campus. I could find a roommate. I can work out how to go on alone. I even know how to divide up the furniture.

BRETT: *(bursting in on her thoughts)* Honey, you know I love you, but I've always had my doubts about this relationship. I'm not willing to give anything up like you have, and I don't think that's fair, but . . . maybe if it was "meant to be" then I would feel differently. The only thing I've ever been sure of is that I want to live in Savannah, and now I feel like I'm never going to get back there. I guess I didn't really think it through.

(the "telephone" scene breaks, and BRETT returns to his position, turned away from the audience)

DEBORAH: *(walks back toward audience)* So, less than three weeks later we are at the same point. A few random boxes and bare walls are the only signs that we're newly moved in. The day after this phone call, Brett called to let me know that he wanted to "stick it out." I felt ambivalent about Brett's wonderful news. Was this a change of heart? A turning point? Or is it just a pattern—one I'm not willing to live with?

BRETT: *(returning to the scene)* When I'm with you, it's wonderful. You're the most precious, loving, giving person I've ever known. But when I feel frustrated with my job, or anything, my mind keeps going back to the past, and I feel like I've made a terrible mistake.

DEBORAH: But you keep making it. This would have been so much easier to deal with three weeks ago before I moved down here. YOU decided you wanted to stay in Houston. You told me that staying with me was much more important to you than living in Savannah without me. That's why you agreed to even look for a job down here in the first place. *(to audience)* I feel like screaming, "You picked ME! You always pick me, so how can you torment me like this?!"

BRETT: It's just that, when I do something that takes me away from what I want—like moving down here—I can't handle it, especially when I think someone else convinced me to do it.

DEBORAH: *(quietly)* God, it hurts when you talk about feeling taken away from "what you want"—because I know you're not talking about me. *(to audience)* It's simple. He doesn't want me.

BRETT: All I can think about at work is whether the things I'm doing there can get me back into my old job. I don't care about these people. *(pause)* I was doing what I wanted to do, where I wanted to do it, with people I care about, in my community. . . . I feel like I'm lost. You're my best friend . . . and I keep hurting you. I don't know what to do because it hurts me so much when I cause you this pain, but I don't know . . . what to do.

DEBORAH: *(to audience)* What have I done? What a mess. I've tried to be the perfect girlfriend, the perfect wife. All this time, have I been ignoring what Brett really wants and needs? Did I really, somehow, force him to marry me?

BRETT: I know that if I go back to Savannah, it will be bad for us. I know it will hurt so much.

DEBORAH: Brett, if you have to leave, then I won't blame you for it. Don't stay with me because you think it's the "right" thing to do or because you're afraid of hurting me.

BRETT: That's not what I meant. It also hurts me to hurt you. Isn't that what it means to love someone?

DEBORAH: *(to audience)* I don't know, is that love? *(to BRETT)* Listen, you need to make a decision about this, and I can't help you. I think you should go and talk to a counselor. We can't keep doing this. *(to audience)* I can't keep doing this.

(BRETT walks to center stage and sits on one of the chairs)

(DEBORAH walks to the hat rack and dons the jacket) So, while this is going on at home, I'm studying and teaching interpersonal communication. As I stand before my students, I am aware of my wedding ring and my double-barreled married name. As I speak to them, I know that my words are weighed and filtered through the lens of my femaleness and my married-woman status.

(walks to the lectern)

Good morning, everyone. In the last class period, we discussed communication messages and meaning. Today, we take that idea a step further to talk about messages operating at two different levels simultaneously. If you learn nothing else in this class, it is essential that you understand the concepts of content and relational levels of meaning. Gregory Bateson was the first theorist to suggest that any utterance provides both a content level, called the "report," and a "command" level that tells us how to respond to the message content.

(moves toward the audience as she addresses her "class" more directly)

Why is this such an important idea? Well, think about this. You find yourself arguing with a family member or spouse. Somehow, you know that what you're arguing about is not the real issue, but you just keep arguing. Or maybe you feel like you're having the same conversation over and over again—the words are different but you keep going over the same ground. Those are relational patterns at work, and they are insidious because they are often out of our awareness. Marriage researchers have identified a correlation between relationship satisfaction and the ways that couples talk to each other. In the conversations of couples who have been identified as "distressed" or "abusive," patterns of enmeshment and negative reciprocity can be identified at the relational level of their interaction. Negative patterns appear even when these couples are talking about something simple, like what happens during their average day! This is important research because marriage remains the desired state for adults—despite the enormous difficulties associated with attaining the ideals of the modern marriage, and despite the fact that divorce is statistically normal.

(forcing a lighthearted tone)

Seems like we all want to live happily ever after, but we're not necessarily aware of what we're doing—or not doing—to contribute to our own happiness or distress.

(DEBORAH steps out from behind the lectern and slowly takes off her jacket)

Talking to my students, standing at the lectern, I am bearing witness to my painfully flawed union—but I fall short of baring myself. Instead, I take cover behind the research, and the dialogue I usually enjoy in the classroom gives way to monologue. I know that the storyteller is infinitely more vulnerable than the scientist. And I'm not willing to be that vulnerable in front of my students.

Scene 2

(DEBORAH returns her jacket to the hat rack during the ANNOUNCER's speech)

WEATHER ANNOUNCER: Well, just like I predicted, Tropical Storm Fred has moved west and seems to be gathering some intensity out there in the Gulf. He's churning up some waves *(ocean sounds for the following scene can begin at this point)* but isn't doing anything definitive yet. Looks like we have to wait and see if Fred is ready to come ashore.

DEBORAH: *(to audience)* Brett went to see a therapist last night. We walk in the dark as Brett speaks and I listen. Like waves through the flow of Brett's words, phrases pound me, one after another.
(both BRETT and DEBORAH stand side by side and deliver the following lines to the audience until DEBORAH addresses BRETT directly after his speech)

BRETT: I told her how we met doing the graduate school thing, and how we got married primarily for convenience—

DEBORAH: *(to audience)* The first wave knocks me to the sand.

BRETT: I told her how every month or so I would bring up something about your weight to try to motivate you to do more stuff, and how I know that hurts you a lot—

DEBORAH: *(to audience)* And again.

BRETT: I told her that you always knew you wanted me, but I just tended to take the path of least resistance, so I never really decided if I wanted you or not—

DEBORAH: *(to audience)* I try to struggle to my feet.

BRETT: We talked about the time we were dating long distance and I broke up with you. I couldn't see the point of a long-distance relationship. I told her I wasn't unfaithful, but I let myself get emotionally attached to someone else. I got back together with you because it was Christmas time, and it didn't seem right to break up with you then. She said it sounds like I didn't think it through enough—

DEBORAH: *(to audience)* The waves break over my head.

BRETT: She asked me if I would put a hundred dollars down right now on whether I would stay or go. I said, "Listening to this conversation, I'd bet that I would go." She asked me if my love for you had grown since we got married and I said, "Yes," and she seemed to stop and think. She said, "That's one sign of a strong relationship—it grows."

DEBORAH: *(to audience)* At this point, we stop at a water fountain. I drink the tepid water, tasting rust.

(BRETT and DEBORAH turn to each other; ocean sounds stop abruptly)

Brett, do you think for one minute that I would be standing here right now if you hadn't convinced me time and time again that you desperately wanted to be with me?

BRETT: *(pause)* No. I don't.

DEBORAH: Then how in the hell do you reconcile that with the fact that you say you have never made a decision about us? Were you lying when you said you wanted to be with me?

BRETT: No, I wasn't lying. I guess I see what you mean.

DEBORAH: *(to audience)* We start walking again. Brett talking. Me listening.

(BRETT slowly walks circles around DEBORAH as he delivers his lines)

BRETT: Maybe all I have to do is learn to appreciate what I have instead of obsessing about all the things I don't have. I guess I don't appreciate the pain I put you through, but one day I'll grow. I'll finally realize that pain— but you may not be around anymore when I finally wake up. I've done this in every important relationship I've ever had—I take what I have for granted. I broke up with Amy three times until she finally wouldn't have me back again. I'm doing the same thing with you. I know that if I'm ever going to change my attitude, I have to stay with you and work through it. I don't want to keep hurting you.

DEBORAH: Okay!

(BRETT stops walking)

I appreciate that, Brett. But tonight you told your therapist that you'd bet a hundred dollars you're going to leave me . . . and an hour later you're saying that you want to stay and change your attitude?

BRETT: I also told you that I'm stupid and I've done this with every other aspect of my life, so what's to stop me from doing it again?

(BRETT walks away)

DEBORAH: *(to audience)* Well. That's helpful.

Scene 3

(bathroom; morning; BRETT is speaking from the "shower" as he washes himself, standing between the two chairs; DEBORAH is applying her makeup in a mirror, facing the audience)

WEATHER ANNOUNCER: Fred's been downgraded from tropical storm status, and that system seems to be breaking up. Looks like this isn't the big one after all. Stay tuned, though, you know how unpredictable these storms can be. In fact, we have a significant depression forming out in the Atlantic, currently southeast of the Bahamas but heading west. We'll keep an eye on that one for you, but, for now, things look sunny.

DEBORAH: *(to audience)* Brett is in a buoyant mood. I am not.

BRETT: You know, honey, I've been thinking about our situation, and I've decided to stay here with you. I'm not going to ask for my old job back.

DEBORAH: *(to audience)* I'm creating my public face. These dark circles under my eyes seem more noticeable every day.

BRETT: I know what a wonderful person you are, and I know we could be happy if I can just change my attitude. I realize that what I've been doing is emotionally abusive, and I'm not going to do it anymore. I love you, honey, and I just know that if I go back to Savannah now, I'll really regret losing you.

DEBORAH: *(pause)* Don't I have a say in this?

BRETT: *(emerges from the "shower," wrapping a towel around his waist, and walks forward to face DEBORAH)* What do you mean? *(pause)* Of course you do.

DEBORAH: Since the beginning of the year—well, really, since the beginning of our relationship—you've been saying that you want to leave me, so I've had plenty of time to think about it. Right now, given this pattern, I know I'll be quite okay if you leave me. But, the fact is, I don't know anymore if I'll be okay if you stay. If we keep this up, I know I won't be okay.

BRETT: You don't trust me anymore.

DEBORAH: That's right. I don't. *(to audience)* Not as far as I could throw you, Brett.

BRETT: *(pause)* Well, if you're going to decide you want me to leave, I'd appreciate knowing that in the next couple of days. I'll need to know so I can make arrangements.

DEBORAH: *(to audience)* Can you believe this? *(to BRETT)* My only point is that there's no point staying together if there's no change.

BRETT: Well, what do you want me to do?

DEBORAH: We've talked about this already! *(to audience)* He's so frustrating! Why am I always the silent party being dumped on, or suddenly in charge? *(to BRETT)* I think you need to see a therapist—regularly. And you should be prepared for your counselor to support your decision to leave. I just want *you* to know what *you* really want.

BRETT: I guess I don't have the confidence in therapy that you do, but I'm willing to give it a try. I'll make another appointment for this week.

(BRETT walks to sit in one of the chairs, facing the audience; he remains in this position during the next scene)

DEBORAH: *(to audience)* So, we got some things out in the open. Then why do I feel disappointed? It would be so much easier if he just made up his mind and left.

Scene 4

(DEBORAH walks to the hat rack; she puts on her jacket and goes to stand at the lectern)

DEBORAH: Let's turn to what Cupach and Spitzberg have called "the dark side of interpersonal communication." Aversive behavior and hurtful messages come in all shapes and sizes. You may not immediately recognize "information" as a kind of hurtful message, but it is! One thing that makes "information" so hurtful is that the receiver of the information cannot refute what is being said.

BRETT: *(still facing audience, not speaking directly to DEBORAH)* I got back together with you because it was Christmas time.

DEBORAH: Also, what may seem to be just one person's behavior or personality can be very hurtful in a relationship—like *indecisiveness*. When someone is indecisive, they tend to violate intimate relationships by breaking promises, changing significant plans, and not being there when the partner needs them.

BRETT: I never really decided whether I wanted you or not.

DEBORAH: There's also *equivocation*, or going back and forth between positive and negative frames of mind. Some research shows that this kind of behavior is a type of psychological abuse.

BRETT: Honey, you know I love you, but I've always had my doubts about the relationship.

DEBORAH: When one partner shifts between statements of love and statements that undermine the other's sense of self, I'm sure you can see how that could start to drive a person crazy!

(BRETT turns his body to face offstage; DEBORAH steps out from behind the lectern and walks a couple of steps toward the audience)

DEBORAH: I can feel my own story encroaching upon the orderly world of scholarly research, threatening to burst out from behind my teeth. In my mind, I hear the voices of other scholars who critique this construction of the "divided self," this schism between the academic and the personal.

They call me to step up and tell my story. But, in the midst of a chaos narrative, how can I tell it? Or, perhaps more to the point, how can I tell my story if I haven't remembered it yet?

(returning her jacket to the rack and turning to the audience)

Time marches on. We're walking again, this time beside the swampy river water: messy, dark, and filled with hidden creatures that could strike at any time. Just like our marriage, really.

BRETT: *(joins DEBORAH downstage)* When I think about staying married to you, I can see you finishing your Ph.D., getting an academic job somewhere far away. I see a house and children—but I don't see myself in that picture.

DEBORAH: *(to audience)* I feel like I've been punched in the stomach. Is this my *husband*? *(to BRETT)* What *do* you see?

BRETT: I don't know. I can't imagine being happy anywhere but where I was, and I see staying married to you as one move after another. I don't see how I can build a career that way.

DEBORAH: Well, what were you thinking when we got married?

BRETT: Like I've said before, I got married to avoid having to make a decision about letting you go—so that you would stay in Savannah for another year or so. That's all.

DEBORAH: *(to audience)* I've heard Brett's version of our marriage before. Charming, isn't it? *(to BRETT)* But what about the vows we exchanged and the promises we made? How could you stand up in front of our friends and family without having any sense of what this marriage meant to you?

BRETT: You're right. I guess I'm just an asshole.

(BRETT leaves the scene; DEBORAH looks at the audience as if to say, "What do YOU think?")

Scene 5

WEATHER ANNOUNCER: Well, three weeks ago I said it couldn't happen, but that depression kept growing. Batten down the hatches Houston, Hurricane Georgia's in the Gulf and heading our way. For those in low-lying areas, sandbags are available at your local fire station, but remember they're in limited supply—

(DEBORAH mimes checking closets, writing a shopping list, general business that keeps her moving through the scene)

BRETT: *(entering the scene, flustered)* They gave my job away.

DEBORAH: What are you talking about?

BRETT: I got an e-mail message from Karen today telling me that they had offered my job to someone else. Of course, the guy took it. It's a great job.

DEBORAH: *(continues looking for supplies and adding to her shopping list)* Did you think they were just going to hold the position open indefinitely? You told Karen more than once that you weren't going to come back.

BRETT: Of course I knew they were going to fill the position. I just didn't know how I was going to feel about it.

DEBORAH: *(to audience)* Grow up and live with it, Brett!

BRETT: *(continues, flustered)* I think that while the job was still open, was still an option for me, I felt better about being here in Houston. And now I've lost my chance. I'm stuck.

DEBORAH: *(to audience)* Yeah, stuck with me. God! How much of this do I take? *(to BRETT)* Look, we have to get sandbags. We don't have time to talk about it now.

BRETT: I've made a terrible mistake. I should've taken back my job when I had the chance.

DEBORAH: Well, why didn't you?

BRETT: *(pause)* Oh my God, I knew it. I should have gone back. I've made a big mistake.

DEBORAH: I am so angry with you right now, I could . . . you are NOT going to do this. No matter what decision you make you turn around and fixate on whatever it was you didn't choose. We've spent weeks talking about this. You made your choice for whatever reason, and now you're going to forget all that and make us both miserable.
(BRETT turns away from the audience)
(to audience) So, we drove to the fire station. I slammed my way out of the car just as the rain started to come down.
(sound effects of rain begin here and can continue into the beginning of the next scene)
We worked filling and lifting fifty-pound sandbags as the rain fell. Brett's mood lifted as he engaged in the physical activity. I used my anger to keep up a good pace with the shovel. We finally got back in the car, wet and covered with gray-black sand.
(BRETT and DEBORAH turn the chairs to face the audience and sit side by side in the "car")

BRETT: I'm sorry. I didn't mean to dump all that on you. It was just the shock of having my job given away. I need some time to adjust.

DEBORAH: I just wish you'd think about what you say and the kind of negative rubbish that invades your mind. And take some fucking responsibility for your choices.

Scene 6

(sound effects of rain from the previous scene can be faded into background music for the car radio; suggested music: Riders on the Storm *[The Doors] and* Like a Hurricane *[Neil Young])*

DEBORAH: *(to audience)* A few days later, Brett and I are driving. The car is becoming the habitual venue for our relational discussions.

BRETT: I guess no matter what I have, I always think about what I don't have. If I'm with somebody, it doesn't matter who they are or how wonderful they are, I end up thinking about all the things they don't have.

DEBORAH: *(to audience)* He means me. I'm not thin enough, pretty enough, athletic enough, competitive enough—

BRETT: I've always been a perfectionist, I guess. Nothing and nobody is ever good enough. Whatever I have, I can always imagine it being better; that is, of course, until I lose it and then I regret it.

DEBORAH: Wait a minute. All these years, you've said you're a perfectionist. But you're not talking about wanting to make yourself a better person— you mean you are never satisfied with *other people!* You're always finding fault. My God! How do you live with yourself? How does it feel to never be satisfied with anything?

BRETT: It's terrible! I'm never satisfied. I'm never happy with what I have.

DEBORAH: *(to audience)* I feel like I'm talking to a stranger. *(to BRETT)* You know what? That's so fucked up I can't even begin to tell you. . . . You know, you've talked about wanting to have a family before, and I just want to tell you, until you sort through that shit, you have no business bringing a child into the world. I can just imagine how screwed up your child would be, growing up around a father who is never satisfied, putting all kinds of conditions on your love. . . . Whether it's with me or with someone else, you'd better sort that shit out or you're going to really fuck some little kid up. *(fade out music and rain effects as WEATHER ANNOUNCER begins)*

Scene 7

WEATHER ANNOUNCER: Well that was a close call. Looks like Georgia's decided to hang out in the Gulf for a while. That's good for all you frustrated surfers out there, but be careful. We're going to continue to feel the effects of Hurricane Georgia, with plenty of wind and rain in the Houston area, until she decides to do something definite.

(back in the apartment; BRETT and DEBORAH stand; BRETT is turned slightly away until DEBORAH addresses him)

DEBORAH: *(to BRETT)* I'm not very happy.

BRETT: Tell me how you feel.

DEBORAH: *(to audience)* He asks me this, now? It's like a bad joke! *(to BRETT, calmly at first)* I'm so frustrated. You say you don't want me and you don't want to be in this marriage, and I can't believe that I've committed my life to a man who doesn't want me. I know you didn't take our wedding vows seriously, but I did! You tell me that you want to understand how I'm feeling, but anyone who hears the things you say knows how painful they are. Why don't you? You haven't ever admitted to *wanting* to be in this relationship, to *choosing* to be here, but I *am committed to you*, so I let you keep hurting me, and I keep forgiving you. I've never told you what I want. I've never asked for what I need. I want to be able to talk to you about the future, to build a future. I want to talk about building the kind of relationship that will sustain us throughout our lives. I want to talk to you about what kind of husband you want to be. I want to feel loved, and cherished, and precious to you—but I'm not! You're supposed to be my soul mate, my supporter, but you're not. You're too busy thinking about how miserable you are with me.

(DEBORAH is overcome with the awful truth of her disclosure)

BRETT: *(pause)* I'd like to be able to do those things. But before I can talk about what kind of a husband I want to be, I think I'd better decide if I even want to be a husband.

DEBORAH: *(to audience)* It's taking too long. My body is screaming with pain. I can't keep doing this week after week. When's it going to end? *(to BRETT)* Please . . . please DO something.

BRETT: *(pause)* Don't you ever think you deserve someone better?

DEBORAH: No. I just deserve to be treated better.

BRETT: *(pause)* You know, honey, if I could just stop looking at other women, then I reckon we'd have a marriage.

DEBORAH: *(to audience)* My God, can you believe this! He's saying this to make me feel better! *(to BRETT)* No, that's bullshit. Everybody *looks*, but you see other women and you resent the fact that you're not free to date them. You see your desire for them as evidence that our relationship is inadequate—that *I'm* inadequate—and THAT'S the problem. *(to audi-*

ence) He stabs me in the heart then steps right over my body, oblivious, without even blinking. My God! I've heard this enough times. You'd think I'd build up a little immunity! I have to get away from him. *(to BRETT)* I have to get to work. I don't know when I'll be back.

BRETT: I love you.

(DEBORAH exits the scene as though she hasn't heard, and moves upstage to get her jacket; BRETT moves back to sit in the "car")

Scene 8

DEBORAH: *(standing at lectern)* As we learned in our lecture about relational patterns, it takes two to tango. Sometimes a partner may respond to hurtful messages by acquiescing or withdrawing regardless of what she feels. The partner may do this because she feels she is maintaining the relationship by not responding with hurtful messages of her own. Also, if women feel more responsible for the success of the relationship, we will resist expressing our dissatisfaction. However, one of my favorite theorists—Carl Rogers—offers what I think is some great advice on this topic. He suggests that any persistent feeling, even if it is negative, needs to be disclosed. He states, "If this is not done, what is unexpressed gradually poisons the relationship." However, if you're a person who tends to avoid conflict, or if you're stuck in a cycle of attack and retreat, expressing your feelings may be something that's easier said than done. But what's at stake if a couple can't "get it together"? Some researchers suggest that establishing a shared reality—a story about the relationship that both parties can agree with—is *the* most important goal of an intimate relationship. People assume that living together or being married will provide a clear definition of the relationship for both parties, but that's certainly not the case. So do you keep struggling until you reach consensus? If so, for how long? When do you stop struggling?

(during her next line, DEBORAH enters the scene, still wearing her jacket, and sits beside BRETT)

(to audience) Two weeks later. We're in the car, again, on our way back from a university social event.

BRETT: I want to ask you something, but I'm not sure of the best way to put this. How would you feel about—

DEBORAH: *(to audience, interrupting)* Oh my God. He's moving out but he wants us to stay married, or he wants to separate so he can date someone else—

BRETT: How would you feel about me not making any drastic changes soon but staying on in the relationship to see what happens, to give it a chance?

DEBORAH: *(to audience)* That's *it?!* That's the big revelation? *(to BRETT)* What do you think? Not happy! It means this limbo would continue—of not knowing when you're going to go or to stay.

BRETT: I guess I understand that—you don't trust me anymore. But I want to do something to try to make this work out. I know I'm responsible for causing you all this pain, and I really want to know if *you* think this relationship's worth saving? If there's anything left to salvage?

DEBORAH: It's not that I think you can't understand me; it's just that I know I can't *teach* you that, and I don't know if I can handle being around long enough to find out if you eventually change.

BRETT: You couldn't bring me up to your level so I drag you down to mine. Interesting—

DEBORAH: *(to audience)* He's blaming himself, again. *(to BRETT)* Listen, I'm responsible for this, too. I thought I could take up the slack in our marriage, at least long enough for you to step up and make a commitment. I never stopped to think about what *I* needed.

BRETT: Why don't you just put up a wall? When anybody says something bad about me or to me, I just put up a wall. "Fuck them!" Why don't you do that with me?

DEBORAH: Because I care what you say to me! I still believe in the Brett that everybody meets and likes on sight. I believe in the Brett who nobody could say a bad word about. *(pause)* Look, I just want you to know that if you want to build your home in Savannah, with someone who never wants to leave there, then *go in peace.* I give you your freedom with my absolute blessing.

BRETT: Why are you saying this to me now?

DEBORAH: *(to audience)* Have I not been telling him this for months?! *(to BRETT, with accelerating anger)* Before we were married, I gave you a chance to back out. When you called me from Houston three months ago, I told you to ask for your old job back. This is not new, Brett. This just might be the first time you've taken me seriously. You're not doing me any favors by staying around here being miserable and taking out your frustration on me.

BRETT: *(pause, thinking)* I can't make this decision. I'm too afraid I'll make a mistake.

DEBORAH: *(to audience)* Perhaps that's it. I'll be the one to make it for him.

Epilogue

(BRETT leaves the stage for the final scene; DEBORAH stands alone address-ing the audience)

DEBORAH: When the moment finally came, it was not earth shattering, or momentous. Brett came in from work one evening and began to talk about how close he had come to quitting that day. He told me he had never been more miserable and depressed in his whole life. He said that there was only a small part of him that could see himself being happy in our marriage in the future. He said the only way he could see himself back on the right track would be if he returned to Savannah to start again. I thought, "Here we are. Back to square, fucking, one." Something snapped. In less than twenty-four hours my conversations with Brett changed from "What would separation be like?" to "I'm looking for apartments next weekend." I'd been to this point so many times in the past four years that it seemed strangely anticlimactic. Perhaps I didn't allow myself to fully realize what I was doing. Perhaps I was just really tired of the whole thing. One thing was very clear to me. The time for dialogue was gone. The repetition of our words had eroded their meaning, anyway. Hurricane season was over.

The Practice

BY MATTHEW J. MEYER

Editor's Introduction

There are times when drama has an overt pedagogical purpose intended by the playwright. Matthew J. Meyer, a Canadian teacher educator with a background in theatre, employs the art form with his pre-service students and in-service professionals. He labels his work "Theatre as Representation" (TAR) and describes it as a

> reality-inspired dramatic scenario where the participants [such as students, teachers, or administrators] participate either as a reader or viewer. This experience of participant self-reflection within a group context serves as a mechanism for administrator and/or professional development in the realm of leadership and decision-making. It is hoped that after participation in such a project these future administrators will be better prepared to make more complete complex decisions than they were able prior to the experience. (2001b, p. 150)

TAR provides dramatic simulations of actual problems adults may encounter when they work with students or peers. Also known in human communication methods as "trigger scripting," this dramatic scenario propels its readers to reflect on the conflicts presented and ask themselves, "What would I do if I was in this situation?"

Meyer's repertory of TAR scenarios includes such conflicts as teachers burdened by their inability to meet administrative expectations; personnel conflicts during faculty meetings; disagreements over school board policy development; and a principal dealing with difficult parents in his office. These scenarios are authentic because Meyer develops them from observations of school culture and through interviews with teaching professionals. Field notes and transcripts provide collective data for reconstructing and writing "what if" scenarios with real-life concerns woven into the dialogue.

The Practice, according to Meyer (2003),

> is based on an actual event in an urban Canadian secondary school. The author had first and second account conversation data from many of the actual participants of the event. They have been fictionalized in this scenario. . . . There are many questions and issues that concern morality, professionalism and mutual respect that arise from this scenario. [Pre-service education] students in either small discussion groups or in a large forum discuss them after the scenario has been presented in class. The class discussion began with the open question by the professor, "What just happened here?" (p. 17)

The female adolescent character-participants in *The Practice* speak candidly during a stressful situation, and their teacher, Coach Mark, is faced with difficult decisions to make in the heat of the moment. (Readers who want to know how the incident develops further with the school principal, a teacher's union representative, and one of the girls' parents in TAR scenarios, can access Meyer (2001a).)

Meyer asserts that TAR is a more relevant and emotion-evoking stimulus than the traditional narrative case study for teacher education purposes. Discussion does indeed flow intensely from participants after reading these scenes aloud, based on presentations Meyer has made at conferences of the American Educational Research Association, and his analysis of audience response during professional development seminars. Though overtly pedagogical, theatre is used purposefully here as a novel, arts-based teaching method.

The Practice

Characters

The Girls' Basketball Team: ADRIENNE, JILL, BES, MARTHA, KAREN,
MIFFY
COACH MARK JACKSON

(SCENE: the final practice of the Senior Girls' Basketball Team late in the afternoon, just before the final tournament of the season; it is after a break; all the team members are female and consider themselves "high overachievers"; MARK JACKSON is a veteran teacher and has coached for many years; in the scenario, "Jappy" is a slang expression for Jewish American Princess)

JILL: We don't need this practice.

ADRIENNE: You can say that again. He nailed us last week with that lame "beat the press" drill. Shit, why don't we just cancel this practice, we're all just too busy.

BES: Fat chance.

MARTHA: Regardless—We demanded to be in this tournament and the school's arranged all types of schedule changes—the play rehearsals, some due dates for papers . . .

JILL: OK, OK, let's just get it over with. We all have a million things to do.

MARTHA: Fine. I missed Banggor's class yesterday—does anyone have the notes?

KAREN: *(to ADRIENNE)* Yeah, we know. We also know that this practice isn't going to be canceled. That's not going to happen, so let's just deal with it. That tournament is this weekend. Every little bit might help.

ADRIENNE: Come off it—you need the practice, I don't.

KAREN: What's that supposed to mean?

ADRIENNE: Exactly that, Karen. You're the weakest member of the team. You have two left feet and you can't dribble worth shit. We're here to support you.

MIFFY: Come off it, Adrienne. If I recall, you haven't been shooting anything close to 50% for weeks. At least Karen hasn't been giving Coach any crap. If you're so pissed off, then quit and stop with the Jappy attitude, it's giving us all a bad name.

JILL: *(to MARTHA)* Not again. *(to MIFFY and ADRIENNE)* Can you guys just stop? Give it a rest. We're sick of hearing you go at each other . . .

MARTHA: . . . all the bloody time.

ADRIENNE: *(ignoring JILL and MARTHA, focuses on MIFFY)* Don't get so high and mighty with me, bitch. I can play you under the table anytime, anywhere. Talking about losing time and not being with it—if you weren't screwing Bobby every hour on the hour, maybe your game would improve a bit.

MIFFY: Who the fuck do you think you are? My game is on and—furthermore, Miss "I'm the greatest thing since sliced bread"—at least I'm getting some. I hear you've been dry for months since David dropped you.

ADRIENNE: You slut! *(lunges at MIFFY; a fight begins; other players try to break it up)*

KAREN: *(pulling off MIFFY who is besting ADRIENNE; BES pulls away ADRIENNE)* Enough! You guys want to get suspended? The Coach would do anything to cancel this trip. Grow up. Fighting will get you off the team.

ADRIENNE: *(screaming at MIFFY)* Just stay away from me, slut! That goes for all of you. Without me you'd all be nowhere.

(the group all stares at ADRIENNE; no one speaks; ADRIENNE realizes what she has said and attempts to apologize)

Look, I'm sorry. I didn't mean that, really. I didn't— I'm sorry, Miffy. I just lost it. I've just had it up to here and . . .

(COACH enters)

COACH: OK, girls, let's get going. Bes—start the pattern drill. *(no one moves)* Girls, I said move! *(they begin to move toward the center of the gym)*

ADRIENNE: Coach, I really don't want to practice this stupid drill anymore— we know it cold.

COACH: I disagree with you, Adrienne—you don't. And we play our first game against Cliffordville. They'll cream us unless we get our defense up.

ADRIENNE: Oh, come off it, Coach, we won this tournament last year.

COACH: No, Adrienne, we barely squeaked through the round robin last year. Cliffordville was the team that beat us—and we've lost to them twice this year already. Now, if you don't want to practice today, don't bother getting on the bus tomorrow after school when we leave. Understood?

ADRIENNE: That's not fair! I work 300%. How dare you talk to me that way? *(everyone stops and stares)*

COACH: I don't agree. You haven't been working, cooperating, or contributing. You've hogged the ball all practice and, not just this one but all season your shooting has been abysmal, and you don't pass the ball. Frankly—and I've told you this many times before—your heart is not in this team.

ADRIENNE: How dare you say that? Give me one example of how I haven't contributed!

COACH: Adrienne, we have no time for that. Now, *(to everyone)* can we please finish off this practice?

ADRIENNE: No, we're not going to finish off this practice until you give me an answer.

MIFFY: *(aside to ADRIENNE)* Adrienne, stop it, you're pushing him.

ADRIENNE: Bullshit, Coach, I'm waiting for an answer!

COACH: I'm not going to respond to you. *(to the team)* Now, let's start drill pattern Omega.

ADRIENNE: I'm not doing this stupid, lame drill.

COACH: Adrienne—you're benched for the remainder of the practice.

ADRIENNE: You can't do that!

COACH: Yes, I can.

ADRIENNE: How dare you? Who do you think you are?

COACH: *(after a few moments and staring her down)* You know the rules— if you're not going to work, you sit.

ADRIENNE: *(screaming at COACH)* Well, if I sit, we all sit!

COACH: What is that supposed to mean?

ADRIENNE: Well, if *you* bench me, the team walks!

COACH: *(to the team)* Is this true? *(no one responds)* Then you've decided. Fine. The tournament's off, and so is the team. I'm withdrawing the team from the conference. Leave your uniforms in the gym office. *(he turns away and begins to walk out)*

ADRIENNE: You have some goddamned nerve! You can't just drop the team! Who the hell do you think you are?

COACH: *(exasperated)* The coach, Little Miss Bitch.

ADRIENNE: Well, this "Little Miss Bitch" is pissed off, Coach Asshole. I'm going to nail you with the Principal.

MIFFY: Stop!

KAREN: Please, both of you—this is out of hand!

BES: Adrienne, chill! Sir, please, I'm sure Adrienne didn't mean what she said.

KAREN: Sir, please—I'm sure you didn't mean to call her a "bitch." We really do want to go to . . .

ADRIENNE: Listen, he called me a "bitch" *(turns toward COACH)* and my parents are going to get you fired, Coach Asshole, and that's that.

COACH: Just because you're a spoiled Jappy bitch who can manipulate your friends and parents, doesn't equate to manipulating me. Now—all of you—the team is finished, the season is ended. Leave your uniforms in the office. I'll inform the Principal.

Wearing the Secret Out

BY JENNIFER CHAPMAN,
ANNE SWEDBERG, AND HEATHER SYKES

Editor's Introduction

Wearing the Secret Out portrays "the real-life experiences of nonheterosexual physical education teachers, and is performed in teacher education classrooms to discuss homophobia and heterosexism in teaching and learning environments" (Chapman, Sykes, & Swedberg, 2003, p. 27). The play's specific pedagogical purpose during performance and post-performance discussions is to examine "identity politics and how they play out in schools, particularly in relationship to sexual identity," and to analyze how the ideologies of heterosexism and homophobia "exist in subtle and overt forms among teachers and youth" (p. 28).

Sykes, a professor of kinesiology and physical education (also known as exercise science), conducted life history interviews with eighteen gay, lesbian, and queer physical education teachers as part of her ongoing research in relationships between sexual identity, teaching, and learning. She originally intended to publish her findings in her discipline's journals in standard article formats. But at a curriculum theory conference she witnessed ethnodramatic presentations in reader's theatre formats (Goldstein, 2001a). Excited by this method of presentation and representation for her own life history research, she collaborated with Chapman and Swedberg, two trained actors and theatre education specialists, all of whom instructed at the University of Wisconsin, Madison.

The three worked together on the development of the piece during rehearsals, and found themselves in continuous dialogue and debate over the content, structure, and staging of the research. Most notable was finding the proper balance between research as art and art as research—a tension that surfaces when nonartists in education and social sciences apply the criteria and rhetoric of "scientific" ethnographic writing onto artistic, dramatic form. One solution that emerged during rehearsals (which was to prove later in performance as a brilliant concept) was to discard the reader's theatre approach "because of our desire to involve the body as text, to find these embodied metaphors for the scripted text, and thus to move rather than remain seated throughout the piece" (p. 31).

Reader's theatre has the potential—and danger—for creating didactic work. This is the "talking heads" syndrome in which the writer feels that the focus on text permits and justifies the inclusion of philosophical and theoretical content, resulting in a stagnant, nondramatic narrative. Actors are trained to express not only with their voices but also with their bodies, and are thus freer and more comfortable moving in front of audiences. In fact, the impulse to move is indoctrinated into the trained performer who eventually senses intuitively when the character's monologue and dialogue justify the need to gesture or traverse the performance space to communicate the character's objectives and emotional states. Directors and acting teachers sometimes coach their students by prompting them, "Trust your body—it knows what it's doing," a principle developed and cultivated by the acknowledged founder of realistic acting methods, Constantin Stanislavski. Chapman and Swedberg, as the performers of *Wearing the Secret Out*, trusted what their bodies and artistic impulses were telling them. During rehearsals, the actors explored how the participant's stories could be physically realized—not through realistic movement, but through choreographed, symbolic gesture. In retrospect, Sykes noted that "[our] focus on physical education—a body of knowledge and a knowledge of body—has a curious resonance with performed ethnography" (p. 32).

When I saw *Wearing the Secret Out* performed at the American Educational Research Association conference, I was impressed with the production's elegant artistry and visual impact. Chapman and Swedberg presented the participants' stories simply, directly, and with utmost respect. The physicality of the production was arresting—the symbolic movements, gestural motifs, and writing on their bodies elaborated on the participants' narratives. The play *in perfor-*

mance "evokes resonances between the body and the methodology, between the research focus and its embodied representation" (p. 32). Readers may not receive the full impact of *Wearing the Secret Out* since its ideal presentation is a live performance, not a printed script. A videotape recording of the production is a second-preference mode since the intimacy and humanity of the piece may be lost through electronic mediation.

As I stated in the anthology's introduction, the collaboration between qualitative researchers and theatre artists has the potential to develop a stronger artistic and ethnographic product than if either developed the work on their own. From my perspective, Chapman, Sykes, and Swedberg created what theatre practitioners call "a perfect gem" with *Wearing the Secret Out*.

Wearing the Secret Out

Production Notes

The structure of this performance piece lies somewhere in-between a play, performance art, and classroom teaching. We are both authors and performers of this piece, and so the dialogue of the text is designated for Heather, Anne, or Jennifer. We prefer to perform *Wearing the Secret Out* in a large classroom with students sitting in chairs that are pushed back to give us a bit of room in order to give us an intimate relationship with our students/audience, and also to emphasize the fact that the performance is only a part of the whole experience. The discussion that we lead following the performance is an integral part of the teaching/learning experience.

In the text that follows, our first names are used to indicate who is doing what (we don't play continuous "characters" throughout the piece, so it's easier to simply use our own names). The actions and explanations are in italics. Although the text is divided into sections based on themes and/or performance techniques, all of the transitions throughout the performance should be fluid. The text below refers to a "stage" (downstage, center stage, etc.), describing the area of classroom space that we perform in. The "stage" should be set up with a table upstage center and two chairs facing one another at an angle in front of it. Both Anne and Jennifer wear sweatpants, tennis shoes, and white tank tops with three white t-shirts worn in layers that will be taken off during the performance. Heather is not physically present during the performance, though her voice is heard on a recording. She is, however, an important part of the introduction and following discussion.

We begin by describing the research project that led to this performance: Heather Sykes interviewed many people who teach and/or coach in the field of physical education who self-identify as "nonheterosexual" about their life experiences that affect pedagogical choices. We explain that it is important to protect the anonymity of the interview participants. Stories and statements are placed so that the audience should not be able to locate an individual at a specific school or region. However, because we want the audience to understand that the interview subjects occupy different identity locations than us, we "wear" information about the interview subjects on our various t-shirts that are removed in performance. Finally, we explain that the agreement that Heather made with the Human Subjects Committee at the University of Wisconsin-Madison required that we keep all interview material intact. So, everything the audience is about to hear are verbatim statements and stories, though we occasionally omitted an "um" or a pause to keep things moving along.

Wearing the Secret Out was initially funded by the University of Wisconsin-Madison's Virginia Horne Henry fund for studies in Physical Education. If you would like a DVD copy of the performance, please contact Jennifer Chapman at jchapman@albion.edu.

(stage/classroom space set with a table up center and two chairs, stage right and left, facing each other on a diagonal; ANNE and JENNIFER stand back-to-back center stage; as the recording of HEATHER's voice begins {below}, they fall into one another's bodies; for most of the recording, ANNE and JENNIFER engage in contact improvisation)

HEATHER: *(a recording of 2 minutes, 30 seconds)* One of my worries about the piece is that we had to leave out so much. There were so many stories that we wanted to include, and indeed interviews, um, with other people in the project, that haven't been shared in this piece.

(ANNE and JENNIFER push off from each other; ANNE moves to the upstage left corner and JENNIFER moves to the downstage right corner; during the remainder of the recording, JENNIFER turns and faces ANNE who blows the gym whistle, signaling "start")

(both performers walk around the performance space, moving in a figure 8 pattern on a diagonal between upstage left and downstage right; ANNE blows the whistle when she and JENNIFER are across the space from each other; both freeze; ANNE looks at JENNIFER, who faces the audience; JENNIFER removes her first white "identity" t-shirt with PROFESSOR, BIRACIAL, LESBIAN written across the front in a list; she performs the gesture sequence: crosses her arms over her body once in a hug; raises her right hand, elbow out, to shield her face, which she turns to the side; when she completes the gesture sequence, ANNE blows the whistle, and both begin to move again)

(this time, ANNE blows the whistle when JENNIFER is in the downstage left corner of the stage; both freeze; JENNIFER removes her next t-shirt with MIDDLE SCHOOL, WHITE, LESBIAN written across the front in a list; JENNIFER does the gesture sequence and ANNE then blows the whistle, signaling "start" again)

(the third and final time ANNE blows the whistle, they are very close, with ANNE positioned just behind and slightly to the side of JENNIFER; the front of JENNIFER's t-shirt now reads PROFESSOR, LATINA, LESBIAN; but this time, JENNIFER turns and faces upstage toward ANNE, who is behind her; this allows the audience to see the fourth interviewee identity, written on the back of the same t-shirt: GRAD STUDENT, WHITE, QUEER)

(ANNE blows the whistle; JENNIFER faces the audience once again and removes the third t-shirt; she has a plain white tank top underneath the three layers of shirts; ANNE scoops up all three t-shirts from the floor, walks upstage, and throws them under the table as JENNIFER repeats the gesture sequence for the last time; ANNE freezes as she faces downstage toward the audience; when JENNIFER makes the gesture shielding her face, ANNE watches; at the end, both freeze for a beat; this final moment should happen about the same time that Heather is finished speaking on the recording {below})

HEATHER: *(the recording continues during the action above)* And I'm not sure whether the piece manages to strike a balance between the difficulties that homophobia creates in students' and teachers' lives in physical education—and those are very real—versus the pleasures and the rich experiences that lesbian, queer, bisexual, and gay teachers bring into the profession. I'm not sure whether we've managed to strike that balance. As a researcher, this has been challenging for me, because after conducting the interviews, typically I think about them a lot, I do a lot of reading, and write for a long period of time making interpretations about what was said in those interviews. Those interpretations focus on gender relations, how identities are formed over lifetimes, and the politics of education. And in this piece those interpretations haven't been included. This is focused only on what was said in the actual interviews. So that's been very challenging for me. But ultimately, my hope for this piece and the reason, um, it's come into being, and I've been working with people in drama education and in theatre, is that it will give us a safe way to start talking about homophobia in physical education. So that really is my hope and we'll see whether the piece manages to do that for us.

(ANNE crosses to sit in the upstage left chair; JENNIFER crosses upstage and sits on the table)

JENNIFER: I do this life history research because I'm in teacher education and I'm trying to understand how change happens in Phys Ed.

ANNE: And the big question I'm after is, how do we change homophobia, especially within this profession?

JENNIFER: Some people are just beginning to say, well maybe we should have something in the curriculum in teacher education, so that student teachers are made aware of the fact that there are lesbians in sport, there are lesbians in schools and in the world, and maybe that awareness will help them down the road.

ANNE: *(stands and walks downstage center)* I mean, there have been some efforts to make schools safe for lesbian, gay, transgender children. *(ANNE crosses to the downstage right corner and addresses the audience)* But that seems a long way from what we do in the gym sometimes.

JENNIFER: *(stands and begins to speak the same line; she crosses to the downstage left corner)* I mean, there have been some efforts to make schools safe for lesbian, gay, transgender children. But that seems a long way from what we do in the gym sometimes.

ANNE: *(repeats the phrase as she begins to walk backwards along the stage right side of the space)* But that seems a long way from what we do in the gym sometimes.

JENNIFER AND ANNE: *(repeat, vocally overlapping as they back diagonally across the space and bump into each other; ANNE and JENNIFER gently collide, breaking off in mid-sentence)* But that seems a long way from what we do in the gym sometimes.

* * *

(JENNIFER crosses upstage left, ANNE upstage right; JENNIFER walks downstage, straight along the left edge of the performance space, and starts speaking)

JENNIFER: We're just starting the second interview with, um, Donna and we were just chit chatting about the class she's just taught and now we're getting into talking about teacher-student crushes, so that's where we're gonna start right now.

ANNE: *(moving downstage along the right-hand edge of the performance space)* Since we discussed that in class today.

JENNIFER: *(backing toward the upstage left corner)* Let me make sure I'm on, yeah, and we've got new batteries so we should be set. Um, carry on with what happened in the discussion this afternoon in the class with Special Ed students.

ANNE: *(from the downstage right corner)* Today, conversation started with a presentation that students put on in regards to Down's Syndrome. And the conversation somehow twisted to sexuality, *(ANNE starts backing diagonally toward upstage left, JENNIFER starts backing toward downstage right, so both are backing into each other along the diagonal)* or I helped guide it in that direction, to discuss that the students we work with are not asexual, *(both pivot, avoiding contact with each other, and continue on diagonal to their corners, so that ANNE arrives upstage left and JENNIFER arrives downstage right)* that they do have relationships—and we were talking about adults and some of the adult programs and stuff, then one of the students asked,

JENNIFER: *(speaks as if she is a student)* Donna, have you ever dealt with a student having a crush on you?

(ANNE makes "crush gesture": hand to mouth, sharp intake of breath, knees slightly bent)

ANNE: And I said, "As a matter of fact, yes, and the first time it occurred was during my student teaching." *(ANNE walks from upstage right to downstage left, along the left-hand edge of the performance space)* I asked them did they want to discuss it—we'd talked about certain things in their curriculum they may have been missing out on, and they decided they had never heard anyone in the Ed department discuss what do you do if a student has a crush. *(JENNIFER makes the "crush" gesture)* I've told them on many occasions, if something comes up that they're missing, let's go there, you know, and so one of them basically said,

JENNIFER: *(raises her hand as if she is a student in class)* This is missing in my curriculum, I've kind of been curious.

ANNE: *(continues, walking toward the downstage right corner)* And I'm like, okay, let's go there, and so we all moved our chairs around, got into a circle and just did a seminar kind of thing on what do you do if a student has a crush. *(JENNIFER repeats "crush" gesture)* So I told them about my scenario. I told them that yes, you know, I did have a student that had a crush *(JENNIFER repeats "crush" gesture)* on me. I basically just gave them the scenario and said that it did blow me away, absolutely blew me away, the crush *(JENNIFER repeats "crush" gesture)* that did occur.

JENNIFER: How old were you both?

ANNE: She was 17 and I was 22, 23 at the most—that's pretty young, within 4 years of one another.

* * *

(JENNIFER crosses upstage to grab a sheet, which she drops over ANNE's head, encircling her body as ANNE reaches center; ANNE picks up the megaphone and crosses to center, speaking the following line into the megaphone)

ANNE: Of course there are lesbians on our basketball team and our coach was lesbian, but of course people didn't talk about it publicly but everyone knew.

(at the end of the line, ANNE freezes as the sheet comes around her; she bends slowly to set the megaphone down and rises in slow motion as the tug-of-war begins and JENNIFER begins speaking)

JENNIFER: I guess I don't think it would be good for my students to know—it's like, what more of a role model could they have, if they've already decided they like me. They make statements like, "I've never met a gay person," and I make statements like, "Yes you have, you just don't know it." *(raises sheet to shoulder, then high above head, pulling in opposite directions, ANNE facing downstage and JENNIFER facing upstage)*

ANNE: *(twists her end of the sheet around her body, turns upstage to face JEN-NIFER, turns JENNIFER to face out and supports her weight as she goes all the way down to the floor, face down, and then ANNE pulls JENNIFER back up to standing again)* I'm out as somebody who supports all marginalized groups of people, so basically I don't tell everybody, "Hello, here I am, I'm gay." But I'm out to them as somebody who celebrates diversity in all ways.

JENNIFER: But I do have a fear, I do have a fear of being in a group and saying, "Hey, I'm your teacher and I live with a woman." I think I would have a hard time doing that.

ANNE: I'm queer. If I have to say it, I'm queer. And so it's really hard for me, there's dissonance when somebody says, "Well, are you a lesbian?" To say yes means you're putting me in this category where I don't know if I belong. I'm in a relationship with a woman though I may not identify as a lesbian.

(at about this point, ANNE is pulling away from JENNIFER, facing upstage toward JENNIFER, gradually lowering herself to the floor with both hands holding the sheet between her legs as ANNE sits)

JENNIFER: I'm at a different stage in my pride as a Latina than I am in my pride as a lesbian. If I were at a cocktail party I'd be happy to contribute to a conversation based on my standpoint as a Latina. Depending on the crowd, I wouldn't so readily say, "Well, as a lesbian this is how I feel."

(JENNIFER pulls ANNE back to her feet, then ANNE takes the other end of the sheet from JENNIFER as she pulls it around her neck, so the sheet is crossed behind JENNIFER's back—this "strangling" pose usually occurs as JENNIFER is talking about being silenced as a high school teacher—then JENNIFER works the sheet down her body and bends backwards, as though about to do a backbend, but not all the way to the floor)

ANNE: Usually I have my rainbow bracelets on. And it becomes apparent where I'm coming from. I know the students are sitting there and they're looking at me, and I've got the short hair, and the polo shirt, or whatever. So I come at it kind of in an underneath way where I'll give them all the clues, and then they'll make the connection.

JENNIFER: I think I'd make one hell of a high school teacher if I could be as open with high school kids as I am with college kids, and I think I just need to deal with the fact that at this time society's not ready for me at that level.

ANNE: I have never used the words "lesbian" or "homosexual" in my class.

JENNIFER: I think I pick and choose my battles and I don't think the lecture hall is the best place to do it.

ANNE: I have to try harder to be me, to be my natural me.

(at about this point, JENNIFER has returned to standing, and ANNE releases the piece of sheet extending to her left, or JENNIFER's right, snapping the sheet into the full tug-of-war)

(JENNIFER and ANNE are now circling each other in the tug-of-war, the sheet extended between them)

JENNIFER: So what I tell people is that, you know, I, the first time that I like totally came out, it was out of anger because I'd had it, I'd had it with things being yelled down the hallway.

ANNE: I knew you couldn't be fired for being gay in California.

JENNIFER: I don't really know who knows and who doesn't know.

ANNE: I'm fairly visible when there is a gay function.

JENNIFER: It was never hidden, it just was never explicitly stated.

ANNE: I think being out would help a lot of people. You know, I think it would help a lot of people.

(JENNIFER simply drops her end of the rope, releasing all tension, exchanges a glance with ANNE as she begins to speak and moves to the chair upstage; ANNE moves into downstage right chair in audience, drops the sheet under the chair and removes her whistle)

JENNIFER: All the students know. I've been that way now for about six years. . . . I think that I just sorta came to the whole topic of being out, 'cause you were asking, how out am I at my school? About six years ago it was a week before school let out or two weeks before school let out . . . I had walked out of my classroom over to my office to get something and a student yelled from a doorway, "Coach Schneider's gay!" and I kept walking 'cause there were two teachers standing right outside the door talking and the child yelled it again, and when I got to my office, rather than turn around, out of the corner of my eye I could see that the adults had continued their conversation, they'd never interjected at all. So when I got what I needed out of my office I went back to the classroom and I went right to the child sitting right by the door and I said, "I need to see you outside." And I said, "Okay, who yelled that about me from your class?" "I didn't, I didn't!" And I said, "No, I know you did not. I want to know who did because I know you were sitting there and I know if I could hear it as far away as I was, you heard it and you know who it is." And so she told me what boy so I came back to the door and I called them outside. I think I called like one or two and they gave up the third guy who had been standing there. I pulled them outside and I said to them, "I don't have a problem with the fact that I'm gay. I have a problem when I'm disrespected for it." And I said, "I don't disrespect you, I don't expect you to disrespect me. Does that sound fair?" "Yeah." Then I went back to my classroom and on the walk over, I just thought, okay, do you go back in the room and say, "I'm sorry it took me longer, I had to deal with something," or do I tell them what I had to deal with. And I got back in the room and I decided to tell them what I had to deal with, so I brought them all and I sat them down on the floor and I said, you know, I basically just repeated it . . .

ANNE: Right.

JENNIFER: . . . to the class. And then kids asked some questions. Which I can't specifically recall, I just remember being rather impressed with what they did ask because a lot of it was, you know, "When did you know?" and "Does your family know?" and "How are they about it?" and, of course we got to, "Do you have a girlfriend?" and "How do you do it?" At which point I said, "Okay, well, that's not appropriate for the classroom."

ANNE: Right.

JENNIFER: Well, this is a group of sixth graders, and when they left the room they went over to their room, uh, and started the buzz talking about it. And about an hour later my principal comes out to my room and says, "How's it going?" I said, "Good." He said, "Oh. Did you happen to talk about your personal life today in class?" I said, "Yes, a situation came up and I felt it was appropriate to comment on it." And basically I told him what had happened. Well, what he told me was that, I guess several of the students got back to the classroom and they were talking about it and the teacher sent them up to him, and what he was being told was that I had said to the kids was that I get all hot and bothered in the locker room, uh, when I'm watching the girls. And, I said "No," and I told him, "Well, apparently not only do your students need to be educated but apparently your teachers also need to be educated. Because there's just no way I would ever have said anything like that and they should have responded differently. They don't need to validate what the girls were saying by sending them up to you, you know. . . ."

ANNE: So, just to clarify a bit, after you had gone back to your room and had that conversation with them, they had gone back to their own room and they were sent to the principal because they were saying you get all hot and bothered?

JENNIFER: Well, they were telling the kids what I had said in class, basically they were telling the kids that I came out in class and they were repeating the conversation and that was—

ANNE: But why were they sent to the principal's, because the teachers just heard them talking about the fact that you'd come out?

JENNIFER: 'Cause the teachers didn't know how to deal with it.

ANNE: Or because they were disrespecting you and saying that—

JENNIFER: 'Cause the teachers don't know how to deal with it. The teachers don't know to say, "Well I don't know what Coach Schneider said in her class but right now you're in my class, this is what we're focused on and I will talk to Coach Schneider later about what, what happened in class." The teachers don't know how to deal with it and that's what they chose to do.

. . .

ANNE AND JENNIFER: (*in unison as they walk center stage and stand side-by-side, JENNIFER stage left, ANNE stage right*) How do you cope with all that stuff when you're in the moment of teaching?

ANNE: (*crosses to downstage right corner, saying*) I'm trying to understand . . . I'm trying to understand . . . I'm trying to understand how change happens in Phys Ed.

JENNIFER: (*vocally overlaps, repeating the phrases*) I'm in teacher education. How do we change homophobia?

ANNE: (*removes her first identity t-shirt which reads ELEMENTARY SCHOOL, WHITE, GAY MAN in a list as she moves into chanting*) There are lesbians in sport . . . there are lesbians in schools . . . there are lesbians in the world. (*each time ANNE removes a shirt, JENNIFER mimes doing the same*)
   (*ANNE removes her second identity t-shirt, which reads PROFESSOR, BIRACIAL, LESBIAN; the identity on the third t-shirt beneath it reads: PROFESSOR, LATINA, LESBIAN*)

(ANNE turns her back to reveal the fourth identity: ELEMENTARY SCHOOL, WHITE, LESBIAN-MOTHER and says) I mean, there have been some efforts to make schools safe for lesbian, gay, transgender children. But that seems a long way from what we do in the gym sometimes. *(ANNE walks to the upstage right corner and repeats)* But that seems a long way from what we do in the gym sometimes.

JENNIFER: *(in downstage left corner, vocally overlaps)* But that seems a long way from what we do in the gym sometimes.

(JENNIFER mimes removing the shirt; ANNE matches her with removing the third identity t-shirt; at the end, ANNE moves to sit in the upstage left chair)

* * *

ANNE: She was 17 and I was 22, 23 at the most—that's pretty young, within 4 years of one another.

JENNIFER: That's a young teacher!

ANNE: And I'm sure I looked pretty young, too. So anyway, she wasn't a student of mine, she just found out about me and knew I had a similar background. So she would come to the gym and just hang out. This student was really very articulate, I mean, most of the time when she'd leave my office I'd be looking up a word that she said that I didn't understand. Very smart, very well read, more so than myself. And so we would spend a lot of lunchtimes together, and then she started coming to my softball practices, so I thought maybe, hey, she's got an interest in softball. So I'd encourage her to come play. And then notes started showing up via my softball pitcher. And I went, oh, that's a little odd, but I didn't really say anything, they were very innocent, there was no . . . idea of any kind of crush within them at all. They were just, "how's your day," you know, "didn't get a chance to see you," you know, kind of thing. So that was very innocent, but I was sorta like, hmmm, what's up with that? . . . With her staying at practices and stuff I finally went up to her and said, "Are you sure you don't want to play softball, you're always here watching, you'd probably be really good. You're very athletic, why don't you try it out?" She goes,

JENNIFER: *(as if she is the student, walking downstage center)* That's not what I'm interested in. *(JENNIFER begins a gesture sequence: hug chest, then turn face away from audience and shield face with right hand; repeat three times; this should overlap with ANNE's dialogue below)*

ANNE: Just flat out said it and I just said, "What do you mean?" I was clueless, and she goes,

JENNIFER: *(as the student, still down center stage)* That's not what I'm interested in, I'm interested in you. *(JENNIFER continues gesture sequence)*
ANNE: Just a 17-year-old kid.
(JENNIFER falls back—should look like a "trust fall"; ANNE quickly moves behind JENNIFER as she continues speaking, so that ANNE is in position to catch JENNIFER as soon as she falls)
I mean I had not experienced that with any other woman or any other man to that point in my life. Anybody that straight out with me and that straight up with me.
ANNE AND JENNIFER: *(in unison, repeated)* How do you cope with all that stuff when you're in the moment of teaching?
(the "trust fall" ends in a freeze, then both actors move to their chairs; ANNE moves her stage left chair slightly downstage center so it will be in position at the end of the writing sequence)

. . .

JENNIFER: *(seated in stage right chair; looks up from the journal she is already in the process of reading silently and begins to read out loud)* Inner City Middle School, California, 1993. My principal, he already knew because the year I got back from San Diego I was in science and then he wanted me to go back out to P.E. and I told him, I said, "I don't know if you're aware of it or not but I am a lesbian and I'm probably gonna get a lot more politically active so I don't know how that figures in your decision of where you want me to be." He looked at me and he said, "Well, I am aware of it and I'm not worried about it because I expect you to behave as you have been and this is professional and I don't see it being an issue." And I said, "Fine."
(JENNIFER closes journal and remains seated, listening to ANNE)
ANNE: *(looks up from her journal and begins to read it aloud)* First year of Coaching Cross-Country and Track, State College, Nevada, 1990. I had a class with some of them and one night—it was February 'cause it was a cold time of the year—a number of the assistant coaches said, "Why don't you come out with us, you never go out and have a beer with us" and I said, "All right." So I go out and it's a favorite spot in this little town and we were having chicken wings, I remember, and beer. And we're sitting and talking and I remember clearly thinking, "All right, these guys aren't so bad, you know, I just thought they were assholes but they're not so bad." And I remember him coming over and sitting next to me and starting up

this conversation about how it was for me to be back and coaching and how I liked it.

(JENNIFER crosses over to ANNE, who is seated, stands behind her, places a hand on her shoulder, and looks at the journal, as if reading, as ANNE continues speaking)

He says, um, "You know when people heard you were coming back there was a lot of excitement, you know you're really well thought of and I'd heard a lot of good things about you," and I'm just kind of sitting there thinking "okay, okay" and he says

(JENNIFER leans both arms on ANNE's shoulders so that she is in a position of dominance)

JENNIFER: Uh, you know, there's one thing, boy, everybody's, everybody's asking, you know, she's coming back here and the one thing nobody knows is do you eat men or do you eat women?

ANNE: And, and I remember just feeling warm and there I was, I mean there's like ten people at this table. I was just stunned, and out of the corner of my eye someone stood up and yelled, "What the fuck are you doing? You don't talk to her like that!" And he was like—

JENNIFER: *(resumes speech, as if talking to others in the bar)* No, sit down. I want her to answer this question. I want her to answer this question. People want to know—does she eat men or does she eat women?

ANNE: *(breaks free, stands up, moves downstage center as JENNIFER backs away)* And I, I just, I just, I panicked and I, there was a pitcher of beer and I threw it and got up, I let the chair fall and I ran and they, he and two other guys chased me home. I got home, had to call the police. And they were outside yelling, you know, "Come out!" and "Fucking tell us!" And it was horrible. It was horrible. *(ANNE looks up from the journal out to the audience)*

* * *

(all of the "writing" in the following section should be done with a large, washable marker; words are written on ANNE and JENNIFER's tank tops as well as their skin that is showing {such as arms, necks, hands, etc.}; the writing should be big enough to be seen by the audience)

(JENNIFER grabs a megaphone and positions herself at center as she broadcasts; ANNE grabs two markers, uncaps them, kneels in front of JENNIFER, and writes THAT'S SO GAY on JENNIFER's chest as JENNIFER speaks her lines below)

JENNIFER: *(speaking into the megaphone)* You ask a gay man what's the most homophobic setting in your middle, your high school experience, what does he say? It's not music, it's not art class, it's not English, it's P.E., it's in the locker room, it's in the gym teacher, the macho, you know, domineering, toe the line or you'll be a sissy, you know. In P.E.
(JENNIFER bends over, puts the megaphone on the ground, and freezes; ANNE writes the word FAG on JENNIFER's back as she speaks her lines below)

ANNE: When is it okay to take a stand and call something unacceptable?
(ANNE freezes; JENNIFER writes DYKE across ANNE's breasts as she speaks her lines below)

JENNIFER: I observed a student call another a fag, right literally five feet from the teacher, and the teacher said nothing. I mean, turned his back and walked away. It was a male teacher. Now the question is, I'm going to give him the benefit of the doubt . . . that he didn't know what to do, he didn't know what intervention to use, so he walked away. *(JENNIFER freezes; ANNE writes CARPETMUNCHER on JENNIFER's right arm, LESBO on her chest, RECRUITER on her left arm, SISSY on her back, and IT'S A STAGE on the back of an arm while she speaks her lines below)*

ANNE: We were talking about sexual orientation in my class and how would you work with a teenager in the trades, and in areas like that, in Ag, in P.E., in art. You tend to have kids tell you things, and that's what we were discussing, you tend to have kids tell you things that you may not necessarily want to hear. What do you do if a kid comes out to you and tells you he's gay? And my student raises his hand and he goes, "Well, first of all, I'm an Ag-Ed teacher and there aren't any gay kids. And if somebody did say they were gay I would just basically tell them that I love them as a student but that I believe in God and I believe in the Bible and they're wrong and they're going to hell. But I love them because they're a student in my class."
(ANNE freezes; JENNIFER holds ANNE's arm out and writes BUTT-FUCKER across it while she speaks her lines below)

JENNIFER: So this needs to be an environment where we can say what we're thinking and we will think before we say it and make sure we're not being hurtful to someone in particular. But we need to be able to say what we're thinking and deal with these issues. *(JENNIFER freezes; ANNE writes UNACCEPTABLE and DYKE on whatever space is left available on JENNIFER's body while she speaks her lines below)*

ANNE: Because the thing of it is, you can say "no name calling," but there isn't any ability to educate about the humanness of the people that are behind those names. Because I can't stand up to them and say, "Well, I'm a lesbian." For whatever reason, I don't feel that's acceptable as a professional person for me to do, that I would then be called a recruiter—I don't feel like I can do that.

(ANNE freezes; JENNIFER writes FAGGOT on whatever space is left available on ANNE's body as she speaks her lines below)

JENNIFER: You're not going to be able to give a course in tolerance to students when you can't even say "gay and lesbian" in a North Carolina middle school or high school. So the only thing you can do is use behaviors, and hopefully the teacher behavior is going to be modeled by the students, or that's the goal.

* * *

(JENNIFER speaks as she moves to the chair center stage and stands on it; ANNE moves in front of her so that they are both standing/facing the same direction, but on different levels; both face downstage and make eye contact with audience members as they speak)

JENNIFER: See, this is what I'm really interested in . . . how your experiences influence your decision to go into the profession and then translate into pedagogy and your philosophy.

ANNE: I really don't want another kid to have to grow up in the ignorance I grew up in.

JENNIFER: Because, you know, you want to treat, or I want to treat, all the students in the class as I would like to be treated if I was in that class.

* * *

ANNE AND JENNIFER: *(in unison as JENNIFER steps off chair and moves to center stage)* How do you cope with all that stuff when you're in the moment of teaching?

JENNIFER: *(repeats gesture sequence from earlier: hugs herself, turns her face away from the audience, shields her face with her right hand; completes the sequence before she begins her line)* That's not what I'm interested in. I'm interested in you.

ANNE: Just a 17-year-old kid.

(JENNIFER crosses and sits in the chair in the audience, in the downstage right area; ANNE directs all her lines to JENNIFER, as if in an interview)

I mean I had not experienced that with any other woman or any other man to that point in my life. Anybody that straight out with me and that straight up with me. And my students were like, "What did you do?" And I said, "Well, that's where the people skills just sorta showed up." And thank God they did. And I explained to the class what I said to her . . . basically I told her it was inappropriate for her and I to have a relationship because I'm a teacher and she's a student and she's going to my school. I basically told her that I believed that someday she's gonna find somebody that would be wonderful for her and that she's gonna make a great partner for somebody someday. I validated who she was.

ANNE AND JENNIFER: *(in unison)* How do you cope with all that stuff when you're in the moment of teaching?

JENNIFER: That's an amazing response considering, you know, you had no sense that this was coming, this was your having to do a whole lot of processing in a split second and then to come up, I mean that is an incredible response to give her.

ANNE: It was just working with people and being sensitive to people and that's what I said to the class, that I didn't want to tell her that no, that's not right, you know, freak out on her and leave her at this softball field by herself. *(MUSIC begins softly underneath ANNE as she continues to speak)* So that basically flattened my class when they asked it and I told them the truth, the whole nine yards—that the first experience with a crush just happened to be a woman.

(the volume of the music comes up a little as JENNIFER and ANNE begin their final figure 8 movement, reaching out to touch each other, across the shoulder on the first cross, the cheek on the second cross, and then move to the final pose: JENNIFER stands on the chair, ANNE in front of her; ANNE bends her left arm across her body, her right hand shields her face {same as gesture sequence} as JENNIFER bends around ANNE in a hug; freeze)

Ethnodramatic
Extensions

The final section of the anthology presents departures from conventional ethnodramatic texts by illustrating how realistic monologue and dialogue can be extended using a repertory of theatrical elements, devices, and techniques. The stage directions for *Wearing the Secret Out* in Part II describe how the actors juxtapose natural, verbatim interview passages with choreographed, symbolic movements and gestures. In Part III, these ethnodramas' texts, structures, stage action, and scenographic approaches are vividly "theatrical," for lack of a better term. But that should not imply that style replaces substance, or that the artist's creative vision supersedes ethnographic rigor and credibility. On the contrary, the theatrical elements in these plays—the mix of prose and poetry, unexpected departures from realism, mood music and sound effects, actors sculpting themselves into evocative images onstage—intensify character-participant representation while enhancing the presentation aesthetics of research.

All three ethnodramas in Part III utilize monologue and dialogue extracted from fieldwork, and each play exhibits variations in form and genre within itself. Jim Mienczakowski and Steve Morgan's *Baddies, Grubs & the*

Miranda Lilley, Christine Klein, Jess Sari, David Ojala, and Kate Haas as the homeless youths in *Street Rat*

Nitty-Gritty demonstrates how direct address, audience interaction, parody, irony, farce, and satire heighten the critical scrutiny of a serious social issue. Johnny Saldaña, Susan Finley, and Macklin Finley's *Street Rat* illustrates how dramatic and poetic narratives interweave, and how a narrator's function can extend beyond exposition and into Brechtian social commentary. Michael Rohd and Laura Eason's *Hidden* shows how a professional theatre ensemble, Sojourn Theatre, collaboratively developed a collage of vignettes using research as a catalyst for artistic inspiration and social change, rather than as a template for mere descriptive reportage.

Baddies, Grubs & the Nitty-Gritty

BY JIM MIENCZAKOWSKI
AND STEVE MORGAN

from *Stop! In the Name of Love*, an Ethnodrama Research Team Project

Editor's Introduction

Jim Mienczakowski, pioneer of contemporary ethnodrama and one of the subject's most prolific essayists (1995, 1996, 1997, 2001, 2003; Mienczakowski & Morgan, 2001; Mienczakowski, Smith, & Morgan, 2002), researches health issues in Australia as topics for his dramatic constructions. He and his colleagues have explored such areas as attitudes toward schizophrenia, drug and alcohol abuse and detoxification, and recovery of sexual assault victims, by interviewing patients, clients, and victims as well as the professionals involved with their care including nurses, psychologists, and police officers. Mienczakowski, Morgan, and their research teams

> use a form of critical ethnography as a means of promoting student learning, but more importantly as a mode of debate and inquiry concerning

123

health issues. Borrowing from [theatre and social activist Augusto] Boal and, at a more theoretical level, [Nobel prize-winning playwright and political satirist] Dario Fo, we attempt to give our audiences opportunities to interact with our actors, actions, and content in post-performance forums. (Mienczakowski & Morgan, 1998, p. 3)

Thus, ethnodrama is a stimulus for constituency discussion ranging from ethics to professional demeanor to problems within the health care and justice systems.

Baddies, Grubs & the Nitty-Gritty is just one portion of a larger ethnodramatic research project on trajectories of sexual assault recovery in Queensland. The focus of this act is on the police officers' perspectives. Due to its controversial content, Mienczakowski and Morgan's presentation of the play at a 1998 symposium in the United States was carefully prefaced with the history and evolution of the work:

> The core of the research has involved work with counselors and recovering victims of sexual assault. This has led us to the undeniable recognition that for many victims the reporting of a sexual assault to police represents a major milestone along the trajectory to recovery. This is not to suggest that women who decline reporting assault do not recover—a point that is made elsewhere in the script—simply that "the Police" represent a key theme. (p. 3)

The original research team consisted of a number of female respondents and researchers, yet it became imperative to examine how the police environment operated. The team noted that the ratio of male to female police officers working in Queensland's special sexual assault units was about 7:1.

Tension emerged and continued virtually throughout the project over the way the counseling staff of Sexual Assault Services felt they were depicted— even in the verbatim interview transcripts and with repeated participant checks for comment and validation. The research team had to negotiate and accommodate the rewriting demands of staff participants in a vulnerable position with possible funding cuts to their agency, and thus wanting to appear in the best possible manner for an audience of government officials and health groups. Mienczakowski and Morgan report that

> the researched support unit of Sexual Assault Services believe that their role should be revised to show them as being highly proficient and effective

counselors. They alter and "formalise" the language used in the script. We recognise their plight and are extremely concerned for their well-being and for the integrity of the research. The new script is a misleading PR exercise. The new script reads like a politically correct handbook of ideal situations and idealised outcomes. We, with the help of Sexual Assault Counselors, edit the text and agree on the validity of only part of the script. (p. 6)

Despite the commendations from sexual assault *victims* in the audience over the portrayal of their perspectives, the working relationship between the counselors and the researchers grew "cold."

The next stage of the project interviewed officers from the Police Sexual Assault Services who also displayed suspicion, mistrust, and initial resistance to the research team. Professional relationships between sexual assault staff counselors and the police were already "fragile," at best, and they again did not want to be presented in a "negative light" through this stage of ethnodramatic script development. Confronted with these ethical dilemmas, the researchers eventually secured the officers' cooperation, and the result is a portrait of "baddies" (sex offenders such as rapists or pedophiles), "grubs" (the worst and cruelest of sex offenders), and the "nitty-gritty" (detailed victim statements of the abuse and/or attack) within the culture of Queensland's Police Sexual Assault Services (Mienczakowski & Morgan, 2001, p. 226). Levity was added to the script based upon police experiences of assault interviews.

Mienczakowski and Morgan provide one final disclaimer. *Baddies, Grubs & the Nitty-Gritty* is "part of an overall project and is experimental and fluid in its construction and meanings. We are presenting data . . . and are not expressing views, characterisations or opinions that we in any way agree with. We are offering a form of data presentation and cultural critique" (Mienczakowski & Morgan, 1998, p. 4). Harsh as it may sound, the editor tells his graduate students that if they cannot study the human condition in its entirety—from its triumphs to its atrocities—then they have no business being ethnographers.

Baddies, Grubs & the Nitty-Gritty

Acknowledgments

Jim Mienczakowski and Steve Morgan extend special thanks to Kelly Wilks, Di McLeod, Amanda Smith, Amanda Curry, Jennifer O'Brien, Kirsten Fritz, and the staff and clients of the Southport Sexual Assault Support Services, Queensland.

Characters

ROB WILKINS: a police officer
SALLY: a victim of assault
COL GOLIGHTLY: an officer in charge of a sexual assault unit
PLANT: a female cast member secretly planted in the audience

Scene 1

(ROB's scene; lights down; music up)
(SLIDE: Support the person—protect the system)
(lights up; enter a 30-ish male, dressed only in underpants with a towel draped over one shoulder; there is a table stage right and one wooden chair; ROB towels himself dry and then combs his hair as if he is looking into a full-sized mirror; he speaks with the Greek/Italian accent of "hip" inner Melbourne; music out)
ROB: You're still beauutttifuull Rob. *(turns and speaks directly to audience)* Oi! Oi! *(walks into audience almost menacingly; glares aggressively at a particular audience member)* Oiye! I know you! *(relaxes; smiles)* Howyaz goin' mates? Didn't I see you down at Stars and Stripes last night? What'a night, maaate. . . . Did you see that blonde I was with—a honey, mate. With the legs all the way up. She wanted it baaaaad, mate. We were practically screwing in the club. I had me hand right up her skirt—call it a fucking skirt, mate. This security bloke came and told us to "cool off or go outside." So we did. Only fucked her on the beach—then I went back and finished me beer. I wasn't going to waste that on a fucking loose moll. She was a bit pissed off but she went away in the end. Stupid bitch. *(combs his hair again; is still in the center audience aisle; smiles.)* I know what you're

thinking—"Rob's not very nice to women"—but that is bullshit. I know how to take a woman out, mate. Show them a top time. Hire a limo, expensive restaurant, nice aftershave, expensive watch. *(makes his way back onstage)* Flash the wallet early mate—tell her she pays for nothing—ever, with Rob. Treat them special—they love it. I always tip the waiter at the beginning a $10 or $20 to make sure they treat you right and let the moll know you are serious. They love it—the slags. *(whispers)* But—you know, the funny thing is—that I find these gorgeous chicky-babes and treat 'em sweet, but after a while I just get bored, so I get 'em to do all this weird shit—you know, get them to talk dirty, filthy—say these amazing things, be like real whores, lick me balls, anything that comes into my head. And they do—the dirty filthy molls. Then I get mad and want to slap them down *(violently gestures "slapping down" a woman)*—they repulse me and I go off, mate. I don't want to go out with any girl that will agree to do what I want them to—and they all fucking do. Dirty fucking molls, the lot of them. . . . So that's why I don't ever live with them. *(in disgust)* Never know where they've been!

Some women is all right. Me mother, me sister. Good sorts. But they are hard to find and when you meet one they want marriage, kiddies, mortgages—and you know the worst thing? They got religion and they go off at you all the time. And in me sister's case, she ain't no oil painting. Know what I mean? *(laughs)* I know, I know—You think I'm a bit fucked up. But hey—I'm young and I have a bloody good time.
(puts on police officer's uniform and leaves the stage)

Scene 2

(SALLY enters; she sits on a chair center stage)
(SLIDE accompaniment)
SALLY: Well, when I was initially sexually assaulted it was around the Christmas period and I couldn't get help. I don't think funding was very good at the time but, eventually, I did speak to somebody in Brisbane, um. . . . I rang as many different organisations as I could—people were either on breaks or no one was available, so in the end I was forced to ring the police.

It was very intimidating, and the police officer I saw, er, whilst he befriended me, um . . . he actually eventually crossed the line of his professional role. Ah. . . . Well. . . . Started to come around. . . . *(long pause)* We eventually had a relationship for a while. I think he found my vulnerability and dependence, all of those things, he found them erotic.

When I went to the police . . . I wasn't . . . It wasn't offered to me to see a woman, and retelling the whole saga took eight hours. The first four hours . . . oh shit. . . .

Finally I saw him, I think I saw him about a week after it had occurred. He took me into an interview room and, ah . . . didn't record anything or anything, the door was open. I had to come back the next day and make my statement in a public office and you could have heard a pin drop—so it was quite intimidating really. Everyone could hear and there were lots of interruptions. He very kindly came in on his day off, the next day, to take my statement 'cause he saw my genuine distress. Ah, it was still pretty intimidating. I would have much preferred to talk to someone . . . a woman in an office in a sexual assault clinic. . . .

Look, the first positive thing I did after the assault was to go to the police, well before that, the first positive thing was to physically run away and hide from my assailant, the second positive thing was to go to the police. That was a really big step because it was putting all of my eggs in one basket and publicly saying "It's not my fault" . . . in front of a lot of uniformed men. So I think it was a big step in the healing process . . . and going through with the stalking charges was a big step, too, because it meant that I was saying that I count and have rights and the law should protect me.

(lights fade; SALLY exits)

Scene 3

(lights up; spot center stage; music: Down Under; enter narrator/officer COL)
(SLIDE sequence of rural and remote Oz whilst COL speaks)

COL: Baddies and Grubs, that's what we call them. Blokes who put their pants where they shouldn't—and it is our job to get them out of circulation as fast as we can.

I'm getting ahead of myself a bit there—perhaps I can give you some background . . . I'm Senior Detective Inspector Col Golightly and this is Canungarra regional police station, and you are in the headquarters of the Sexual Assault Squad. Office, desk, interview equipment, cells and files—all the usual malarkey. All the usual trappings. Canungarra is an aboriginal name meaning "evil water" or "bad spirits" or something similar. One tribal elder said that the closest interpretation of the name was "water tastes like piss" and that because of all the tannin coming down the mountains nearby from the rain-forests, it looks like piss, too. I think he was having me on.

We are right beneath Mount Warning or Wollamaharra, the storm maker or cloud gatherer. Anyway, you can always tell the quality of a place in Australia by its name. If it has an English type name it means that the first white settlers wanted it, and if it has an aboriginal name, well, the settlers thought it was crap.

So, both the first nation peoples and the first settlers thought Canungarra was crap but there are now around 350,000 people living in this region. Leastwise, people come and go around here. New population growth. 1,000 people a week were moving to Queensland not so long ago. Moving here for a few years before moving on. Moving here from foreign places or just moving away from the unemployment down south. You could buy 3 houses by the sea for the price of a town house in Melbourne or Sydney. Sun, sand and easy living—that's Queensland. Beautiful one day and perfect the next, or so they say. And it is for some. But with such a growing and fluctuating population it is hard to develop any sense of community. Malls, condominiums, canal front lifestyle. 133 golf courses—100 more courses then we have schools—it is endless. Everything must be new. Nobody wants to buy used housing stock or secondhand lifestyles. *(end SLIDE sequence)*

And there is crime and hurt, like there is anywhere. And we deal with a specific element of that, you know? Now, SA, sexual assault, is a weird type of environment for a bloke to find himself or herself in. Me? Well, I'd have to say that it was a good promotion and I was interested. My partner is also in social services and we've worked together on some cases.

If I'm really honest, I think we do the best social therapy possible. We put the grubs away. Get them off the streets—if we can stop the sexual assault counselors from stuffing up the investigation! If we can get a confession from a grub before it gets to court then that is sweet. *(ROB enters)*

But excuse me. I've got a new bloke joining the team today and we are in for a busy shift.

ROB: G'day, sir. *(salutes)*

COL: G'day. Call me Col. You're Robert Wilkins, aren't you? Where have you been stationed before, Robbo?

ROB: Did a year in Olaladullah.

COL: Shit. Hot out there—bugger all serious policing to do.

ROB: Only on a Friday night when the locals get on the grog and beat the shit out of each other. But I've spent the last 2 years on the Gold Coast.

COL: What duties?

ROB: General, lot of traffic patrols and beach patrolling.

COL: Strewth! Lot of young blokes would give their teeth to get amongst the Bay Watch parade down on the coast. All those topless bars and nude beaches. Supposed to be bloke heaven down there. Why leave?

ROB: Professional development?

COL: Really? *(pause)* Have you ever worked with a Sexual Assault Squad or on a rape case before, Rob?

ROB: No, sir.

COL: So, come on then, why did you want to come and work here?

ROB: Oh, you know—care for oppressed, fight for rights of women in society.

COL: Bollocks. Quick promotion to full detective?

ROB: Yeah, that too. But ambition isn't a crime is it?

COL: Nope. Promotion was in my mind when I joined the squad. Says here you are not married. Any plans?

ROB: I'm putting the job first until the right one comes along. Is that a problem?

COL: Hmmm. No, but "married" helps at times. "Married" keeps you on an even keel.

ROB: So, what's the go today?

COL: Glad you reminded me. Well, we had a lady making a sexual assault complaint just come in. The duty officer has taken details. She is in an interview room awaiting the arrival of the doctor and the forensic team. We'll interview her shortly to get a quick statement and then again after she's been seen by the forensic team—providing she agrees to the examination, of course. Many don't. Now you might find this interesting, this woman is complaining of being raped outside a nightclub by a guy she had been dancing with and had never met before. *(pause)* Now why would that be slightly unusual, Robert?

ROB: Most rapes are committed by relatives or friends, sir. I know, I've done the training. Anyway, it sounds suspicious to me. . . . Why has she got it in for the bloke? I know that most complaints are not vindictive but 1–6% of all complainants are found to be lying! That's still a lot, though . . .

COL: Is it?

ROB: About 30% usually withdraw when they realize what court will involve. So, what do we do?

COL: Yeah. We get a short statement from her. If we know who the baddie is we get him out of circulation first. My philosophy is that we play it softly: we are kind, polite, thoughtful, caring and considerate to victims, but we want to process the victim quick in order to get enough evidence to get the offender. We must focus on the evidence.

ROB: Will we offer support? Counselors, Sexual Assault Services? You know?

COL: Robert, in my experience the system supports a woman best by finding a perpetrator guilty which means we have to get the evidence and quickly. The special room for this stuff is downstairs. It's got a video and triple deck tape recorder. I like to get them giving evidence on video—so that if we can get that as evidence we can see her give her story—the expression on her face—see how she feels about it—see if she breaks down and cries. When that goes to a jury—pow! We will also have to ask about the nitty-gritty. So, Robert, what did they tell you on your two week training about the way we conduct interviews?

ROB: Well, let's see. Let's say a rape and fellatio and cunnilingus have occurred and all the bits and pieces . . . then we don't want her to have a cup of coffee or a cup of water. Now, she would probably like coffee or water—but if there are sperm in the mouth then we don't want to lose evidence. If she has been raped we don't want her to take a shower or get out of her clothes. So most want to go down the track of changing themselves from the event, refreshing themselves—but we want them to stay with the event until our scientific people arrive, the doctor arrives. Stay with it until we can get the drop sheet for them to put their clothes on . . . we get pubic hairs, other shit that is transferred across because of the contact. So if the man says "I never been there"—but you get 2 or 3 of his pubic hairs or something else to tie him to it or his blood group on his collar—you don't need much. Wham! And we got him!

COL: And DNA?

ROB: Or even saliva—if he had spat on her or given her a golden shower—pissed on her. With DNA that can be conclusive. This evidence can be got in a couple of hours.

COL: But the victims are naturally keen to get cleaned up. Another thing is we need to get this done quickly in order to get to the baddie before he gets a story lined up or gets away.

ROB: So we have a female cop for this interview then?

COL: No. Not one available today. Look, I might as well put you straight on this. I reckon that this women—woman stuff is all bullshit. I am a professional person and so are you, the lawyer, the doctor even. . . . I can't guarantee a jury of women only so why start now? Strewth, if this was a rape-murder and we were looking at the naked body of a deceased female victim nobody would be expressing these sensibilities. I want to be there when they gather evidence, if I'm allowed, to be able to direct the investigation. To be able to say, "Photograph that bruise," "What's made that scar?" "Take a shot of that."

Her body is a crime scene and I'm gathering evidence—to try and piece the story together and make sure it fits. Anything at all to get enough evidence for a watertight case.

Think of another crime where you have to ask permission to gather evidence or gather it secondhand through a Connie? Sometimes I'm allowed in. Sometimes I have to get a Connie, a female constable, to go in my place. It makes me sick. I don't like it. It's bad police-work.

ROB: You don't feel embarrassed for them, you know? Watching them naked with the forensics team doing their thing?

COL: Shit no. Apart from the science I'm curious about the victims, too. *(smiles knowingly)* I want to have a look. Don't you? Anyway—don't ever lose sight of the fact that our core business is just this—to gather admissible evidence! And we do it in a statement, through forensic tests on the complainant or through collecting other data like semen stains with this little gadget. *(picks up an infrared/ultra-violet torch)*

ROB: I have heard about these. How does it work?

COL: Like infrared, this special light is calibrated to show only semen stains as blue marks, when you point the light at something.

ROB: Let me see. *(points it at wall, then at COL's groin, who scowls and covers up; points at ceiling and back to COL, peering closely)* What have you been up to then? *(shines it at audience members; tries to embarrass whoever the light lands on)*

COL: All right—put that back. There are more than enough officers whose marriages are on the rocks because they've secretly taken one of these home for the weekend. . . . Curiosity isn't always a good thing.

ROB: Er, sorry. Now—in the interview, what about another female, a counselor or friend? Just for support?

COL: Maybe, but well, I reckon after 10 minutes of chitchat I have enough rapport to do this, to get the nitty-gritty. *(quieter)* Usually anyway.

ROB: So we want the nitty-gritty?

COL: Nitty-gritty, mate! The ins and outs. Who stuck what in where and how big it was and whose juices were spilt. The nitty-gritty may cause offense and can be a shock in court, but it can also make the difference between a baddie getting a 5 year or a 7 year sentence. *(puts on a sequined green jacket)*
(ROB exits)

Scene 4

(lights down; a follow-spot on COL; cabaret music in background; we are now in a Cabaret Review Bar setting)

COL: *(picks up microphone)* Ladies and Gentlemen, just while we have a chance I'd like to go over a few things with you. What a wonderful audience you've been so far. Anyone here tonight from this wonderful [city in which the performance is held] town? Wonderful. *(applause)* You have a wonderful town here and it's great to be here, isn't it everybody? *(forces applause)*

Wheewweee! What a great group of folks you all are. Anybody here from my home town? Any Australians? *(if so, what part of Australia are you from?, wonderful town, etc.)* No? No Australians? Any New Zealanders? *(if yes, where from?, wonderful town, etc.)* Great place, New Zealand, where the men are men and the sheep are nervous. . . . Only kidding. Bit of local humor.

What a great looking audience you are. Just look around this room. Such interesting looking people. I just have to learn more about you. *(comes down from the stage and finds a likely looking member of the audience)* You, sir. You are from . . . [name of place mentioned by audience member]? Now that sounds like a fine place. And how are you liking [city in which the performance is held]? *(finds another audience member)* Madam. You look like you are having a good time. And where are you from? Are you married? Do you have children? How many? *(forces audience applause)*

And when did you last have sex? Oh, come on now, this is sooo interesting. But I'm just trying to learn more about you. Come on. I'm sure you can be a little more sharing. But sorry. It's just the old policeman in me. *(goes back to the stage)*

Let's make this easy on us all. Please, everyone, sit back, close your eyes, and just relax. I want you to think about those warm, sharing moments with a loved one—or whoever. Yes. Please, all of you. Think back to the last time you had great sex—you know, fantastic sex. Earth tremor, window rattling sex—with someone else, that is. I know for some of you this will be a big memory effort, but please try. If nothing memorable stands out in your minds, try thinking back to your first sexual encounter. *(takes off jacket and resumes police officer role)*

OK. Now go over the details. Where was it? Why was it? What had you been doing beforehand? Who did what to whom? How did it start?

Who initiated it? Was there foreplay? What? How much? Who unbuttoned, caressed, or touched what first, second, third? Who parted or penetrated what?

Think hard . . .

Were you both ready to go? Was it your usual Thursday night once a month arrangement, or was it passionate, fiery and instant? Did one of you have to put the other in the mood? If so, how was this done? What were the signs, the cues?

How many partners were involved in this act? Know what I mean? Did anyone's tongue do anything to anyone else?

OK. Now I want the sharing to continue.

I'm going to ask folks to tell us all a little about these special moments. Share with this group of strangers some of your intimate moments. Shouldn't be too hard should it? After all, we are talking about something you really enjoyed aren't we? Well, all right then!

You, Madam. Could you tell us about a special recent event? *(to a cast member audience PLANT)*

PLANT: Well, it was at home. I had been to a party without my boyfriend and I met this footballer. He was really cool. A real spunk. We fooled around a little but I thought he was quite shy. I was a bit drunk . . .

COL: Fooled around?

PLANT: You know, kissing and cuddling and things?

COL: "Things"? You mean touching? What? Who? Was it reciprocal?

PLANT: Well, everything and then . . .

COL: Yes?

PLANT: He drove me home as he was going the same way. I invited him in for coffee, thinking nothing special about that. I went to the bathroom for to freshen up a bit, but he must have followed me because the next thing I knew he put the lights out—threw me face down on the floor and, well, we made out. It was like the wildest thing ever . . . because, it was, like, *so unexpected?* Good job we had carpet on that floor and not ceramic tiles!

COL: Hang on a minute. How did we get from kissing and cuddling to a state of undress? Ladies and Gentlemen, are we missing something out here? Were you naked to start with or simply not wearing any underclothes? He entered you from behind? How did you know it was his penis?

PLANT: Of course it was his penis!

COL: So, you knew it was a penis. Had you experienced sex often before that occasion? Are you experienced?

PLANT: No! Yes! Huh?

COL: So, how did you know that it was a penis then? You were in the dark—
it could have been a finger, a zucchini, or another guy all together!

PLANT: But . . .

COL: Thank you, Madam. A round of applause for the little lady, everyone.
Now who is next? What? No volunteers? OK. Turn to your neighbor and
tell them all about your experiences . . . only kidding. . . . Think about
this, then. If it is so hard to share a few joyous, intimate moments with a
group of strangers—how hard would it be to talk about something really
unpleasant?

Put yourselves into another scenario all together. If you can't discuss
this with one other person, how would you feel to be describing an hor-
rific personal violation to strangers? You've been violently, sexually
assaulted. Terrified and abused. Traumatized and now you have to face a
strange group of police officers, doctors and forensic scientists as well as
tell us all the details about something you are trying your hardest to forget. This is information that will be used in court and later the details of
your violation will be in the hands of journalists and your relatives, neighbors and even your mom and dad will be reading about what, exactly, was
done to you.

Your best hope is if a baddie confesses and we can save you from going
to court. And to do that we have to put pressure on with the amount of
evidence we have—so victims refusing the examination is a disaster if we
want a conviction. But—either way we do it nicely with the grub. We are
nice to them to soften them up, to get them to confess. Two-faced folk—
that's what we gotta be.

So we treat the baddies like Lord Muck from Turd Island. And it
makes me sick, underneath, of course. We apologize for having to pull
them in. We are blokish about it. Give it the old "nudge-nudge"—could
happen to any one of us—routine. Let us demonstrate. *(returns to stage where
ROB is reading a newspaper)*

Scene 5

COL: Robbo. I will play the part of a baddie and you'll interview me. Let
me get into role now. Nervous, shaky. Me mates don't know and me wife
doesn't either. Never been up in front of the police before—because no
woman has ever had the nerve to report me before. Just take me through
what we do. Suck me in, lead me on and get me talking so I trap me'self?
OK? Just like in training.

ROB: Just like in training. Sorry to have to bring you in for this, mate. Smoke? Tea? Coffee? I have to tell you that a female has made a complaint about you maybe putting your pants somewhere they shouldn't have been, so we have no choice but to follow it through. You understand, don't you?

COL: Who is this bitch? I haven't done nothing!

ROB: 'Know what you mean but there it is. Trouble is we have to follow up these allegations no matter what. . . . Anyway, would you like to tell us what happened?

COL: What she say about me then?

ROB: Can't say, wasn't the one who interviewed her. What did you do that she didn't fancy then?

COL: I don't know the woman!

ROB: Take us back to the disco. You were dancing with her then?

COL: Drinking mostly.

ROB: So you were at the disco? And did you dance with her?

COL: Maybe.

ROB: And she was friendly? What happened next?

COL: Nothing. I didn't hardly touch her.

ROB: So you did touch her then? And she didn't like it?

COL: Wasn't that way. She was begging for it. *(mimes the dancing and groping)* Grabbing at me butt and rubbing herself up against me. Pissed and horny. We both were. The security guard told us to "cool it" or "go outside." She was dying for it. What else can I say? We were pissed and horny and that was about it. Nothing more to say. *(COL mimes the dancing and groping)*

ROB: Ah. And what happened? *(ROB also acts out the scenario, increasingly becoming manic in his depiction; both ROB and COL are now depicting the assault)* Let's see: you went outside to kiss some more and she put her hand on your trousers and you put yours up her skirt, but she said "no" but went on kissing you—so you thought she must mean "yes" and then you grabbed her, pulled her on the ground, pulled her knickers down—and played "hide the sausage" and *"bury the bone," "bury the bone," "bury the bone"!* *(ROB and COL stand center stage enacting pelvic thrusting)* But she made a drama out of it afterwards and you thought, "I ought to slap her down, the dirty filthy whore! Slap her down!" *(violently enacts beating the victim down—in this case, COL) SLAP HER DOWN!* *(pause)* Sorry mate, don't know what came over me there.

COL: *(gets up)* Thanks, Rob, little too empathetic there for my taste but probably effective. *(aside)* Don't know what they teach them in training these days!

Of course, it won't be so straightforward because if the baddie is able to get an alibi lined up or get his story straight it will take far more work to trap him.

ROB: Maybe.

COL: Of course! If you were looking at a 4–5 year stretch in the bin wouldn't you try to sort something out? But, if I am nice as pie to him when he is in the interview room, as big a turd as he is, then he will do time. I'll give him anything he wants—but he can't go home.

ROB: Do you crack them all like that?

COL: You'd be surprised how many, mate. Remember, plenty baddies don't want to go through the trauma of court either.

ROB: OK. That's the baddie, so what about this woman in the interview room? What female support have we got for this woman we are about to interview?

COL: You keep banging on about support, don't you? Maybe her mother—if she sits still and shuts up. She can sit there and shut up. Say nothing. Evidence just walks out of the room. Counselors give them words and language that a decent lawyer would shoot holes through. Give them ideas about dropping charges. And they are so cowardly that most of them won't go anywhere near a courtroom. . . . But some are really good. They know the score. It's the young idealistic feminist types that are the problem. It's hard to deal with contamination of story after support service intervention.

ROB: They probably just want the person healed.

COL: Us too. We are the real bloody therapists in this.

ROB: How come?

COL: Seeing a baddie caught and sent to court to answer publicly is part of the recovery. Most victims need to hear "Yeah—you are right—he did rape you." And some of the nitty is very gritty. Back in the '80s I had a case of a Maltese bloke who'd had sex with his 2 daughters, 2 sons, and a dog. I went to pinch him and the bastard did a runner. Both the girls ended up in Sydney as prostitutes—no support services made a difference to them.

   When he finally turned up a few years later and the day of reckoning came—it all came out. D-day, they let it build up and just let it go. Anal sex, golden showers, threesomes, selling them off to mates—stuff they'd never told us in interview. Court and conviction was their best therapy.

ROB: And the dog?

COL: I reckon it got better support than the family did!

ROB: (pause) Well, I suppose we'd better interview this woman then?

COL: You'll do. I'll bring her in for you.

(COL sets up desk and chairs and walks down into auditorium, comes back with the female audience PLANT)

ROB: What happened leading up to the alleged assault outside the nightclub?

PLANT: It was assault.

ROB: Did you kiss? Cuddle? Inside the club?

PLANT: *(no answer)*

ROB: Did you dance with him, you know, closely? Did you agree to go home with him? Why did you leave the nightclub with him?

PLANT: *(still no response)*

ROB: Did you agree verbally to have intercourse with him?

PLANT: *(still no response)*

ROB: Did you contemplate intercourse with him?

PLANT: *(still no response)*

ROB: Could you be accused of leading him towards a misunderstanding?

PLANT: *(still no response)*

ROB: When you decided you were being assaulted how far had your physical relationship gone?

PLANT: *(tears)*

ROB: Had you let him touch your breasts? Buttocks? Vagina? Were you clothed or unclothed? Who had done the undressing? Did you resist? Did you open the labia? How far? Had you touched his penis? Did you voluntarily spread your legs? Did you call for help? Did you struggle or did he *just slap you down! (glares at the audience as he mimes slapping the victim) Just slap you down . . .*

(blackout)

Street Rat

ADAPTED BY JOHNNY SALDAÑA, SUSAN FINLEY, AND MACKLIN FINLEY

Editor's Introduction

It is estimated that between 500,000 and 1.5 million young people each year in the United States have run away or been forced out of their homes, leaving between 200,000 and 300,000 living homeless on the streets. *Street Rat* portrays a day in the life of five of these young people facing problems with alcohol, drugs, pregnancy, and a lack of compassion from adults around them.

Educational ethnographer Susan Finley and her son Macklin developed several pieces from their fieldwork and experiences with homeless youth in New Orleans in the mid-1990s (Finley, M., 2000, 2003; Finley, S., 2000, 2001; Finley & Finley, 1998, 1999). Their published work and presentations of their research at arts-based educational research conferences caught the attention of Saldaña who saw ethnodramatic potential in their body of work. Though a reader's theatre piece based on interviews with the homeless teens had been developed earlier (Finley & Finley, 1998), the arrangement was a collage of excerpts organized by category, rather than a single storyline. The article "Sp'ange" (Finley & Finley, 1999)—a contraction of "spare change"—portrayed a day in the life of these runaways through a composite short story creation.

This version provided the plot structure necessary for a more theatrical adaptation. Macklin Finley's evocative book of poetry, *Street Rat* (2000), inspired his integration into the play as an omniscient Brechtian narrator who comments, in poetic form, on the harsh reality of street life around him. Most of the dialogue of the play was written by Macklin, but he contextualizes it in the setting and plot structure of "Sp'ange" and other publications produced as research documents.

Saldaña, as director of the production, had made regular annual trips to New Orleans as part of summer in-service teachers' workshops, but he had never been in the area during January, the time period of the original "Sp'ange" story. He had also strolled through the French Quarter frequently, but as a tourist, not an ethnographer. The staging of *Street Rat* called upon his casual knowledge of New Orleans culture, and some of that knowledge—such as tourists decked with layers of Mardi Gras beads drinking from opaque plastic beer cups in public—worked itself into the play.

In order to develop a more authentic staging and production, Saldaña conducted "quick ethnography" (Handwerker, 2002) to become better familiar with the setting and the participants' world. So, before casting and rehearsals began, he visited New Orleans in January 2004 to assess the climate and how it affected what tourists and local citizens wore; this influenced the costuming. He revisited some of the places mentioned in Finley & Finley's research, such as Jackson Square and Rampart Street, but this time with an ethnographer's eye; this influenced the scenic and properties design. He talked to locals to learn where street kids regularly hung out and chatted informally with a few of them to get a sense of their personalities, dialects, vocal tones, and appearances; this influenced characterizations by the actors.

Informal interviews with the homeless teens posed questions and topics that would further inform the production, such as "What kinds of actions do you do when you're sitting with friends?" (smoking, pointing at and making fun of passersby, drinking), "If I went to a squat, what would I see there?" (blankets, used condoms, feces), and "Tell me what other homeless kids might wear" (lace-up boots, chains, tattoos). A stroll down Bourbon Street, coincidentally on the night trash was to be collected by the city, inspired the visual concept for the production: a narrow, street-like performance area in the center of the studio theatre with the audience seated on blankets on both sides, flanked with piles of garbage. Since the premiere performance was to take place in Arizona, Saldaña's New Orleans colleagues assembled a collection of regional "trash" such as Winn-Dixie plastic grocery bags, empty containers of traditional southern foods (e.g., grits and gumbo mixes), and old Bell South phone directories for random distribution throughout the set and audience seating area. Only one of the nine-member acting company had ever visited New Orleans and none of them had ever experienced homelessness, so they viewed documentary videos of the Louisiana region and homeless teens, and read and discussed articles about homelessness including Finley and Finley's original research. The principal actors, on their own initiative to get a better understanding of their character-participants, "sp'anged" downtown, talked to homeless youth in the area, slept outdoors with them for a night, and gave up showering and grooming the week before and during performances.

The purpose of all this description is to emphasize that, aside from the careful development of the ethnodramatic text, ethnotheatrical production has its own kind of preparatory research and fieldwork, display of artifacts, and representation of social life through carefully selected details of human action. If one of written ethnography's primary goals is to give the reader a sense of "being there," ethnotheatre should also strive to do no less through authentic reproduction onstage, as much as time, budget, space, and human resources will allow. But no ethnodramatic production is credible or trustworthy on its scenography alone. The narration, monologue, and dialogue must also ring true to life and evoke the world of its participants. The live, intimate, real-time nature of ethnotheatre gives the audience member not a sense of "being *there*" but, during performance, "being *here*."

Street Rat

Production History

Street Rat premiered at Arizona State University (ASU) April 6–8, 2004. The production was staged and directed by Johnny Saldaña and featured the following cast: Chris Marley (Mack), David Ojala (Roach), Jess Sari (Tigger), Christine Klein (Quiz), Kate Haas (Jewel), Miranda Lilley (Genie), Adam Bauer, Daniel Charns, and Wilana Ortega (Adult Ensemble Members). Production Assistants: Amy Crater, Justin DeRo, and Laura Hutton. Production support was provided by the ASU Department of Theatre and Katherine K. Herberger College of Fine Arts (J. Robert Wills, Dean).

Characters

MACK: male, early 20s, a street poet
ROACH: male, 19, a street rat; spider web tattoo on half his face
TIGGER: male, 22, a street rat; ROACH's best friend
QUIZ: female, 16, a street rat
JEWEL: female, 17, a street rat
GENIE: female, 16, a 7-month pregnant street rat
THREE ADULT ENSEMBLE MEMBERS (two male, one female) to portray: Tourists, Waitress, Drug Dealer, Gay Leatherman, Business Man, Conventioneers, etc. When needed, they also assist with the staging of the production.
One Male Adult Ensemble member is African American; all other characters are White

Setting

The French Quarter and a homeless squat in New Orleans; a Friday in January, 1997

Dedication

To the street rats

Preshow

(music: a collage of New Orleans Cajun and Zydeco; ROACH, TIGGER, QUIZ, JEWEL, and GENIE sit on the ground by the entrance to the theatre or house; the STREET RATS hold their hands out to audience members and ask as they enter, "Spare change?" "Spare change for alcohol?"; MACK is nearby reciting his street poetry; inside the theatre, ADULT ENSEMBLE MEMBERS in Mardi Gras masks offer beads and other Mardi Gras souvenirs to incoming audience members)

Scene 1: Free Live Poetry

(house lights fade and stage lights rise; the set includes various street signs from the New Orleans French Quarter and suggestions of a condemned yet lived-in property; trash is strewn throughout the set and audience seating area; MACK, dressed casually, enters; he sets a cigar box on the ground, pulls a one dollar bill from his pocket and drops it in the box; he stands on an upturned milk crate and shouts to two TOURISTS passing by, both wearing Mardi Gras necklaces)

MACK: Free live poetry! All's you have to pay . . . is attention!
(the TOURISTS stop to listen as MACK recites to them; music fades out; MACK speaks with an easy passion)
I find my definition
in storm patterns—
A change of energy.
I can feel it underfoot—
The sky is flecked
light with grey,
I think I may
feel partly
cloudy.
Like a thunderclap
I am deafening in
fierce self-proclamations.
Like the sky I am poisoned
by industry; the city's smokestacks
choke me, and the five o'clock
traffic jam is burning
holes in me with its
bitter exhaust.

(one of the TOURISTS raises her camera and takes a snapshot of MACK)
I think I may—
I think I may—
feel partly cloudy.
(TOURISTS smile at each other, shake their heads and walk off as one drops a coin in MACK's cigar box; MACK speaks to them as they exit)
And I don't want to
be a rain of history
on your day-in-the-park parade—
but I'm vaporous, controlled by
the elements raining
heard words on deaf
ears—
(Cajun/Zydeco music up; as MACK continues to recite, ROACH, a 19-year-old street rat, enters, empties a milk crate full of trash, turns it over, sits on the crate and glances both ways for people; MACK looks at ROACH, then to the audience as he speaks)
you're walking
down a street of gutter
punks, starving,
wise children,
coast to coast wanderers—
and all this petty extravagance
has been hung on poles of
degradation: for your benefit.
Somebody tell the children
with their fiddle stories
and longtime bad habits,
that these neon beer
gardens are cesspools
of wasted minds
and lives of no
reward.
I think I may—
I think I may—
feel partly cloudy.
(through the rest of the play, MACK sits, leans, rises, and walks across the stage, as necessary, while commenting on the action; music out)

Scene 2: Spare Change?

(BUSINESS WOMAN in a dress enters, walks by ROACH)
ROACH: Spare change?
(BUSINESS WOMAN catches a quick glimpse of ROACH then looks away, clutches her purse tightly and keeps walking until she exits; BUSINESS MAN in a blue suit and tie enters, carrying a briefcase, walks by ROACH)
Spare change?
(BUSINESS MAN does not acknowledge ROACH and keeps walking until he exits; ROACH shakes his head, says half to himself, half to BUSINESS MAN)
Mr. Blue-suit-on-his-way-to-work-business-maaan never even look my way. You got money in your pocket, actin' like you don't see me. You see me, mother-fucker!
(a GAY LEATHERMAN enters, walks toward ROACH)
Spare change?
(GAY LEATHERMAN stops, glares at ROACH, reaches into his jeans, pulls out three pennies, drops them one at a time at ROACH's feet, then walks off; ROACH mutters to himself)
Gay-yuppie asshole.
(he picks up the pennies and pockets them; MACK looks at ROACH, speaks to him and to audience)
MACK: Three pennies
fall like
rain in
the thunderous
silence after.
Remorse is
a court word
holding no
tender in the
lives of men.
(as MACK continues, TIGGER, a 22-year-old street rat and ROACH's best friend, enters and crosses to ROACH, sits close to him; ROACH mimes talking to TIGGER about the GAY LEATHERMAN who gave him the coins)
As one
more chokes
into the
nameless
void and

one more
skirts
St. Claude
outside the
street light.
Eyes not
guilty,
but
free will
be blessed
with the
splendor
of another
southern
dawn.

ROACH: People try and trick with me for money all the time. I just say, "Fuck off, I'm not a whore." People figure that if you're in the gay district, you *are*. I'm not going to sell my ass.

TIGGER: I know plenty of fucking straight up prostitutes. They're cool as hell, but that's not something I'm going to do.

ROACH: It makes you compromise yourself. People who do it have to be comfortable with doing it. Sometimes people get caught up in it, when they aren't comfortable doing it, but they do it anyway. That causes so many problems.

TIGGER: That, and the simple fact that people who hustle—not the people who hustle, but the people who hustle them—it's like, the only reason why these rich fuckin' guys are doing this shit, lots of times, the simple fact is they know they can grab a guy off the street and just say, "Come home and fuck me!", "Come home, do this with me," and just take control. I don't know, it's just fucked up.

ROACH: And then they act all disgusted when you tell them, "No." Like you're nothing if you don't do something like that to earn money.

TIGGER: Like you don't have any choice in the matter.
     (a WAITRESS on her way to work passes by)

ROACH: Spare change?

TIGGER: Spare change?

WAITRESS: *(smiles at them, pulls a coin from her apron pocket, and puts it in ROACH's outstretched hand)* There you go. *(exits)*

ROACH: Thanks.

TIGGER: Thanks.
(*ROACH and TIGGER leer at the WAITRESS as she leaves*)
ROACH: Now, if a woman wanted to pay me to have sex with her, I would.
TIGGER: Well, depends on the woman.
ROACH: Yeah. If it's some Nancy Reagan–looking woman, then no.
(*a GAY TOURIST enters, wearing Mardi Gras necklaces and with a clear plastic cup of beer in hand, walks past the boys*)
ROACH AND TIGGER: Spare change?
(*the TOURIST glances quickly at ROACH, shakes his head "no," and sets his half-empty cup on the sidewalk by a trash can; exits; TIGGER goes for the beer*)
ROACH: Fuck him. Sneakin' peeks at my facial tat.
(*as TIGGER gets the beer, ROACH smiles and starts a private joke between them*) Just say "No!"
TIGGER: No! (*he drinks from the cup, offers ROACH the last swig*)
MACK: We stand
on the
corner
amidst
the buzz
the flow
their cash
inextricable.
The flow
on which
we prey
which
invariably
covers us in
a film
of spilled
broken
bottles.
TIGGER: (*rooting through the trash can for food*) We better make quick work of the schwillies, man. We gotta sp'ange enough for all weekend today; it's gonna rain tomorrow.
ROACH: How do you know that? Are you a weather man now?
TIGGER: I read it in the paper. Town is gonna be packed and we can make bank. The Clover has a sign welcoming some conference, so there's plenty of green around. We just gotta get it while the weather holds.

ROACH: *(looks down the street)* I've gotta meet that guy in a couple hours. *(pulls out some partially smoked cigarettes from his pocket, gives one to TIGGER; they both light up)*

TIGGER: *(worriedly)* Right. I don't buy it. I don't trust him, Roach.

ROACH: *(tries to reassure TIGGER but sounds doubtful)* I'm not going to have anything on me. The guy holds the stuff. I just go find customers. I take them to him and he gives me a runner's fee. I'm not going to have the stuff on me.

TIGGER: Never in my life have I fucked with the needle.

ROACH: *(insistent)* I'm not using it, Tigger. I'm just running it.

TIGGER: You've done it before, now you'll want to do it again.

ROACH: No! It's only a job. I'm going to get money so we can get a place and we can eat. *(TIGGER does not look at him; impatiently as he sits)* I'm a fuckin' slinger, man. I sell drugs on occasion.

TIGGER: Being around the needle, talking about the needle, makes me very uncomfortable. Fucks with my head. But if someone's gonna do it, they're gonna do it. I've seen it—friends dead.

ROACH: You snort coke with me, but if I try heroin with the guy I'm going to sell it for, that makes it wrong? You're such a fucking hypocrite!

TIGGER: No I'm not! You know what I think's going to happen? You're going to start slammin' it again.

ROACH: *(singing the end of Neil Young's song to TIGGER)* "I've seen the needle and the damage done, a little part of it in everyone, but every junkie's like a setting sun." *(laughs; pulls TIGGER by the arm)* C'mon, let's get outta here.

TIGGER: *(yanks his arm away from ROACH's grip)* You do what you gotta do, I'll catch ya later.

ROACH: Tigger, . . .

TIGGER: *(as he exits)* I'll be on the Square. Hook up with me when you're through.

ROACH: Tigger! Damn. *(shouts after TIGGER)* I hate it when we fight! We fight just like a couple of fucking married people!

MACK: The heat
has descended.
Surely another
night will
follow, long,
sleepless,
dusty.

(ROACH pulls a flask from his pants pocket, takes a swig)
How many
have been
lost?
How many
mothers'
sons
choke
gasp
and
die
as
three pennies
fall like
rain in
the thunderous
silence
after?
(ROACH exits; MACK recites to audience; transition music rises)
We walk
a fine
line
down
Rampart's median,
unwanted
on either
side.
Nothing can
be done
as
three pennies
fall like
rain in
the thunderous
silence
after.
(lights fade on scene)

Scene 3: The Fortress

(lights rise and music fades as JEWEL and QUIZ enter, escorting GENIE, about 7 months pregnant and a worn tote bag strapped on her shoulder; they are orienting her to the life of a street rat at The Fortress, their squat)

JEWEL: Sometimes it takes a while before you find a squat.

QUIZ: You'll look around and find a place, and then find out that somebody's already squatting there.

JEWEL: Either that, or a place will be really dirty and you have to clean an area, pull all the trash.

QUIZ: Try to find a squat where there are already other squatters and then stay, because it's safer, as long as there aren't too many people.

GENIE: *(sitting and looking at the property)* The first place I stayed was this cool old house. It was abandoned. We slept in the attic.

JEWEL: This complex is condemn... The city is supposed to tear it down eventually.

QUIZ: Roach decides who can live here.

JEWEL: That means he can decide what'll happen to you. He kicked his girl-friend out during a raid, and she was afraid she would run out there and get arrested.

QUIZ: Most people don't give a fuck what Roach does. For one thing, he won't even hit girls. If he just dislikes you, he doesn't care if you stay here, but if you do something to piss him off, you don't even *want* to stay here. Roach and Tigger had to chase three people out last week. They beat Scooby up a couple of days before that. *(showing GENIE)* All these holes in the wall? They put his head through it.

JEWEL: Roach owns The Fortress. But you *want* some protection, some kind of squat boss. Every single room is open—take your pick. We call the courtyard the pit. If you're going to fight, you take it to the pit.
    (TIGGER enters)
    Tigger! This is Genie.

TIGGER: *(beat; smiles at GENIE)* Hi.

GENIE: *(smiling back)* Hi.
    (ROACH enters and all stare at him; uncomfortable pause as he glares at GENIE)

QUIZ: *(half defiant, half pleading)* She wanted to know where she could stay.

GENIE: *(rising; as if anticipating his concern)* The cops ask me my name. I have a clear name so they just let me go.

ROACH: *(staring at GENIE's pregnant stomach)* Fuckin' cops out here are fuckin' evil. *(beat)* You can stay with us. *(ROACH approaches GENIE and speaks roughly)* I'm not a squat Nazi or anything like that. But I like my home to be peaceful and relaxing. When people fuck with my shit or fuck with me, I consider it disrespectful and I'll fight over it. We protect ourselves, and we try to protect our stuff. We try to make sure we're all safe and nobody's going to get us all busted. Some people think they can do whatever they want. *(shakes his head "no")* We go down. We'll bust your ass.

(ROACH exits, motioning for TIGGER to join him; TIGGER follows, but looks back at GENIE)

JEWEL: *(calling after ROACH)* You fucker!

GENIE: *(shaken, sits, starts crying; the girls go to GENIE)* This is Boy Scout's fault. When I met him, he was a squatter. He had a tattoo on his cheek and a carving out of one of his ears. I used to let him come to my house and take showers. I tried to convince my aunt to let him stay, that he needed a place for the night. My aunt was, "No!" So, I just said, "Fine, I'm going to spend the night with him." First night, we slept on this guy's porch.

(looks at her stomach)

QUIZ: When I went home for Christmas, my mom beat the shit out of me and told me I couldn't come back to her house anymore. It ended up with me in a hospital and yelling at my mom that she was a fucking bitch because I nearly had a heart attack because of crack cocaine. *(to JEWEL)* Remember when I had stitches on my chin? I couldn't fight back because I was too high; I couldn't really stand up.

JEWEL: *(to GENIE)* I ran away from home when I was 12. Came back, got put into rehab, got out, ran away again, came back about three months later. *(gets a paper bag from the floor)* I've been in and out of 11 rehab centers from the time I was 11 years old. *(pulls a pint of vodka out of the bag)* That was a big mistake on my parents' part.

QUIZ: *(to GENIE)* Have you danced?

GENIE: Huh?

QUIZ: You can make good money dancing. I know a girl who does private parties.

GENIE: Yeah?

QUIZ: *(touching GENIE's stomach)* Well, she's pregnant.

JEWEL: That's a fetish. Turns some guys on—you know, dancing pregnant.

GENIE: Makes a lot, huh?

JEWEL: Every month more pregnant, the price goes up. These guys like it best when they're ready to deliver.

QUIZ: One girl who did it has her own apartment now. She's already got her kid, but she never quit doing drugs so he looks a little strange. Seems a little slow. I'm careful. I'm not having kids until I can take care of them. *(takes a drink of vodka)*

GENIE: My sister has a friend who went to cosmetology school. She made a lot of money as a beautician. You have to get your own chair, though. Otherwise, it's minimum and by the hour. Without a degree I couldn't get a job or an apartment and stuff. Just the fact that I'm young, and I don't have anywhere to go.
(ROACH and TIGGER enter, listen to the GIRLS)

JEWEL: I made close to 35 dollars last night and plan on making more tonight. I figure I'll make twice what I made last night because it's Friday and everyone will be getting their paychecks and getting drunk off their asses.

ROACH: *(to GENIE)* "Nawlins" is a good city to panhandle in. You can make 40 to 50 bucks a day. It's variable; it doesn't always work, but you can make that much. Weekends are good when there's no rain. Conferences make weekdays feel like weekends.

TIGGER: *(sitting by GENIE)* Roach has been making tons every night. It seems like I only make money when I'm with Roach.

ROACH: We sp'ange in the gay district. Guys can make money down there.

TIGGER: Yeah, but the bigwigs in the gay community wants us to get the fuck out of there. They say we scare tourists.

JEWEL: *(to GENIE)* Work closer to the bars. A good spot is next to The Bourbon Bar.
(ROACH starts walking off)

TIGGER: Where y' goin'?

ROACH: *(a lie)* I'm . . . gonna go hustle at the market, find a truck to unload 'til I got enough to make schwillies. If ya wanna job, sometimes ya gotta take care of the nasty shit. *(exits)*

QUIZ: *(to TIGGER)* I hear Roach is slingin'.

TIGGER: *(picking up a book to read)* I don't care, so long as he fucking stays clean, doesn't fucking rob anybody.
(lights fade and transition music rises)

Scene 4: Needles in Veins

(lights up; as MACK recites, the DEALER, a short nervous Jamaican, about 30 and going bald, enters and waits nervously; ROACH enters; they meet covertly and mime talking to each other; music fades out)

MACK: Lobotomizing without tools,
    tubes in noses,
    paper on tongues—
    Constant escape,
    circular streets
    around and down,
    scraping gutters,
    sleeping in abandoned homes
    watchful of peripheral motion—
    Always taking chances
    With motions like
    a train.
    (the DEALER passes ROACH a baggie of heroin packets, a cell phone, and a piece of paper with phone numbers written on it and mimes talking the directions for hook-ups)
    Needles in veins
    Needles in veins
    Needles in veins.
    Pink blood, diluted
    blood, blocking the
    works blood, cramming the
    artery blood. Metallic tastes
    numb tongues, prickly eyes
    watery walls—
    unaware a thousand
    tomorrows rusty machines
    around like turnstile justice.
    (the DEALER pulls out a joint from his pocket and lights it, drags, passes it to ROACH who also takes a hit)
    Like a train rhythm—money
    burning—like a train rhythm—
    bondsmen and pushers
    bondsmen and pushers
    bondsmen and pushers—
    Insane on floors—
    Spinning—Hot hairy Middle-
    Aged hands—Gotta pay somehow—
    like a train rhythm:
    Shaking at dawn

for another,

another,

another.

DEALER: *(keeps and continues to drag on the joint)* For every hook-up you
   make with a customer, you take a 10 dollar cut, whatever size the sale.

ROACH: Thas' OK. There's nobody lookin' to me for more than an evening's
   entertainment anyways.

DEALER: You use?

ROACH: No. Well, I have. I don't anymore, not now. *(laughs)* Tell you the
   truth, I'm back on that shit all the time.

DEALER: *(reaches in his coat pocket, pulls out a packet of heroin and places it in
   ROACH's hand)* That one's on the house. Gift to newcomers from your
   Neighborhood Club. *(he laughs through his cough and flicks the joint down
   on the ground)* Meet me here tomorrow. Same time, same place. We'll set-
   tle accounts then. *(he turns and walks away briskly, exits)*
   *(as MACK recites, ROACH looks at the heroin, slips it in his pocket, picks up
   the joint the DEALER flicked to the ground, snuffs it out to save for later)*

MACK: In and out

dusty phone booths

dying young with bad lookin'

yellow, inflated corpses.

Dusty back-alleys

risks like a train rhythm,

needles in veins

needles in veins

needles in veins

blood wash spoon

nicotine

chasers

there will be a change.

*(ROACH dials a phone number written on the piece of paper on the cell
phone, mimes talking as he looks about nervously)*

Gotta pay—born in debt—hot

hairy—Clorox clean-up

committee—phone call

to Jimi/Janis—shot up—

Put down—hung on last

generation's sellout

ambitions—song of

somebody else—
Phone call to Walt Whitman—
Unlisted—sanity—sobriety—
Change—will there be—
Is there an I—change—
Sanity—train rhythm—
Ran risk stop sign—
Clean-up committee—
Zero tolerance—
Heard words—symphony.
Phone call to William
Shakespeare—heard words—
Othello blackface comedy—
downstairs train rhythm—
(ROACH hangs up on the phone, stuffs it in his jacket, and thinks deeply)
It's very drug culture—
I don't know if I can
hang with all the smoke
up in here.

Scene 5: Doc Holliday

(lights suggest an isolation from real time and "reality"; MACK stands on a milk crate)

MACK: *(to ROACH)* Free live poetry! All's you have to pay . . . is attention!
(ROACH takes a swig from his flask, walks toward MACK and stops to listen as he recites)
Doc Holliday
spat a little
shriveled lung in
his kerchief,
straightened
his hat—
found the next
whiskey—
savored the irony.
His boots
were always
shined to

a bright
black glow—
matching
his eyes.
He was a
wizard
of a kind.
He was a
wizard
way ahead
of his time.
Doc Holliday
was wise
to the
plans of
the other man—
Doc Holliday
was wise
to the
deck in
hand—
Doc Holliday
was wise
to the
street
before there
was a
street to
be wise
to.

*(pause; MACK smiles at ROACH, they give each other a quick friendly nod;
ROACH reaches in his pocket, pulls out a coin and flips it to MACK; MACK steps
off the milk crate and makes a gesture as if to suggest they trade places; they do so;
MACK listens as ROACH speaks and takes an occasional swig from his flask)*

ROACH: I started drinking in 7th grade. That was the only reason to go
to school—drugs and alcohol. Pot, cocaine, heroin. I dropped out in
7th grade, never been to high school. Teachers don't care, but they were
nothing like the kids. I lived in a trailer park in Texas; it was the worst. I was
kind of small. Kids who didn't live in the trailer park used to chase me home.

If I made it to our trailer, I wouldn't get beat up. A lot of the time, I didn't make it and they'd beat the shit outta me. I missed school whenever I could.

MACK: *(walks to a second crate)* Doc Holliday
stood—thin—
shakin' in the
too hot sun—
He was dying
and he knew
it didn't
matter—
the country was
growing—
modernizing.
He would be
an anecdote—
if he made
it that
far—

(MACK sits on the crate, ROACH steps off his crate and crosses to MACK)

ROACH: I pretty much taught myself. I listen. I watch. I've got a lot of time under my belt, a lot of experience. I didn't read about survival of the fittest and say, "Wow, that's cool; that'll be me." I've just lived it. But I've still got a lot to learn, just like everybody does. Learning is a life-long process, whether you're in school or not. I have ADD, so I didn't pay any attention at school, I didn't do my homework. My mom would tell me something and I would forget it two minutes later. I've pretty much fixed that. I haven't completely grown out of it, I'm still ADD and all that, but I've learned how to focus when I need to focus.

(MACK rises, stands on his crate)

MACK: The sun
formed
slow
bubbles in
his eyes.
A 15 year old
kid stood a
hundred paces downwind—
A drunken bet
was the cause.

Draw Squeeze—
One shot
a body falls
A boy died
in the street.
It did not
matter.
Doc Holliday's
next drink's
free—

(MACK steps off his crate as the two circle each other, scoping each other out)

ROACH: The first time I was on my own, I ran away to Dallas when I was 13, didn't come home for a long while. I spent a year on the streets selling cocaine. Had a cocaine habit. *(stands on a crate)* Fuckin' slammin'. Needle in the vein, man.

MACK: the fever
worse—he sweats
through his sportcoat—
Saw white horses
ridin' high in
strange black
streets—eerie humming
glowing signs
in impossible
windows.

(ROACH remains on the crate while MACK sits on the ground)

ROACH: I don't really blame my mom. She didn't kick me out. I sort of left, and when I tried to come back, she'd already had enough watching me go downhill and knowing what I was doing and knowing I was lying in her face. Being apart from my mom for so long—having me go out into the world and learn things—helped my relationship with her. I've become more independent. I'm not so needy all the time. I had the problem when I was younger. I always needed her attention and stuff, although I didn't play it off like I wanted her. Deep down I really did. But I'm not like that anymore. My mom and I are good now. I mean, we smoke pot and drink together, because she realizes that I've been on my own for, what, 6 years in January. She's realized that I take care of myself, that, "Hey, you're still alive. You're an adult." I go there sometimes and I get a job to support

myself while I'm living there, because they don't have the money to support me. They don't have the money to support themselves. You know
what I mean? To me, it's just a visit. One day I get up and I leave.
*(he steps off the crate; MACK rises and crosses to him; ROACH stares at
MACK, as if hypnotized)*

MACK: Children squatting
　　on stone walks
　　near the black
　　patch—

ROACH: their
　　hands out,
　　their eyes
　　dead—

MACK AND ROACH: odd
　　bruises, scabs
　　tracing their
　　veins thumping
　　in unison—
(beat; MACK gives ROACH a slight push to bring him to)

MACK: Cough shakes
　　him to—
(MACK sits)

ROACH: Sometimes I think about my family, my mom and my little brother.
　　I give them a call and I keep in touch. My brother just had his 13th birth-
　　day. Sometimes it makes me kind of sad, that I can't visit with them. I can;
　　I can go and visit with them. It's just that it's far and it's cold. My mom
　　lives in Maryland now.
(BUSINESS MAN from Scene 2 passes by)
　　Spare change?
*(BUSINESS MAN looks straight ahead and does not acknowledge ROACH,
exits; ROACH runs after him and shouts)*
　　Mr. Corporate Man! White collared mother-fucker wearing a suit and tie,
　　look me in the face! Remember me? Wouldn't give me spare change. Shoot
　　you in the head—boom, boom!

MACK: Praised be the
　　vision of our murderous
　　Father, Doc Holliday!
(ROACH, angry, crosses to MACK)

ROACH: Fuck you! Every square dad and Arab between here and there gonna look me up and down, hate me, throw me away with their eyes. I don't waste my time on smellin' nice or livin' a lie. I'm not a bad guy, but I'm looked on as a piece of shit, and that's just totally wrong! I don't want to be part of a society that hates me, and wants to assimilate me, that won't allow me the chance to do the things that I want to do, and allow me to live the way I want to live. I have the right, just like any other human being, to do anything I want to do as long as I'm not hurting anybody.
    (ROACH sits on a crate, dejected, looking away from MACK; MACK rises and pushes the other crate with his foot in increments toward ROACH's)

MACK: There's a
    kid down the
    way
    with a finger
    in every pie—
    He's got
    old style
    hustle
    with his
    hat on.
    Majesty
    is nothin' but
    practice for
    comfort;
    the boy's
    a king of
    unthinkable
    consequence
    makin' it
    work—
    (ROACH pulls out from his pocket the packet of heroin and stares at it)
    Night to
    night, day
    to day.
    He's gotta
    take care of
    the
    (MACK shoves the crate forcefully against the one ROACH is sitting on, startling him)

shit
that gotta
be taken
care of—
(MACK sits on the crates, smirking)
ROACH: We have an animal instinct for survival. If you had my reality for
24 hours, your view would change forever.
(grabs MACK by the shirt; MACK grabs ROACH by the shoulders)
On the street, if all shit hit the fan, the Yuppies wouldn't survive.
(they let each other loose)
So where do I fit? Right here, in my heart. That's where I fit. I'm planning
on staying in New Orleans another day, maybe another 20 minutes, maybe
a year from now. *(ROACH starts walking off)*
MACK: *(standing on a crate)* So when
a boy dies
on the
paved streets
of modern day
America—
Everyone knows
it does not
matter.
ROACH: *Fuck you!* *(exits)*
MACK: Boy/king
'round the
corner
lights a
candle
on the
altar for
every soul
he brings down
in grim street
light.

Scene 6: Fugue

*(lights rise back to "reality" level; as MACK calls out, a CONVENTIONEER
with a name badge and convention program book passes by and stops to listen)*

MACK: Free live poetry! All's you have to pay . . . is attention!
    (MACK's recitation varies in energy, passion, and anger)
    Young and poor—
    No god to pray to—
    No luck to pray for—
    Nothin' but life chokin'
    on life.
    So whatcha in for?
    Call it "Public drunk," not
    doin' a damn thing. Jus'
    walkin', but th' cop go's
    me figured on a diff'rent
    score—
    Who ain't in the central
    for jus' bein' bo'n?
    Who ain't?
    Some try to sleep it off
    in the late-night
    holding cells,
    no relatives to call,
    no bail to be posted.
    Some stand and pace,
    bitter stomachs
    and torn minds
    toiling against broken
    stamina.
    What next? What next?
    Bullshit tournaments in
    the corner—
    Who's the baddest?
    In this last-stop
    dead-end cell he
    with loudest voice
    is booming his
    notorious command—
    "You be my bitch in the house!"
    And it's misplaced anger
    for that last five minutes
    of out time

that went so
wrong.
There will be a change.
(*a second CONVENTIONEER with a name badge and convention program
book passes by and stops to listen*)
Nights that plague
reality, poking holes
in it, setting it
to purple flames
of delusion—
Mystified, pinned
on walls in pale
street lights—
passing smiles in
choking voiceless
rooms and unconscious
connections
forming lines
at money burners
Begging for a little
escape
(fast set down
fast money
for fast connections),
Itching at the corners:
Escape! Escape!
Making kissing noises
at the passing faces—
Gotta pay somehow—
need a ride—
need a bed—
need a hot, hairy, middle-aged
hand on your thigh—
"Cause you look a little
cold, and I could use a
little company."
That little wedding ring
don't mean a damn thing 'cause
I can buy out the sentiment

behind it.
Besides, if it's not you it's
some other beer-starved
mouth.
You need the fix,
po' white trash, nigga,
spic, queer, li'l boy with
no one to talk with, and
no bed to sleep in, never
mind your confused sexuality—
I got a big green paper
dick for you to suck on—
and once you have, you can
get high.
Won't that be nice?
Wake up, middle-aged
whore monger,
there will be a great day
of reckoning.
*(a third CONVENTIONEER with a name badge and convention program
book passes by and stops to listen)*
Living on broken bread-crust
promises—
Telling her I'll be
fine.
Struggling to get a
foothold outta bed—
Bleak—slow—blurry—
No comfort—itching
at the corners—
Struggling for control
of the headboard—
You can't have it
'till you cut me—
Red/brown bedsheets,
grinding—in/out
sweating/reeling/
needing/releasing
gentle song

neighbors complaining
springs—
Needing—itching at
the corners—confusing
desires—wanting—metallic
tastes.
(TIGGER, GENIE, JEWEL, and QUIZ enter and stop to listen with the crowd)
Needing
Needing
Needing
Hot Hairy Middle-Aged
Hands
Gotta pay—
Gotta pay somehow—
Is there an "I"—
Am I all that I am?
I want to keep the promises,
but, y'see there's this
train rhythm.
(one CONVENTIONEER looks at his watch, leaves the crowd)
So, who am I?
is there an "I" that stands
out as more than a cog
in this rusty old machine?
Who Am I—
Who Am I—
Who Am I?
Am I the junk in veins—
The wine in skin—
An inebriate forming
consciousness cocktails—
scotch and soda handcuffs?
Happy Hour
Happy Hour—
3 for 1 Happy Hour—
Who wants sanity—
Who wants sobriety?
*(a second CONVENTIONEER leaves the crowd as she reads her convention
program)*

Neon-rendered
Uncle Sam points
fingers at fine
foreign slaughters
and I know—
I know who
doesn't.
Corporation
America with its
indirect democracy
has bred a
quarter generation
of dead-end
addicts;
the children beg
your spare
change for
alcohol—spare
change for
alcohol.
(the third CONVENTIONEER leaves the crowd; the four STREET RATS listen)
Give this generation
An uncoated tongue.
We will do what the
hippies sold out on.
Give this generation
one night, one night
to come up sober,
and we will change
these things that
have been done.
Hey, mid-line easy
solution conservatives,
it's time to
light another flare
of audacious contempt,
honesty is for those
too weak to invent

a history of
victory:
(MACK *becomes passionately angry*)
Fall into goose-step
formation
Horatio Alger.
These porch-step
children
starve for your
legacy,
and those in
steadfastly
full states and
sensible
shoes bypass with
biting
remarks.
Emotion is for the gays,
The artists, and other
enemies of the state.
Callous is the
call to arms for anybody
with anything to
speak of.
And poverty?
"Poverty
is the rising tide of laziness."
So rise to the
occasion
heads of state,
there's a new generation
to screw over,
and they're too
atrophied to resist.
All it should take
is the offer of
a Big Mac to pull
them into line.
Or a simple co-optation

of their heroes,
maybe.
Bend this generation
and
pump them
hard with their MTV
reality.
There is no
movement,
just look how
hard
you banged the baby
boomers
with theirs!
(pause; MACK breathes heavily, exhausted; he and the STREET RATS stare at each other in silence as lights fade; transition Cajun music up softly)

Scene 7: This Country Is Fucked Up

(lights rise, music out; back at The Fortress, QUIZ is looking carefully through GENIE's hair; JEWEL is drinking from a pint of vodka; GENIE is writing a poem in a worn spiral notebook with a blunt pencil)

QUIZ: I think Ferret was the only squatter I ever knew who was clean. His name was Ferret, and he had a ferret named "Human." Everyone—except one or two of us—in this squat has head and body lice, plus scabies. Thank God, I don't.

GENIE: I had body lice, once.

QUIZ: I would have, but they sprayed me down when they arrested me for loitering. After I went to jail I got an apartment. I went in with this girl. I even paid the rent for that month, but then after two weeks, I just thought: I don't want to live in a house.

GENIE: I'd like to be set up in an apartment somewhere.

JEWEL: I could go to Covenant House, but they'd make me come in every night at nin . I couldn't do that. And while I was in jail, some stupid ass-hole gave The Blitz away. A lonely girl without her doggie is all I am now. But, alcohol's treating me good. *(cheering the GIRLS with her pint)* Smile. It's good for you, too.

QUIZ: *(jokingly admonishing)* Just say "No!"

JEWEL: No! *(takes a swig from her pint; QUIZ crosses to join her)* I love to drink, but not so much that I'll have no liver in three years. *(QUIZ takes a drink; to GENIE)* We've gotta teach you a game! Ever hear of the Straight Edge Band? Every time the lyrics say "drink,"

JEWEL AND QUIZ: you gotta drink!

(ROACH and TIGGER enter, in the middle of an argument)

TIGGER: I believe in monogamy because I have respect for people! Personally, I haven't gotten laid in two months or so. And if I don't have sex for the next five months or so, oh fuckin' well.

(crossing to GENIE)

I want to have someone who I can wake up to and rub her hair and hold her and all that.

ROACH: I'm 19, man. I go through that shit for about two days and then I get sick of the bitch. I'm a beer slut and proud of it.

TIGGER: Yeah, but you'd never force anyone.

ROACH: No, I wouldn't force her. No way, but I'd make her want to. *(intimidating, to GENIE)* And I'd *fuck* the hell out of her. *(exits)*

TIGGER: *(to GENIE, almost apologizing)* I'd never force anyone. We're not rapists.

GENIE: *(smiling, but nervous)* Yeah, go to jail for a long time for that.

(TIGGER sits and talks with GENIE as MACK recites; JEWEL and QUIZ speak on their own and start playing a card game; GENIE sets her spiral notebook and pencil by her side)

MACK: I was just

too shy

to ever

do or

say the

right thing.

So a timid

virgin went

down in flames

while being

chased by

a deep brown,

Mexican

horse—

She didn't

scream or
fight, and
ten stories
were more
than plenty
to render
her limp and
lifeless.

GENIE: *(as if continuing a conversation)* I'm willing to deal with society. Society is just a group of people interacting with each other. I live in a society. We have our own society.

TIGGER: I'm not anti-society, I just don't consider myself part of society at all. I've just been in jail—30 days for sleeping in Jackson Square. Little Hitler, this beat cop who gets his kicks from arresting people for not really doing anything at all, that's who got me.

GENIE: I don't think America works as it should, but it's not like I can say, *this* is the way it's going to work.

TIGGER: This country is fucked up.

GENIE: There's too many people trying to run it; too many people trying to say, "You have to do this," "You have to do that."
(ROACH enters and listens to the conversation)

TIGGER: I think you have to fight for what you believe in.

GENIE: I'm a pacifist.

TIGGER: I don't believe pacifism works. I'm willing to die for my convictions.

ROACH: Ah, beat me! Pacifism subjects you to a lot more abuse than anyone needs to take. *(mimes masturbating)* Yeah, I "pass a fist" all the time.

TIGGER: *(pointing to ROACH, as if it's hard to believe)* This guy's my best friend.

ROACH: *(grabs and holds onto TIGGER from behind)* Doesn't matter who's around, doesn't matter what's going on, doesn't matter what or where. Whatever's goin' down, Tigger is always Tigger and he'll always be my brother.

TIGGER: He's my fuckin' best friend.

ROACH: Patience and tolerance is what it takes to get along. We fight like we're fuckin' married, people say, we've been together so long.
(they wrestle on the floor)

TIGGER: We've been hanging out long enough that we have the right to fight like a married couple.

ROACH: He's my family. We're fucking married!

TIGGER: And I'd better never catch anybody fucking with him. I'd fucking kill 'em. Straight out just kill 'em. I'd take a knife and just stab 'em through the eye!
(ROACH and TIGGER howl and give each other five; ROACH sits with JEWEL and QUIZ and drinks; TIGGER and GENIE continue their conversation; TIGGER picks up GENIE's spiral notebook and pencil and starts sketching)

MACK: Timid, little
tough girl
struggles
for the
love of
a barred-in
street king,
and I guide
her to the
bottle-gets-
y'to-the-
backroom
bars—
Talking
of bail,
she goes
down on
Hope,
and I am just
too shy
to tell
her that
Hope is
for Hollywood.

TIGGER: *(as if continuing a conversation)* My dad kicked me out when I was just 17. When I graduated from high school, he said "Congratulations." Then he gave me two weeks to get out. That was six years ago. When I first left home, I lived in Chicago, in the subway. I did what I had to do to survive. It's all about survival. You either survive or you die. *(he tries erasing his drawing error, but there's no eraser on the pencil; he turns to a new page in the spiral notebook and starts sketching again)* People who live here, the professionals, the fucking little yuppie people, they don't even see this side of life. They don't see it, they're blind to it. That's why they ignore me when I ask them for change. But how am I going to stay fed, other than asking people for money? I hate it. I'm free, but things aren't free. I need things so I have to get money. I want a regular job. *(stands)* When I go job hunting I dress smart, wear button downs most of the time. If I had a tie, I'd wear it. But, I mean, just look. Who the fuck is going to want some nasty lookin', dirty lookin', someone who hasn't taken a shower in God knows how long, handling their food, or ringing them up on a cash register, or whatever? I've got over a hundred goddamn applications out in this city. I've got a voice mail number. Nobody ever calls. I make plans, but anytime I make plans, they always fall through. *(sits)* So, I take things day by day, don't make plans too far in the future. Every minute of my life is another minute of my life. *(he messes up his drawing again, rips the page angrily from the notebook, crumples it and throws it; pause; he looks at the next page of the notebook curiously)*

GENIE: Oh. I write poetry. Would you like to hear some?

(TIGGER shrugs; GENIE takes the spiral notebook and reads aloud)

Once in a while I awaken, asking myself "what am I doing?"

    Am I going to live my life like this forever?

Have the streets really become my home,

    a permanent way of life?

Is this what I have chosen, or can I not do better?

    For I am finding myself truly unhappy.

Spare change, leftovers, or just anything

    to survive on a daily basis.

Day by day. One day at a time.

    Not knowing where my next meal will come from.

Wishing for a better life.

    Not knowing where to start.

(pause)

ROACH: *(sarcastically)* Aw, poor little runaway! *(cruelly)* We're not your fuckin' counselors.

(JEWEL angrily moves away from ROACH and gets a chess set, joins TIGGER and GENIE; ROACH laughs and holds onto QUIZ, looking uncomfortable; JEWEL arranges pieces on the chess set; GENIE looks forlorn, closes her spiral notebook; TIGGER tries to comfort her but she pulls away and exits by the end of MACK's poem)

MACK: The only

    one that

    ever mattered

waits,
protruding;
a baby
breathes
between
her belly
and her lap—
And I
tell her
we can
do it,
together,
but every
face informed
shakes—
And I am
not a
father
figure—
How well
we know
the words,
but settling
into a
room rendered
gray and
smoky
by too
many
hangers-on,
I am just
too shy.
(*TIGGER and JEWEL start their game of chess*)

ROACH: (*rises*) C'mon, Tigger, it's almost 10 o'clock. Let's go.

TIGGER: (*glares at ROACH, then moves one of his chess pieces; JEWEL moves a chess piece*) I want to stay and play chess, man.

ROACH: No, have to panhandle, Tigger.

TIGGER: (*moving a piece*) I want to stay and play chess.

ROACH: (*moving closer to TIGGER*) No! We gotta get out and make money. You're forgetting the time factor, man. It's Friday night.

TIGGER: *(getting angry)* I know what fucking night it is. I don't want to make money. Right now I want to fucking play chess!

ROACH: You have to get out there! It's just like fucking Christmas, man. I want to do this so we're going to do this.

(grabs TIGGER'S arm, TIGGER yanks away)

TIGGER: *(looking at ROACH; pointedly)* No, it's *not* like Christmas!

(TIGGER turns his attention back to the chess board; ROACH kicks the chess set)

ROACH: We fight like we're fucking married!

(ROACH goes to QUIZ, who now has an empty liquor bottle, and takes her by the arm) I've got enough for another pint. Whaddya say?

QUIZ: *(hesitantly)* OK.

(QUIZ rises and walks off with ROACH, who glares at TIGGER)

JEWEL: *(once ROACH is out of earshot)* That fucker!

(lights fade; transition music into next scene: slow Cajun dance music; TIGGER and JEWEL exit during transition)

Scene 8: Why Do You Want to Beat Me Up?

(lights up at low level; music fades to low volume and continues; a ROMANTIC COUPLE wearing Mardi Gras masks and necklaces strolls slowly past MACK; the COUPLE slow dances and exits by the end of his poem)

MACK: Does my name
sound different
on your lips
now that I'm
not with you?
Does the water
miss the sun
it has reflected
when it passes
underground?

(ROACH and QUIZ enter, giggling, laughing, both drinking from ROACH's flask; they fall to the ground and stare into each other's eyes; ROACH strokes QUIZ's arm, they kiss in-between drinks, become physically passionate)

Do the voices
of happy people
fill you with
shame for all
the time we
wasted pretending

to be like
them?
I've never loved,
only feared loneliness.
I sit in crowded places
alone
until they empty
and I must
accept the
solitary state.
I don't mind it
as much
now that I
have the
comparison
of your
company.
The lessons of
silence are
now open
to me.

(*music fades out, segues into distant thunder through the remainder of the play; the BUSINESS MAN from Scenes 2 and 5, now drunk and holding a plastic cup of beer in one hand and briefcase in the other, enters, mumbles softly, walks unsteadily, stopping now and then to collect himself; ROACH and QUIZ stare at him; ROACH smiles and whispers to QUIZ*)

ROACH: Let's roll 'im. Knock six kinds of shit outta him.

(*QUIZ giggles; they sneak toward the BUSINESS MAN; ROACH blocks his way while QUIZ stands behind the MAN*)

Hey, man—spare change?

BUSINESS MAN: (*stares blankly, shakes his head*) No.

(*beat*)

ROACH: Hey. I know you. Mr. Corporate Man!

(*ROACH knocks the beer cup out of the MAN's hand*)

Got some spare change for me now, mother-fucker?

(*the MAN shields himself with his briefcase as ROACH pounds on it*)

QUIZ: Spare change, mister?

(*she reaches into his coat and pants pockets searching for money; the three physically struggle with the characters overlapping their lines and improvising during the roll, ROACH pounds repeatedly on the MAN's briefcase:*)

BUSINESS MAN: No. Leave me alone. Don't hurt me! Please!

ROACH: C'mon, asshole, give it up. Think you're better than me? Think 'cause you wear a fancy fuckin' suit you're better than me?

QUIZ: Where do you keep your wallet, mister? Got some spare change for me? Spare change?

(suddenly the MAN screams and throws his briefcase to the ground)

BUSINESS MAN: *I don't have any spare change! (ROACH and QUIZ back away, startled)* I lost my job today! *(pause; the MAN crumples to the ground sobbing)* Why do you want to beat me up? Why? Why?

(ROACH and QUIZ stare at him in stunned silence; ROACH looks around as if disoriented, trying to figure out what to do next; he grabs QUIZ by the arm and they run offstage; the MAN rises and tries to collect himself as MACK recites)

MACK: Another head splits
   under the thrust
   of a billy club,
   another wrong-looker
   goes down for this or
   that—and a right-looking
   wrongdoer violates
   the trusting nature
   of a street rat,
   'round the corner,
   knowin' he doesn't
   have a thing to
   fear.
   (the BUSINESS MAN stumbles offstage)
   I've spent six years
   pouring sand
   into a coffee cup,
   watching it overflow
   and add character
   to otherwise sterile
   free verse.
   In an induced dream
   I was kept at the
   bottom of a well
   that filled in
   icy purity around
   me—and all the

while, mice died
in the bare lightbulbs
miles overhead.
(lights fade; distant church bells chime three o'clock)

Scene 9: I *Am* Home

(lights rise to low level; ROACH enters the squat, staggering, drunk, and crashing from a heroin hit; as he walks he knocks over empty beer cans on the floor with his feet; QUIZ, JEWEL, and GENIE are asleep but do not hear the noise; TIGGER, aroused from sleep, sits up; both young men stare at each other)

TIGGER: You OK?

(ROACH shows TIGGER an empty heroin packet and drops it to the floor; he takes a swig from his flask)

ROACH: I'm drinking cognac right now. *(thrusting the flask to TIGGER)*

TIGGER: I don't like cognac.

ROACH: You're drinking it anyway.

TIGGER: *(rising, taking the flask)* No, I'm not a slave to alcohol. I know all 12 steps.

ROACH: Just say "No."

(looks at TIGGER for the traditional response but gets none; TIGGER drops the flask on the floor; ROACH angrily grabs TIGGER)

You know, you're my best friend and you're my brother and all, but I can still whup your ass. You know I can whup . . . your . . . *(he collapses)*

TIGGER: Roach!

(TIGGER catches him and helps him to the floor; ROACH yanks away and pulls his jacket tighter around his chest)

ROACH: This city's always cold for mornin'. Now matter how hot the day, cold for mornin'. All I gotta do is walk through it. *(beat)* I wish I could go home. *(looks at TIGGER)* I can go home. *(beat; to himself)* I *am* home.

(ROACH lies down and mumbles softly; TIGGER pulls a blanket over ROACH's shoulders, sits next to him, cries softly, and watches ROACH drift to sleep; MACK walks to them, strokes ROACH's hair and speaks softly)

MACK: Above it all,
there's this
beautiful sky.
I pray you listen,
as I call:
I'm caught,

brother,
I'm hung down.
Chained. Owned.
My voice doesn't
reach far,
and I can't speak
too long.
But our four
hands together
could break two
chains this strong.
No generals are
needed to strike up
a march.
Just us,
just us, going the same
way.
Let's just move with
a wink, and a nod.
Let's see who winds
up on top, when we
pull the top down.

Scene 10: There Will Be

(lights dim on TIGGER and ROACH; MACK rises, speaks to the audience, his anger rising)
MACK: There will be a change—
    It'll take time—
    It took 220 years for one nation to
    fall this far.
    There will be a
    great day of reckoning.
    It won't be biblical in nature.
    It will be fueled
    on street rat blood.
    We will roll down
    the gutters and
    paint your uptown

condos red.
There will be
as little mercy
as possible.
Your Romanesque
capitols and monuments
will fall about
your presidential
myths
like the levied
pound of flesh.
(lights focus intensely on MACK)
There will be
a great day of
reckoning.
Caste-system
education
will burn
and tumble
on pretty
blonde pep rallies—
dunce cap
wrong trackside
bag search children
will wipe
their names
from the board—
education—humiliation
forced into drop-
out situation—
(beat)
All's you have to pay . . . is—attention.

(lights fade to black; music up: the Cajun Les Flammes d'en Fer—*"The Flames of Hell"; lights up for curtain call tableaux; lights fade and actors exit; house lights up for audience exit as music continues; the STREET RATS sit outside the theatre and ask audience members as they pass by, "Spare change?" "Spare change for alcohol?"; MACK angrily recites his street poetry to the crowd)*

Hidden

CONCEIVED, WRITTEN, AND DIRECTED
BY MICHAEL ROHD AND LAURA EASON
IN COLLABORATION WITH
SOJOURN THEATRE ARTISTS[1]

Editor's Introduction

Michael Rohd's *Theatre for Community, Conflict and Dialogue* (1998) was a breakthrough text in the field of drama education and applied theatre. In this insightful book, Rohd provides concise methods, based on the legacy of activist Augusto Boal and other artists, for developing trust with a group of community members for purposes of exploring social themes, concepts, and oppression through interactive nonverbal work and verbally improvised activating scenes. His workshops and commissioned theatre performances are well-known and highly regarded for the dignity and respect accorded to each individual involved. Rohd and members of his company, Sojourn Theatre, "walk the talk"

---

1. Ryan Keilty, Jules Bausch, Hannah Treuhaft, Jenn Vann Nice, Jono Eiland, and Bobby Bermea. The text is based on interviews and research with Oregon citizens and project collaborating partners. Additional writing collaboration was provided by Mary Rose, Kenneth Dembo, and Dawn Young.

in terms of community outreach and social embeddedness. Drama emerges from the direct concerns of the participants—developed, shaped, and captured through still and fluid images that crystallize the essence of the ideas; and through simple, direct language that is accessible and thought-provoking.

In 2002, Sojourn Theatre collaborated with the Portland, Oregon, leg of the Anne Frank national touring exhibit to create *Hidden*, an original production about the themes inherent in her narrative, and how they intersect with contemporary United States culture. Members of the company conducted interviews with local citizens and collaborative partners, and conducted research about discrimination, hate, complicity, and the challenges to social justice at different periods throughout history. Close attention was paid to the bystander phenomenon and Maslow's hierarchy of human needs, and elements of this research were woven into the scripted text. The result is a highly physical and sound-scored production that requires readers to imagine how this production might look and sound, suggested by the stage directions and lyric narrative.

Rohd describes and redefines his company's ethnodramatic approach as "a theatre work potentially constructed of multiple scores that include spoken text. Its development includes exploration of metaphor and theme leading to imagistic work not directly lifted from interviews but essentialized from [the] community." In the hands of sensitive theatre artists, ethnodrama reveals to the audience what they may be feeling deep inside, yet are unable or afraid to express out loud. *Hidden* is a play script that reveals our secrets—our secret history, our secret fears, and our secret hopes.

Hidden

Performers/Creators

The performers' visual ethnic read is:
RYAN KEILTY, white
JONO EILAND, asian
BOBBY BERMEA, african american
JULES BAUSCH, white
JENN VANN NICE, white
HANNAH TREUHAFT, jewish
This read affects the meaning of the show.

(SLIDE: Surviving)

(HANNAH and the cast are revealed onstage)
HANNAH: 1945 was 57 years ago

I was 15.
I'm 72 now.

I still go out and speak.
It's exhausting, to go out and tell the story.
But you know it's a good thing.

I'm the only survivor in my family.
I grew up in a small town in Poland
close to Germany, right on the border.
It was occupied, off and on
for the whole war.

During most of the war
I lived in a Jewish ghetto.
About 80,000 of us lived there
in a few square blocks.
The total number of survivors from that ghetto
was about 2000.
400 were children.

I am one of the 400.

In 1944, I was put on the last transport
with my mother.
The last transport to Auschwitz.

After a couple of weeks of this,
daily lines, daily countings,
daily separations,
my mother and I
we were counted apart
different lines
And that was it.

She stayed in Auschwitz.
I was sent to Bergen-Belsen
and then to a work camp in Germany.
Peeling potatoes in an SS kitchen, of all places!
Thank you, Lady,
whoever you were.

When we arrived at this work camp
a German lady, gigantic,
picked 7 or 8
of the scrawniest, sickliest little girls you've ever seen.
We thought this was the end of the line for us.

She put us to work
inside this kitchen
in a locked closet
with a peephole one way in.
We peeled potatoes.
That's what we did
all day.
We were told not to eat any.
The first day,
after we had worked awhile,
this lady came back in,
She was wearing—

It's funny, you know,
how certain things stay with you—
She was wearing a thick black cape.
She stood so her cape blocked the peephole
so guards couldn't see in.
This lady, she was 6 feet tall,
She opened her cape
and on her arm
was a bucket of hot soup.
She said

JENN: "Girls—here's some hot food.
I don't want you to get caught
or me
so I'm putting this bucket by the door
where nobody can see it through the peephole.
Eat one at a time
for only a minute or two.
Be careful."

HANNAH: You know, she looked so mean
you would have thought
she epitomized the Hitler-Nazi era.
But, she saved us.
She truly . . .
I think she gave me the little bit of strength I needed to go on with things.

(MUSIC: all the music in the show was original, and had an ambient, electronic feel, with melody and specific cultural instrumentation at times, as noted; here, music is guitar driven, slow, and repetitive)

(SLIDE: When you're hungry, does anything else matter?)

Soup 1

(we see the cast, all in slow-motion, come down and move through a stylized sequence about hunger that turns into conflict; JONO and JENN confront each other; the cast scatters; they all freeze in their configuration)

(SLIDE: Groups in conflict)
(SLIDE: Struggle for control of resources)

(SLIDE: *Beliefs that clash*)
(SLIDE: *Scapegoating*)
(SLIDE: *Powerlessness*)
(SLIDE: *Division*)
(SLIDE: *Violence*)
(SLIDE: *Hate*)

(*actors watch slides*)

Swallow

JONO: I don't think hate is a useful word.
It's too simple.
It doesn't get at motivation.
That's what I'm interested in . . .
Why people do what they do.
A lot of people who commit awful acts are survivors themselves
of misery
of violence
of not having so many things a person needs.
As soon as you say this out loud
people come back with—
That's no excuse for harming another human being.
Of course it's not an excuse.
But, it can help us understand.
And if we understand
we can talk about change.

(SLIDE: *Why*)

(*choral, with strong sharp motions shifting spatial configuration every noted
line; a different performer says each line below*)
I do not have the life I want.
I live in a place that has no hope.
I'm poor and opportunity seems out of reach.
I watch newcomers prosper while I struggle to survive.
I'm looked down on in my own community.
(*shift*)
I've been taught that my kind deserves more.

I've been taught that caring is a sign of weakness.
I've been taught that different means less than.
(shift)
As a child, I was attacked
physically
sexually
emotionally.
I learned that my life has no value
so I value no life.
(shift)
Anger feels better than pain.
Blame feels better than pity.
Rage feels better than rejection.
(shift)
I feel powerless.
I have no moments of feeling strong.
So I find strength
in having power over another human being—
I take it
alone.
I take it
with a group.
I take it.
And for a moment
the holes in me are filled.

(SLIDE: Once you are fed, you need to feel safe)

*(MUSIC: percussive, wall of sound behind, airy and slightly ominous; this
runs though the whole next few sections until JULES's school story)*

Safety

*(the cast scatters, as though from something falling from the sky; they seek safety
in an abstract, visual, gestural sequence; from this comes the monologue)*
RYAN: In high school, I came out. My science teacher, he was one of my
favorites, started treating me different in class. He wouldn't call on me, or
talk to me, or even look at me. It was like I wasn't there. Other kids picked
up on it. So at this incredibly scary time for me, it seemed they had per-

mission to treat me like that, too. One day after class, I asked him what was going on. He said he didn't want anyone thinking I was his favorite now. He was married and people might talk. He said it was a dangerous situation and that he had to protect himself. Protect yourself?!, I said. So, who'll protect me, if not you, who'll protect me?

(SLIDE: Once you are safe, you need to belong)

(the group begins to walk, grabs newspapers; there's a 90-second complex movement section and all eventually reach out to each other, first in pairs, then in fours, then as the whole group)

(SLIDE: We all understand not belonging)
(SLIDE: It's a shared human experience)

Smell

BOBBY: People say that we all feel difference.
    That we can all walk into a room
    and have the feeling
    of not belonging.
    That it's a universal experience.
    But I think
    there is a difference.

    It has to do
    with what's visible
    and what's not.
    With what can change
    and what can't.
    Like,
    you can change clothes
    you can brush your hair
    you can take a bath,
    you know.
    But I—
    this color, this skin,
    it stays,

no matter what choices I make.
It stays.
And I'm proud,
you know,
I'm proud of it.

But there are places I go
and I will get a look,
or someone will grab their purse tighter,
or someone will lock a door.
It's like the smell that won't come off—
the bath doesn't matter, believe me 'cause I'm clean.

No matter how much we have this talk,
no matter how much you hear me,
and I hear you,
you can't know what it feels like to live with that smell.
The smell someone else puts on you.
(movement section, more pulling away, and reaching out)
JULES: I'm walking down the hall
    and there's a bunch of guys
    just sitting in chairs by the principal's office.
    As I go by
    the guys are watching me approach.
    Then
    they hold up signs with numbers:
JONO: 7.8
RYAN: 8.9
BOBBY: 9.2
JULES: And they burst out laughing.
    They're having a great time . . .
    I'm a senior—
    I've been here before.
    I can handle it.
    But then I see a freshman walk by,
    A girl.
    I know her.
    She's the younger sister of a guy I used to date.
    Really awkward girl,

kind of sad, and shy.
Once, when I was over at their house,
I heard her mom say
JENN: Don't leave the house without makeup on.
JULES: And at dinner, her dad says
BOBBY: Slow down, honey. You're getting big over there. Watch out.
JULES: She was just real quiet.
    Now,
    here she is in the hallway.
    Not skinny.
    She looks healthy, normal,
    you know?
    But not super skinny.
    And she doesn't know what's coming.
JONO: 4.7
RYAN: 5.6
BOBBY: 3.4
JULES: It takes her a moment, but she realizes what's going on.
    And as they start laughing,
    she kind of folds in on herself—
    you know that shape a girl's body can take?
    arms across chest, head down,
    like a mixture of shame and self-defense . . .
    like a physical attack is coming,
    or it's already happened . . .
    Then I notice
    in the group of guys
    is this girl's brother.
    He's there with the rest
    laughing.
    His sister is right in front of him
    looking like she's been assaulted.
    And he doesn't seem to notice
    or mind . . .
    I saw what happened.
    I know how that girl's body will hold that laughter for years.
    She'll hold it as pain
    and I didn't stop it.
    Her own brother sure didn't stop it.

We both just
laughed . . .
with everybody else.

(SLIDE: If a leader makes you feel better)
(SLIDE: In a time of misery)
(SLIDE: In a period of discontent)
(SLIDE: What will that leader lead you toward?)

(people scatter, distractedly reading newspapers, anxious)

Leader

RYAN: This is where we live.
   Our home.
   Is it what you remember?
   What you dreamed it would be?
   Is this what you expected?
   What you wanted?
   What you deserve?
   I can see on your faces, in your eyes,
   The answer is no.
   We all know why.
   You know.
   You see the differences, feel the differences.
   The streets are full of strangers.
   We can't understand what they're saying
   because they refuse to speak our language!
   We're losing our jobs because they'll work for less.
   The town smells.
   The streets are dirty.
   You tell me, is this what you want?
   Is this what you deserve?
   What is left of the life you wanted, your home, your future,
   will be destroyed.
   It will. Unless we do something to stop them. Now.

(SLIDE: Who is watching?)

(SLIDE: Who is watching out?)

(actors slowly move to their Bystander 1 *position)*

Swallow 2

HANNAH: When we use words like hate
 or evil
 we define it as this incomprehensible force.
 This energy.
 We accept the idea that a leader
 like Hitler, for instance,
 can use this force, nurture it and grow it in a whole people.
 That it's possible to build a hysteria that can sweep over a community
 like the wind.

 I think this passes over an important fact—
 When we speak of an event in a place,
 like the Holocaust in Germany,
 more people in these instances are witnesses
 are bystanders
 than are actual perpetrators.

 It's important to consider these bystanders.
 Because by all accounts
 if they speak up
 things can change.

Bystander 1

(the Bystander 1 *sequence is a languorous, slow-motion, lovely full-stage image that catalogs a busy street scene; someone attacks someone as others look away; it will repeat three times in the performance, with a consequence variation each time)*
(MUSIC: techno percussive, with some menace, out as Ghosts *starts)*
(JENN as perpetrator attacks HANNAH as victim)
(then, a slam into positions for the next scene)

(SLIDE: Ghosts)

Ghosts

(RYAN and JONO face out to the audience, not looking at each other)
RYAN: We worked together in the shop every day.
JONO: For years.
RYAN: That's right, for years. Since we were kids.
JONO: He was the owner's son.
RYAN: My dad owned the shop, so even though I was younger
JONO: by a year
RYAN: by a year
JONO: he was still my boss.
RYAN: I was the boss.
JONO: A manager, almost.
RYAN: Yes. A manager.
JONO: Orders would come in, he would fill them out
RYAN: and he would make the clothes.
JONO: Meanwhile, we would talk.
RYAN: All the time, we were talking. It was perfect.
JONO: We worked all day, and we talked.
RYAN: And we enjoyed each other's company.
JONO: We were very lucky.
RYAN: Very lucky.
JONO: Because some people, they hate their work.
RYAN: They do. They hate it.
JONO: Hate where they work, who they work with.
RYAN: Who they work for.
JONO: That's right, who they work for.

JONO: One day, at home, I heard my father talk of change—of his friends
    having meetings.
RYAN: That's right, there were meetings—my father didn't understand what
    was going on, these meetings—
JONO: These meetings were occurring, and men from the outside, from out-
    side the village, men who wore uniforms—soldiers, I think—they were
    telling my father—
RYAN: My father, and men like him, they started to notice change in the village.
JONO: telling my father, and men like him—"You should not be working for
    them—why do you work so hard, and they grow so wealthy?" Men would
    leave these meetings angry, and at work, they would glare at their bosses.

RYAN: Someone left a pig on the doorstep of our shop—a slaughtered pig.

JONO: My father, he seemed nervous

RYAN: A river of blood from the carcass running under our door.

JONO: He seemed not himself.

RYAN: And we, we just kept going to work, enjoying our talk.

JONO: But there was something between our words now

RYAN: There was something not being spoken.

JONO: My father asked me how I liked my job, how I liked the shop where I worked.

RYAN: My father asked if I was comfortable in the shop, with my coworkers.

BOTH: He asked—"Do you feel safe?"

RYAN: I didn't understand . . .

JONO: Safe? Of course, I felt safe.

RYAN: Why would I not feel—

JONO: —not feel

BOTH: safe?

JONO: So one day, my father gets me up early in the morning.

RYAN: Now you have to remember, this is Eastern Europe

JONO: He tells me to be quiet, to follow him.

RYAN: the late 1930s

JONO: We walk out to the center of town in the early light.

RYAN: a small village far from the rest of the world.

JONO: There is a gathering of other men, and boys my age. And women. The women are here, too.

RYAN: No one in our little home knew what was going on in the rest of the world.

JONO: We are standing in a semicircle facing the town square, facing the path that leads up to the finer houses in town.

RYAN: These soldiers have come in, and they have persuaded my friend's father, and many fathers, that things are not as they should be.

JONO: I hear the sound of sleepy footsteps. I see the breath of hundreds of my neighbors making a cloud of mist as they wearily, curiously trudge toward the center of town.

RYAN: You cannot judge my friend.

JONO: And suddenly, I see my friend, and his family in this crowd. And I realize, this crowd—they are all Jews.

RYAN: You cannot hold him accountable.

JONO: And I—I am standing in a mob of gentiles.

RYAN: He was a boy—barely a young man.

JONO: The men around me, workers. They have guns. The women, stones.

RYAN: It was a tidal wave. He was dragged under.

JONO: My father, he stood at the front of our group. He looked back over our ranks—I followed his gaze. Behind us stood a small group of soldiers, sharp, clean young men with stone faces whose eyes took in my father's, then the slowly waking group before us. The soldiers nodded at my father. And I caught the eye of my friend.

RYAN: This is true. In that instant, we locked eyes.

(they look to each other for the first time, for a moment)

RYAN: I had no idea—

JONO: what was coming next.

RYAN: and before I could think to raise my voice, to make a sound

JONO: the guns were raised

RYAN: and the shots began. For an instant—

JONO: —the first ones hung in the air, suspended—a disbelief that seemed to circle the earth and return to this very village—louder, unanswered, and with a fury.

RYAN: And then, the massacre began.

JONO: I saw everyone I had ever known kill or be killed. There was no fight. Simply screams, blood, and reloading.

RYAN: And when the bullets were gone, and the smoke cleared, some of us were still alive. I was still alive.

JONO: I had done nothing—just stood there and watched.

RYAN: Once again, we saw each other.

(they see each other again, a moment)

JONO: In this moment, convinced it was a dream

RYAN: A dream.

JONO: And then

RYAN: those of us still standing were marched several hundred yards to a barn. We were led inside, and told to sit down—to rest.

JONO: A soldier stood with my father. He gave him a lighter

RYAN: and that was the end of me.

JONO: The barn was burned to the ground.

RYAN: No Jew survived the day.

JONO: I watched the flames. I knew my friend was inside.

RYAN: They all had friends inside

JONO: even lovers

RYAN: even lovers.

JONO: We lived in this village side by side for generations, and in a day

RYAN: 60 percent of us were gone. Poof.

JONO: Poof.

    This happened in my village and in at least six others like it.

RYAN: This is a true story.

JONO: Why did I not stop it?

RYAN: How could he have stopped it?

JONO: This story became our secret. Many of us died in the war, and those that lived—

RYAN: they never spoke of that day.

JONO: Never. It was as if it did not happen. A dream

RYAN: A dream.

JONO: We speak of it often now

RYAN: We do. It is the subject of endless conversation.

JONO: I find it impossible to understand.

RYAN: I find it a memory that refuses to loosen its hold . . .

JONO: We talk about it.

RYAN: We talk about it.

JONO: Our ghosts are different.

RYAN: I am his ghost.

JONO: He is my ghost.

    (JONO begins to walk toward RYAN)

RYAN: My ghost waits to appear.

JONO: I am his ghost.

RYAN: My ghost lives in shadows.

JONO: I am his ghost.

RYAN: My ghost begs forgiveness.

JONO: I am his ghost.

    (JONO is standing next to him, and RYAN turns; they stand face-to-face)

RYAN: Yes. He is my ghost.

(MUSIC: similar to last feel, but with Arabic traditional instrumentation on top of the techno sounds . . . almost a wailing-out as Assumption *starts)*

Bystander 2

(earlier sequence repeats; someone tries to stop the perpetrator; he turns at them aggressively, they back off, and he walks away; no one else helps)

(BOBBY as victim and JONO as perpetrator)

(SLIDE: Assumption)

Assumption

JENN: I'm driving down the street in Northeast Portland. I'm going to meet a friend at a party. When I agreed to meet her there, I didn't really think about the neighborhood.

JULES: Did you hear what happened to her?

HANNAH: She totally had this awful experience driving in Northeast.

RYAN: She was telling us all about it Friday night.

JONO: She was really, really lucky.

JENN: Anyway, I'm not exactly sure where I'm going and I miss the street I'm looking for. So, I go down this side street, to turn around. It's a one-way street. And I get half way down the block and there's this truck stopped, just stopped, in the middle of the road. And there are these two guys, two black guys, just standing outside it talking really loudly. At first I don't think they see me. So I wait for a minute, thinking when they see me, they'll move. But then I clearly see one of them look at me. But they don't stop talking.

RYAN: You gotta be careful in the city.

JULES: You never know.

JONO: Anything can happen.

JULES: I've heard about stuff like this before.

HANNAH: Yeah, me too.

JENN: I think about trying to pass them but the street is really narrow. Maybe they were looking at me because they expected me to pass. But no way am I going to risk scratching their truck. And I'm not going to honk. I'm not going to be the white girl honking her horn telling these two black guys to get out of the street in their own neighborhood, even though I think they're being really rude and should move. So I'm starting to get nervous, realizing that they must know I'm lost. Why else would this white girl be driving down this random street all alone in Northeast at 11 o'clock at night? So, I'm trying not to panic, making sure all the doors are locked, trying to figure out what to do and suddenly, I see a couple other black guys join the first two. So, now it's a group of like 5 or 6, all talking and laughing.

JONO: My folks say Portland's changing.

HANNAH: Back in the day, like when my parents were growing up

JONO: you could go anywhere

RYAN: That's what mine say, too.

JULES: Yeah, anywhere.

JENN: And now I'm really scared. There's a driveway behind me, but what am I going to do? Turn around and drive the wrong way down a one-way street? A couple of the guys turn and look at me. Then one of them starts laughing and waving me forward, like to pass the truck. But I'm not going to do it, it's just too close. I'm sure they see it's too close.

BOBBY: Your parents let you drive into town?

RYAN: No way.

HANNAH: Mine do, but they tell me lock the doors.

JULES: Yeah—lock the doors and don't talk to anyone.

JENN: Then two of the guys start walking towards my car, both towards my window. And I just have this really, really bad feeling.

RYAN: She said they had guns, right?

JONO: She said she thought she saw some guns.

HANNAH: She said she was pretty sure.

JULES: I'm sure they had guns.

JENN: So I reverse really fast into the driveway, do a u-turn and head back the way I came, wrong way down the one-way, back to the main road. In my rearview I seem them looking at me like, "What was that about?" But what was I going to do? Roll down my window and see if they were going to help me? My mom always told me to trust my gut and my gut said get the hell out of there.

HANNAH: She sounded scared, when she told it.

JONO: You'd be scared.

JULES: It was a big deal.

JENN: Chances are, it probably would have been fine. But you always hear these terrible stories, you know? I know I shouldn't have been in that neighborhood at that time of night. It's better to stay where you're familiar. People know you and you know them. No confusion about what you're about or what you're up to.

HANNAH: I was in English class when she told it.

JONO: Mr. Blauvelt, he said she was lucky to be alive.

RYAN: Yeah—I heard that—lucky to be alive.

JENN: I don't plan on going to that neighborhood again. I would like to be more open about it, but it's just not worth the risk.
(BOBBY, who has been watching this whole piece from opposite stage, looks at JENN, then looks hard at the audience)
(MUSIC: similar to last two, but larger, and it gathers force; the beats pop in hard halfway, and grows jagged, dangerous, then softens and is simply a

repeating phrase; music fades out under the movement sequence that leads into the first moment of Bed Scene*)*

Bystander 3

(this time, when the perpetrator attacks, all bystanders drop what they are doing, come together and, in slow-motion, protect the victim, corner the perpetrator, and silently scream for help, all pointing at the perpetrator, now on the floor, caught)
(RYAN as the perpetrator and JULES as the victim)

(movement sequence that shifts from the caught perpetrator above, to three couples in bed; a unison image and sequence; the middle couple is BOBBY and JULES)

(SLIDE: September 16, 2001)

Bed Scene

(BOBBY and JULES are in bed; JULES wakes, BOBBY stirs)
BOBBY: I'm going to put a flag up on our door this morning.
JULES: Uh huh.
BOBBY: Really. I am.
JULES: That sounds great. I'm right behind you.
BOBBY: I'm serious.
JULES: Alright. You got me. Flag. Good. I've got one more hour of sleep.
    Please please . . .
    (silence)
    You're serious?
BOBBY: That's what I've been saying.
JULES: We can't put a flag up. What are you talking about?
BOBBY: I don't like being the only house on our street without one. I don't
    like what it says.
JULES: What it says is that we think for ourselves.
BOBBY: No—it says that we don't recognize something has changed.
    Something has happened.
JULES: Yeah—something's happened. And a large part of why something happened is what our government has been doing around the world for a lot
    of years.

BOBBY: You don't have to lecture me on our political history.

JULES: Maybe I do—

BOBBY: You don't. But this week, it's not about history, or right and wrong. It's about what happened. It's about acknowledging that I am a citizen of a country that's been attacked. Viciously. And I want to say to my neighbors, to my fellow citizens, that I feel it. That it's not OK. That I grieve with them.

JULES: Why do you need to say something at all? Why does your grief have to be public? If my mother died, we wouldn't fly a flag.

BOBBY: Your mother didn't die. But you know what? About 1500 people's mothers did.

(she really wakes up)

JULES: How many mothers has the U.S. killed in the last 30 years?

(pause)

BOBBY: OK, you know what—you're stuck.

JULES: What do you mean I'm stuck?

BOBBY: You are unwilling to allow this moment to be anything other than another piece of a history that already makes complete sense to you—you figured it out. It's static.

JULES: That is not—

BOBBY: The world is not static—it shifts. History changes shape in light of new events. People feel something, and the world can be different. Even if just for a moment in time.

JULES: And in this moment, the flag means something different?

BOBBY: It means that saying I feel some commonality with fellow citizens is not a blanket endorsement with our history, or even our current policies. I don't think unity is so wrong at a time like this.

JULES: Right now, that flag means patriotism. And patriotism means rallying around a common enemy. Is that the unity you're interested in?

BOBBY: That's what it means to you. It doesn't have to mean that to me.

(other performers slowly get up and, in a stylized way, become the crowd in story below)

JULES: Last night, I was driving home from work, about 10 o'clock. I'm coming by Pioneer Square, towards the river. Traffic's moving slow, lots of horns blowing . . . I'm not thinking much about it. As I get closer to the square, I see a crowd on the corner facing traffic. They're holding flags, and signs that say "Honk for America." So, I realize the noise is people honking in response to the signs. I get closer still—the crowd is mostly men—early, mid twenties. The driver of the car in front of me, she's looking around, like to see if she can get over and make a turn. I don't know if she sees the sign, or she's distracted, or what—but she's not honking. And all these guys with flags and signs, they start to notice she's not honking. So slowly, they all start to turn their attention to her. They're smiling, calling out to her,

ALL *(except JULES who listens)*: "Hey—honk for America."

JULES: She's still looking around, not noticing. Then, when they see she's not honking as she pulls into the intersection, they stop smiling and stare a little harder. And then, like a unit, they begin to step off the sidewalk and head for her car. They're shouting

ALL *(except JULES who listens)*: "Honk for America."

JULES: They look ugly. With a guy one step from her window, Miss Distracted sees them and instantly hits her horn, I think more in shock than unity, and they cheer. They smile—she passes—they're high-fiving, and they turn to the next car—me.

BOBBY: What did you do?

JULES: I honked. It was a big group. And afterwards, I felt sick.

BOBBY: I'm sorry.

JULES: As soon as that group took a step off that sidewalk, I was in a country I am not proud of. I was in a country of followers—and that is a dangerous place to be.

BOBBY: You were on one corner in one moment. I'm really sorry that happened. I am. But those men do not have the right to take the flag away from me. I can claim it for myself. Otherwise, they win.

JULES: I live here, too. It might mean one thing to you, but I'm convinced it will mean something very different to everyone we know. Unless we put a sign up saying "your flag, not mine," I'm going to be stuck—just like you said. But not stuck in my understanding of the world—I'll be stuck in yours. And that does not feel right to me. Not at all.

(SLIDE: What's the difference between standing up for a belief)
(SLIDE: For what you need)
(SLIDE: And finding yourself)
(SLIDE: In the role of the attacker?)

Soup 2

(the full opening sequence is reprised, super fast; ends with knocking down of half the cast)

(MUSIC: same music as first time this sequence ran at top of show)

(SLIDE: When do we stand up?)
(SLIDE: Who do we stand up for?)
(SLIDE: What do we allow to go on right in front of our eyes?)
(SLIDE: In our own backyard?)

Hate Crimes

(for touring or local productions, the text can be replaced with local statistics)
RYAN: Gresham—January 20, 2001
Anti-gay slurs were scrawled on the front door of a gay man's residence.
JONO: Salem—February 2
Four males were charged with intimidation for allegedly assaulting a security guard because he is black.
BOBBY: Keizer—March 9
Racial slurs were scrawled on a bathroom stall at a local high school.
JONO: Corvallis—April 5
A 38-year-old was charged with aggravated murder for allegedly beating a Hispanic man to death.
RYAN: Portland—May 6
Racist and anti-Semitic graffiti was spray-painted on gravestones in a Jewish cemetery.
BOBBY: Eugene—June 17
A woman was charged with second-degree intimidation and harassment for allegedly yelling vulgar and racist expressions at two men because of their ethnicity. She also allegedly slapped one of the men and tried to remove a religious garment from the head of the other.
RYAN: Medford—July 6
Dozens of Adolf Hitler posters were posted in the downtown area.
JONO: Hillsboro—August 26
A resident of Hillsboro was savagely beaten allegedly because he lived as a woman.
BOBBY: Eugene—September 18
A 33-year-old man was charged with a hate crime after allegedly making a threatening phone call to the Islamic Cultural Center.
RYAN: Portland—October 15
Two eight-foot-tall crosses were burned outside a Jewish cemetery and in a local park.

JONO: Medford—November 19, 2001
A 20-year-old man was charged with third-degree assault and first-degree
intimidation for allegedly assaulting a Hispanic man while yelling "white
power."

Violence against Women

*(women are on the floor, going through a gesture/movement sequence suggested
by the text)*
JULES: More than half the people in the world
are women.
When we talk about groups being oppressed or victimized
a lot of us think about race, religion, ethnicity,
even sexual orientation.
But we don't often talk about this majority
this group
as vulnerable to attack
HANNAH: But rape is a tool of war—
In the recent Balkan conflicts
mass rape was used as a tool of terror
to keep dissent and organizing
at a minimum.
JULES: When we talk about that over here
we feel outrage.
We recognize that phenomenon
as a horror
as a massive injustice.
As we should.
JENN: For most of history,
women have been without power
without representation.
JULES: Now, hate crime law increases the penalty for crimes committed against
people because of their race, religion, or sexual orientation. But crimes
against women are not considered hate crimes.
HANNAH: I don't know that I am in favor of the same crime carrying different penalties based on the victim's background.
JENN: But if we're going to have these laws shouldn't women be covered?
HANNAH: Aren't we the largest group facing crimes that clearly have to do
with what binds us together?

JULES: Right here in our country one out of every six women will be raped in her lifetime.

JENN: One out of three will be a survivor of sexual assault before age 21.

ALL: One in three.

JULES: Sometimes I want to say—

HANNAH: Where's the outrage?

JENN: Where's the standing up?

JULES: When do we talk about that?

(SLIDE: After you have food, safety and belonging,)
(SLIDE: You must be heard)

Physical Sequence of Jono Breaking through the Wall

(JONO tries to break though a wall formed by the cast; he is repeatedly pushed back)

Advocate

(the monologue below happens while JONO and RYAN execute an acrobatic and tense climb over and embrace, which demands from JONO, the speaker, intense physical balance and effort to speak)

JONO: I work with refugees
and immigrants
from all over the world.
I fight for their representation, their rights.
Many are, like myself, Asian.
I fight for our voices to be heard.

It's important in these times.
There seems to be a strong anti-immigrant sentiment
growing.
People wanting to close the doors, so to speak.
But doors can close in many ways.

When Measure 9 was up,
a proposition that
in my mind

would legislate against the rights of homosexuals,
some men in my community
leaders
men who have become conservative as they have become prosperous—
Some of these men saw this measure as harmless
even the moral thing to do.
And I went to these men
and I said
Stop.

See what this is.

If the people here start to legislate
against certain groups of people because of difference
do you think you will be far behind?
You must work for all human rights,
because if you don't
it is your grandchildren that will pay the price.
It is they who will find
closed doors.

I have to remind them,
remind myself,
that having a voice doesn't mean just talking,
it means listening
very carefully.

(SLIDE: How could hate be in the Gospels?)

How Could Hate Be in the Gospels?

RYAN: The reason I went into the ministry
    was because of studying the Holocaust.
    I could not understand
    how that could happen
    in a Christian society.
    How neighbors could turn on neighbors
    and think they were the instruments of God.
    I think every religion at some point
    has an extreme edge

that pushes belief to rule of law . . .
Life and death.
But here I was
looking at my own belief system
and I was feeling that anti-Jewish values
were actually in the Gospels.
How could hate be in the Gospels?
I went to a professor of mine
He was actually Jewish.
I asked him about this.
He told me
It doesn't do any good
to stand outside your religious tradition
and point fingers.
If you're really searching for answers
you have to become more involved.
Find answers.
Make a difference.
From the inside.
And I did.

(HANNAH enters and begins a prayer gesture in extra slow-motion)
*(MUSIC: when HANNAH enters, the sound begins; a slow deep drone that
becomes percussive, and faster, and techno sounding, deep, ominous . . . it is
at its fastest and loudest as the voiceover section after this completes . . . it is a
slow build through RYAN's text until then)*

People come to religion for lots of reasons.
After September 11
churches were filled.
People said they craved answers
but they don't necessarily want to dig for those answers.
(JONO enters and begins a prayer gesture in extra slow-motion)
I think what they really crave
is comfort.
(BOBBY enters and begins a prayer gesture in extra slow-motion)
(JULES enters and begins a prayer gesture in extra slow-motion)
Our ability to forget history—
it amazes me sometimes.
Look at the Middle East.

The ways the Israelis and Palestinians treat each other.
(*JENN enters and begins a prayer gesture in extra slow-motion*)
There are people there
who went through the Holocaust
who were directly involved
whose families were directly involved.
Some of these people are still capable
of prejudice, of violent policies—of oppression.
I wonder if it's part of the human condition.
Maybe I'm weary.
But I don't think we learn all that well
from what came before.
Ethnic divisions, race,
religious beliefs . . .
Cambodia, Bosnia, Rwanda.
The atrocities continue to happen
from the beginning of time
right up until now.
Today.
(*prayer gestures continue at an accelerated pace, so by the time RYAN finishes the above text, the other performers are all over the stage executing abstracted gestures of prayer from major world religions; these get faster, more frantic, as RYAN finishes the text, joins them, the music gets louder, and we hear a voiceover of the text below*)

God Monologue / Prayer Sequence

(*VOICEOVER: multiple voices*)
I have a God, he has a God. Whose God is the right God? Whose God is the real God? There's no way to know who is listening to a voice, or who is listening to his own head.

I can't prove that he is wrong or right but I have to believe that in this world there's no way that God would wish what He has done upon other human beings. If such a God exists, why would I want to exist in that world?

That world can't be a place for a God like mine or a place for me to live. Nor my children, my family, or my ancestors. So what reason could I have for wanting to stay in a world where a man like this could live?

I have no choice, because here I am in a world where a man like this does live. His God tells him what to do, my God tells me to believe in peace. Whose God is real?

My choice is leave and hope he goes away, or look into his eyes and see if I can understand. If I understand, does that mean I have met his God? And if I meet his God, does that mean my God doesn't exist?

I don't want to understand. I have to look in his eyes, look in his eyes and understand. I don't want to understand. What other choice do I have but to look in his eyes?

If I don't look in his eyes, I walk away. I pretend. I imagine the world goes on. It doesn't.
(gestures continue and then morph into images/gestures of violent ways people are put to death; as the text ends, each performer is put to death one by one, and holds his/her body, suspended; on the last word of the text, a beat; and they all collapse)
(blackout for a moment, and then instantly fading up, blue light and SLIDES up as noted below)
(MUSIC fades out during the blackout)

(SLIDE: "Every human life is worth the same as every other human life")
(SLIDE: Do we share this belief?)
(SLIDE: Do we act on it?)
(SLIDE: As a nation?)
(SLIDE: As individuals?)

Contact

(BOBBY gets up, watches the SLIDES, then comes downstage)

(SLIDES: throughout this monologue, gorgeous photographs of culture clash, hope, MLK, a small child, a playground fight, a mosque besieged, a standoff in China, a flower in a rifle, etc.)

BOBBY: Once you know a human being
    and share values with them
    it's pretty hard to imagine them

as the enemy, right?

I think that if people had a chance
to actually know someone from a group
that they don't know and feel uncertain about
or that they hate, even.
If they got to know someone from that group
found out who they were, really
they'd realize they have a lot of the same worries and problems.

I know, my wife tells me
I can sound so Pollyanna.
But I truly believe it.
When someone is unknown, it's easy to blame them.
I work with dialogue groups here in town
bringing together people of different races, religions.
All these different people,
they're committed to sitting in a room
and talking for eight, ten, twelve hours at a time.
Well, the thing we discover is that
we all have many of the same needs
the same hopes.

My version of a higher power
isn't a force that makes everything work out—
It's a light that offers each of us
each one of us
the invitation
to move toward a more loving world.
So I operate
from that
and I look for chances
for myself
and for others
to meet across borders.
Across difference.
To put on the table all the good and bad.
To make known and learn from
what we usually keep hidden.

(MUSIC starts soft, builds . . . sounds like a melodic version of waves and ocean, with guitar playing the changing elements amidst the techno foundation)

Final Physical Sequence

(a repetition of gestures and motions from throughout the show, which winds up with the cast in moments of connection, and finishing in a unison sequence that was seen at some point earlier in the show—everyone ends up in their opening Soup positions, but facing HANNAH center as she starts)

(SLIDE: Surviving)

HANNAH: Our kids, here in this country,
    so many of them are lost.
    They feel lost.
    There is a tremendous amount of meanness in our schools
    between our children.
    The topdog versus the underdog.
    They don't realize what they're doing,
    our kids,
    when they're mean to each other
    just for what they wear
    or what they look like.

    Why do people come together around hate . . . ?
    I don't know.
    Maybe it's the simplest thing—
    they were raised with prejudice
    they were hurt by someone
    they heard a name called
    didn't know what it meant
    and just kept using it.
    People are insecure—
    if they don't feel confident enough
    or strong enough
    to go out on their own
    they might move toward a group that will help give them confidence.
    All we can do is hope
    that by putting something better out there

a few of them
a few of them might drop out of that.

A few years ago
I was at a school outside Oregon City.
I spoke to a group of 8th graders.
I told my story.
One boy—
he had been invited
recruited
to join a hate group in his town—
his first meeting with them was scheduled for that same day.
He wrote me later.
JONO: "You're a Jew?
    I don't think you look different.
    After what you said
    I can't join my friends.
    I don't think that it's right.
    I couldn't look in my mirror
    and look at myself.
    I couldn't face my God.
    What can I do?
    How can I convince my friends not to do this?"
HANNAH: That was the essence of it.
    A very short letter, really.
    I didn't know how to answer him
    but I thought
    Oh, thank you, Lord
    or whoever there is
    for stories
    for what they help us remember
    for what they help us change
    and for people to tell them.
    Thank you.

(MUSIC: same as before this text, and then fades out)
(blackout)

Appendix

DRAMATIC MODELS
FOR ETHNODRAMA

Playwriting instructors also assign play reading to study exemplars of the art and craft. Aside from ethnodramas, literary and commercial play scripts serve as models and stimuli for developing original performance ethnography. I recommend the following titles from dramatic literature but advise that you stay away from their film adaptations. The playwright's original conception and structure of the script may have been altered for the media.

For autoethnography models, read:

- Jo Bonney, ed., *Extreme Exposure: An Anthology of Solo Performance Texts from the Twentieth Century* (New York: Theatre Communications Group, 2000)
- Carolyn Gage, *The Last Reading of Charlotte Cushman*, in Lynn C. Miller, Jacqueline Taylor, and M. Heather Carver, eds., *Voices Made Flesh: Performing Women's Autobiography* (Madison, WI: University of Wisconsin Press, 2003)
- Holly Hughes and David Román, eds., *O Solo Homo: The New Queer Performance* (New York: Grove Press, 1998)

- John Leguizamo with David Bar Katz, *Freak: A Semi-Demi-Quasi-Pseudo Autobiography* (New York: Riverhead Books, 1997)
- Jane Martin, *Talking With . . .* (New York: Samuel French, 1983)
- Jane Wagner, *The Search for Signs of Intelligent Life in the Universe* (New York: Harper & Row, 1986)

For models that examine a principal investigator's relationship with participants, read:

- Mark Medoff, *Children of a Lesser God* (Clifton, NJ: James T. White & Co., 1980)
- John Pielmeier, *Agnes of God* (Garden City, NY: Doubleday, 1982)
- Peter Shaffer, *Equus* (New York: Avon Books, 1974)

For models that incorporate participant interviews into monologue and dialogue, read:

- Michael Bennett, et al., *A Chorus Line: The Book of the Musical* (New York: Applause Books, 1995)
- Jessica Blank and Erik Jensen, *The Exonerated* (New York: Faber and Faber, 2004)
- Eve Ensler, *The Vagina Monologues* (New York: Dramatists Play Service, 2000)
- William H. Hoffman, *As Is* (New York: Vintage Books, 1985)
- Moisés Kaufman and Members of the Tectonic Theater Project, *The Laramie Project* (New York: Vintage Books, 2001)
- Anne Nelson, *The Guys* (New York: Random House, 2002)
- Anna Deavere Smith, *Fires in the Mirror* (New York: Doubleday, 1993) and *Twilight: Los Angeles, 1992* (New York: Doubleday, 1994)
- Studs Terkel's *Working*, adapted by Stephen Schwartz and Nina Faso (New York: Music Theatre International, 1978)
- Doug Wright, *I Am My Own Wife* (New York: Faber and Faber, 2004)

For a model that displays ways of presenting correspondence data, read

- A. R. Gurney, *Love Letters* (New York: Dramatists Play Service, 1989)

For models that include a narrator as a key figure, read:

- Thornton Wilder, *Our Town* (New York: Harper, 1960)
- Tennessee Williams, *The Glass Menagerie* (New York: Dramatists Play Service, 1976)

Playwriting texts recommended by colleagues who practice and teach the art form include:

- Lajos Egri, *The Art of Dramatic Writing* (New York: Touchstone Books, 1972)
- Michael Wright, *Playwriting in Process: Thinking and Working Theatrically* (Portsmouth, NH: Heinemann, 1997)

Bibliography

Ajwang', R. O., and L. Edmondson. (2003). Love in the time of dissertations: An ethnographic tale. *Qualitative Inquiry* 9(3), 466–80.

Alexander, B. K. (2000). Skin flint (or, the garbage man's kid): A generative autobiographical performance based on Tami Spry's *Tattoo Stories*. *Text and Performance Quarterly* 20(1), 97–114.

Armijo, L. M., and K. Lindemann. (2002). *People of the shadows: An ethnographic performance exploring boundary management among the homeless.* Unpublished manuscript.

Bagley, C., and M. B. Cancienne, eds. (2002). *Dancing the data.* New York: Peter Lang Publishing.

Barone, T. (1997). "Seen and heard": The place of the child in arts-based research in theatre education. *Youth Theatre Journal* 11, 113–27.

———. (2002). From genre blurring to audience blending: Reflections on the field emanating from an ethnodrama. *Anthropology and Education Quarterly* 33(2), 255–67.

Barranger, M. S. (2004). Understanding the "new" docudrama. In ed. M. S. Barranger, *Understanding Plays* (pp. 567–16). Boston: Pearson Education.

Becker, H. S., M. M. McCall, L. V. Morris, and P. Meshejian. (1989). Theatres and communities: Three scenes. *Social Problems* 36(2), 93–116.

Bennett, M., J. Kirkwood, N. Dante, M. Hamlisch, and E. Kleban. (1995). *A chorus line: The book of the musical.* New York: Applause Books.

Berg, B. L. (2001). *Qualitative research methods for the social sciences.* Boston: Allyn and Bacon.

Blank, J., and E. Jensen. (2004). *The exonerated.* New York: Faber and Faber.

Boal, A. (2002). *Games for actors and non-actors*. 2nd ed. Trans. A. Jackson. New York: Routledge.

Bonney, J., ed. (2000). *Extreme exposure: An anthology of solo performance texts from the twentieth century*. New York: Theatre Communications Group.

Boran, K. (1999). *Rising from the ashes: A dramaturgical analysis of teacher change in a Chicago public high school after probation*. Unpublished doctoral dissertation, National-Louis University.

Bowles, N. ed. (1997). *Friendly fire: An anthology of 3 plays by queer street youth*. Los Angeles: A.S.K. Theatre Projects.

Bui, D.-M. T. (2001). Six feet tall: A one-person performance. *Cultural Studies, Critical Methodologies* 1(2), 185–89.

Burge, K. B. (2000, February). *Cultures: A play in three acts and seven scenes*. Reader's theatre performance at the 2000 American Educational Research Association Arts-Based Research Conference, Albuquerque, New Mexico.

Butterfield, F. (2002, August 28). More Black men are in jail than are enrolled in college. *The Arizona Republic*, p. A8.

Carver, M. H. (2003). Risky business: Exploring women's autobiography and performance. In ed. L. C. Miller, J. Taylor, and M. H. Carver, *Voices made flesh: Performing women's autobiography* (pp. 15–29). Madison, WI: University of Wisconsin Press.

Casas, J. (2003, September). *14*. Performance by Teatro Bravo, Phoenix, Arizona.

Chapman, J., H. Sykes, and A. Swedberg. (2003). *Wearing the secret out*: Performing stories of sexual identities. *Youth Theatre Journal* 17, 27–37.

Chávez, R. C., C. M. Adams, and B. E. Araujo. (2004). *Struggling for agency: Democracy, equity, and social justice—Two cases from a graduate multicultural education course*. Unpublished manuscript.

Cole, A. L., M. McIntyre, and K. McAuliffe. (2001, April). *All about Alzheimer's: Who can tell what we know?* Performance at the 2001 American Educational Research Association Conference, Seattle, Washington.

Collins, K. (2001). *I came to live out loud*. Unpublished manuscript.

Community-Based Arts Collaborative Course. (2004, May). *To be American: A work in progress*. Performance at Arizona State University, Tempe.

Conover, T. (1987). *Coyotes: A journey through the secret world of America's illegal aliens*. New York: Vintage.

Conquergood, D. (1991). Rethinking ethnography: Towards a critical cultural politics. *Communication Monographs* 58(2), 179–94.

———. (1998). Beyond the text: Toward a performative cultural politics. In ed. S. J. Dailey, *The future of performance studies: Visions and revisions* (pp. 25–36). Annadale, VA: National Communication Association.

———. (2003). Performing as a moral act: Ethical dimensions of the ethnography of performance. In ed. Y. S. Lincoln and N. K. Denzin, *Turning points in qualitative research: Tying knots in a handkerchief* (pp. 397–413). Walnut Creek, CA: AltaMira Press.

Corey, F. C., ed. (1993). *HIV education: Performing personal narratives.* Tempe, AZ: Arizona State University.

Cozart, S. C., J. Gordon, M. Gunzenhauser, M. McKinney, and J. Patterson. (2003, April). *From monologue to dialogue: Negotiating the ethical tensions of performance ethnography.* Paper presented at the American Educational Research Association Conference, Chicago, Illinois.

Crow, B. K. (1988). Conversational performance and the performance of conversation. *The Drama Review* 32(3), 23–54.

De la Garza, S. A. (2000, April). *María speaks: Journeys into the mysteries: Revealing the mother in the shadows of Mexican womanhood.* Performance at Arizona State University, Tempe.

Dening, G. (1996). The theatricality of history making and the paradoxes of acting. In G. Dening, *Performances* (pp. 103–27). Chicago: University of Chicago Press.

Denzin, N. K. (1997). *Interpretive ethnography: Ethnographic practices for the 21st century.* Thousand Oaks, CA: Sage.

———. (2001a). *Interpretive interactionism.* 2nd ed. Thousand Oaks, CA: Sage.

———. (2001b). The reflexive interview and a performative social science. *Qualitative Research* 1(1), 23–46.

———. (2003). *Performance ethnography: Critical pedagogy and the politics of culture.* Thousand Oaks, CA: Sage.

———. (2004, March 22). Lecture. Arizona State University, Tempe.

Diamond, C. T. P., and C. A. Mullen, eds. (1999). *The postmodern educator: Arts-based inquiries and teacher development.* New York: Peter Lang.

———. (2000, October 5). Rescripting the script and rewriting the paper: Taking research to the "Edge of the Exploratory." *International Journal of Education and the Arts,* 1, Article 4. Retrieved September 27, 2002, from http://ijea.asu.edu/v1n4/.

Dillard, S. (2000). *Breathing Darrell:* Solo performance as a contribution to a useful queer methodology. *Text and Performance Quarterly* 20(1), 74–83.

Donmoyer, R., and J. Yennie-Donmoyer. (1995). Data as drama: Reflections on the use of reader's theater as a mode of qualitative data display. *Qualitative Inquiry* 1(4), 402–28.

Donovan, L. M. (2004, April). *Ahh-sess.* Performance at the American Educational Research Association Conference, San Diego, California.

Edwards, G. (1997). *Monologues on Black life.* Portsmouth, NH: Heinemann.

Ehrenreich, B. (2002). *Nickel and dimed: On (not) getting by in America.* New York: Owl Books.

Eisner, E. (1997). The promise and perils of alternative forms of data representation. *Educational Researcher* 26(6), 4–10.

———. (2001). Concerns and aspirations for qualitative research in the new millennium. *Qualitative Research* 1(2), 135–45.

Ellis, C., and A. P. Bochner. (1992). Telling and performing personal stories: The constraints of choice in abortion. In ed. C. Ellis and M. G. Flaherty, *Investigating subjectivity: Research on lived experience* (pp. 79–101). Newbury Park, CA: Sage.

————, eds. (1996). *Composing ethnography: Alternative forms of qualitative writing.* Walnut Creek, CA: AltaMira Press.

Ensler, E. (2000). *The vagina monologues.* New York: Dramatists Play Service.

Farah, L. (2003). Shaping the world with our hands. In ed. L. C. Miller, J. Taylor, and M. H. Carver, *Voices made flesh: Performing women's autobiography* (pp. 282–300). Madison, WI: University of Wisconsin Press.

Finley, M. (2000). *Street rat.* Detroit: Greenroom Press, University of Detroit Mercy.

————. (2003). Fugue of the street rat: Writing research poetry. *International Journal of Qualitative Studies in Education* 16(4), 603–4.

Finley, S. (2000). "Dream child": The role of poetic dialogue in homeless research. *Qualitative Inquiry* 6(3), 432–34.

————. (2001). From the streets to the classrooms: Street intellectuals as teacher educators, collaborations in revolutionary pedagogy. In ed. K. Sloan & J. T. Sears, *Democratic curriculum theory and practice: Retrieving public spaces* (pp. 113–26).

Finley, S., and M. Finley. (1998). *Traveling through the cracks: Homeless youth speak out.* Paper presented at the American Educational Research Association Conference, San Diego, California.

————. (1999). Sp'ange: A research story. *Qualitative Inquiry* 5(3), 313–37.

Finley, S., and J. G. Knowles. (1995). Researcher as artist/artist as researcher. *Qualitative Inquiry* 1(1), 110–42.

Foster, E. (2002). Storm tracking: Scenes of marital disintegration. *Qualitative Inquiry* 8(6), 804–19.

Gallagher, M. (1991). *¿De Dónde?.* New York: Dramatists Play Service.

Gannon, S. (2004). Out/performing in the academy: Writing 'The Breast Project'. *International Journal of Qualitative Studies in Education* 17(1), 65–81.

Geertz, C. (1983). Blurred genres: The reconfiguration of social thought. In C. Geertz, *Local knowledge: Further essays in interpretive anthropology* (pp. 19–35). New York: Basic Books.

Gingrich-Philbrook, C. (1997). Refreshment. *Text and Performance Quarterly* 17, 352–60.

Giroux, H. (2003). *Public spaces, private lives.* Lanham, MD: Roman & Littlefield.

Glesne, C. (1999). *Becoming qualitative researchers: An introduction.* 2nd ed. New York: Longman.

Goffman, E. (1959). *The presentation of self in everyday life.* New York: Doubleday.

Goldstein, T. (2001a). Hong Kong, Canada: Playwriting as critical ethnography. *Qualitative Inquiry* 7(3), 279–303.

————. (2001b). *Astronaut.* Paper presented at the American Educational Research Association Conference, New Orleans, Louisiana.

————. (2002). Performed ethnography for representing other people's children in critical educational research. *Applied Theatre Researcher* (3) [On-line]. Available at www.gu.edu.au/centre/atr/opt6/frameset1b3.html.

Gómez-Peña, G. (2000). *Dangerous border crossers: The artist talks back.* New York: Routledge.

Goodall, H. L., Jr. (2000). *Writing the new ethnography.* Walnut Creek, CA: AltaMira Press.

Gray, R. E. (2003). Performing on and off the stage: The place(s) of performance in arts-based approaches to qualitative inquiry. *Qualitative Inquiry* 9(2), 254–67.

Gray, R. E., V. Ivonoffski, and C. Sinding. (2002). Making a mess and spreading it around: Articulation of an approach to research-based theater. In ed. A. P. Bochner and C. Ellis, *Ethnographically speaking: Autoethnography, literature, and aesthetics* (pp. 57–75). Walnut Creek, CA: AltaMira Press.

Gray, R. E., and C. Sinding. (2002). *Standing ovation: Performing social science research about cancer.* Walnut Creek, CA: AltaMira Press.

Grinker, R. R. (2000, Fall). In the arms of Africa: The life of Colin Turnbull. *AnthroNotes* 22, 12–17.

Handwerker, W. P. (2002). *Quick ethnography.* Walnut Creek, CA: AltaMira Press.

Higgins, C., D. Cannan, and C. Turnbull. (1984). *The Ik.* Woodstock, IL: Dramatic Publishing.

Hinds, J. (2004, April 25). Rumsfeld's 'poetry' surfaces again, this time set to music. *The Arizona Republic,* p. E5.

Hoffman, W. H. (1985). *As is.* New York: Vintage Books.

Holden, J. (2004). *Nickel and dimed.* Unpublished manuscript.

Honeychurch, K. G. (1998). Carnal knowledge: Re-searching (through) the sexual body. In ed. W. E. Pinar, *Queer theory in education* (pp. 251–73). Mahwah, NJ: Lawrence Erlbaum Associates.

Horwitz, S. (2002, March 8). Baring it all: The actor's life in the solo show. *Backstage,* pp. 32–35.

Hunter, D. (2004, February). *Heinz 57.* Performance at the University of Victoria, Victoria, British Columbia, Canada.

Jackson, S. (1993). Ethnography and the audition: Performance as ideological critique. *Text and Performance Quarterly* 13, 21–43.

Jipson, J., and N. Paley, eds. (1997). *Daredevil research: Re-creating analytic practice.* New York: Peter Lang.

Jones, J. L. (1996). The self as other: Creating the role of Joni the ethnographer for *Broken Circles. Text and Performance Quarterly* 16, 131–45.

——— . (2002). Performance ethnography: The role of embodiment in cultural authenticity. *Theatre Topics* 12(1), 1–15.

——— . (2003). Sista docta. In ed. L. C. Miller, J. Taylor, and M. H. Carver, *Voices made flesh: Performing women's autobiography* (pp. 237–57). Madison, WI: University of Wisconsin Press.

Kalb, J. (2001). Documentary solo performance: The politics of the mirrored self. *Theater* 31(3), pp.12–29.

Karaoke is so yesterday: Movieoke debuts in NYC. (2004). *The Arizona Republic,* 14 March, p. E14.

Kaufman, M., and Members of the Tectonic Theater Project. (2001). *The Laramie project.* New York: Vintage Books.

Keck, M. (1996). *Voices in the rain.* Unpublished manuscript.

Kotarba, J. A. (1998). Black men, black voices: The role of the producer in synthetic performance ethnography. *Qualitative Inquiry* 4(3), 389–404.

Kozol, J. (1991). *Savage inequalities.* New York: HarperCollins.

Kulick, D. (2004). Book review: Harry F. Wolcott, *Sneaky kid and its aftermath: Ethics and intimacy in fieldwork. Sexualities* 7(1), 117–18.

Landy, R. J. (1993). *Persona and performance: The meaning of role in drama, therapy, and everyday life.* New York: Guilford Press.

Lincoln, Y. (2004). Performing 9/11: Teaching in a terrorized world. *Qualitative Inquiry* 10(1), 140–59.

Lincoln, Y. S., and N. K. Denzin. (2003). The revolution in presentation. In ed. Y. S. Lincoln and N. K. Denzin, *Turning points in qualitative research: Tying knots in a handkerchief* (pp. 375–78). Walnut Creek, CA: AltaMira Press.

Madison, D. S. (2003). Performance, personal narratives, and the politics of possibility. In ed. Y. S. Lincoln and N. K. Denzin, *Turning points in qualitative research: Tying knots in a handkerchief* (pp. 469–86). Walnut Creek, CA: AltaMira Press.

McCall, M. M. (2000). Performance ethnography: A brief history and some advice. In ed. N. K. Denzin and Y. S. Lincoln, *Handbook of qualitative research,* 2nd ed. (pp. 421–33). Thousand Oaks, CA: Sage.

McCall, M. M., H. S. Becker, and P. Meshejian. (1990). Performance science. *Social Problems* 37(1), 117–32.

McLean, C. (2004, August). *Awareness about aging and autonomy—"Remember me for birds."* Performance at the National Association for Drama Therapy Conference, Newport, Rhode Island.

Meyer, M. J. (1998). *Transitional wars: A study of power, control and conflict in executive succession—Theatre as representation.* Unpublished doctoral dissertation, McGill University.

———. (2001a). Illustrating issues of power and control: The use of dramatic scenario in administration training. *Educational Management and Administration* 29(4), 449–65.

———. (2001b). Reflective leadership training in practice using theatre as representation. *International Journal of Leadership in Education* 4(2), 149–69.

———. (2003). *Theatre as representation (TAR) in the teaching of teacher and administrator preparation programs.* Unpublished manuscript.

Meyer, M. J., and K. J. K. Moran. (2004). *Evidence and artistic integrity in arts-based research: Necessity with a bit of folly.* Paper presented at the American Educational Research Association Conference, San Diego, California.

Mienczakowski, J. (1995). The theater of ethnography: The reconstruction of ethnography into theater with emancipatory potential. *Qualitative Inquiry* 1(3), 360–75.

———. (1996). An ethnographic act: The construction of consensual theatre. In ed. C. Ellis and A. P. Bochner, *Composing ethnography: Alternative forms of qualitative writing* (pp. 244–64). Walnut Creek, CA: AltaMira Press.

———. (1997). Theatre of change. *Research in Drama Education* 2(2), 159–72.

———. (2001). Ethnodrama: Performed research—limitations and potential. In ed. P. Atkinson, A. Coffey, S. Delamont, J. Lofland, and L. Lofland, *Handbook of ethnography* (pp. 468–76). Thousand Oaks, CA: Sage.

———. (2003). The theater of ethnography: The reconstruction of ethnography into theater with emancipatory potential. In ed. Y. S. Lincoln and N. K. Denzin, *Turning points in qualitative research: Tying knots in a handkerchief* (pp. 415–32). Walnut Creek, CA: AltaMira Press.

Mienczakowski, J., & Morgan, S. (1998). Stop! In the name of love: Baddies, grubs and the nitty-gritty. Paper/performance presented at the SSSI Couch Stone Symposium, Houston, TX.

———. (2001). Ethnodrama: Constructing participatory, experiential and compelling action research through performance. In ed. P. Reason and H. Bradbury, *Handbook of action research: Participative inquiry and practice* (pp. 219–27). London: Sage.

Mienczakowski, J., L. Smith, and S. Morgan. (2002). Seeing words—hearing feelings: Ethnodrama and the performance of data. In ed. C. Bagley and M. B. Cancienne, *Dancing the data* (pp. 34–52). New York: Peter Lang Publishing.

Miles, M. B., and A. M. Huberman. (1994). *Qualitative data analysis.* 2nd ed. Thousand Oaks, CA: Sage.

Miller, M. (1998). (Re)presenting voices in dramatically scripted research. In ed. A. Banks and S. P. Banks, *Fiction and social research: By ice or fire* (pp. 67–78). Walnut Creek, CA: AltaMira Press.

Miller, L. C., J. Taylor, and M. H. Carver. (2003). *Voices made flesh: Performing women's autobiography.* Madison, WI: University of Wisconsin Press.

Montano, L. M. (2003). Death in the art and life of Linda M. Montano. In ed. L. C. Miller, J. Taylor, and M. H. Carver, *Voices made flesh: Performing women's autobiography* (pp. 265–81). Madison, WI: University of Wisconsin Press.

Nelson, A. (2002). *The guys.* New York: Random House.

Nethercott, S. S., and N. O. Leighton. (1990). Memory, process, and performance. *Oral History Review* 18(2), 37–60.

Norris, J. (2000). Drama as research: Realizing the potential of drama in education as a research methodology. *Youth Theatre Journal* 14, 40–51.

Ocklander, M., and G. Östlund. (2001). Comments on the *Brad Trilogy* [Letter to the editor]. *Qualitative Health Research* 11(6), 725–27.

Ollerenshaw, J. A., and J. W. Creswell. (2002). Narrative research: A comparison of two restorying data analysis approaches. *Qualitative Inquiry* 8(3), 329–47.

Paget, M. A. (1995). Performing the text. In ed. J. Van Maanen, *Representation in ethnography* (pp. 222–44). Thousand Oaks, CA: Sage.

Park-Fuller, L. (2003). A clean breast of it. In ed. L. C. Miller, J. Taylor, and M. H. Carver, *Voices made flesh: Performing women's autobiography* (pp. 215–36). Madison, WI: University of Wisconsin Press.

Patton, M. Q. (2002). *Qualitative research and evaluation methods.* 3rd ed. Thousand Oaks, CA: Sage.

Pelias, R. J. (1999). *Writing performance: Poeticizing the researcher's body.* Carbondale: Southern Illinois University Press.

———. (2002). For father and son: An ethnodrama with no catharsis. In ed. A. P. Bochner and C. Ellis, *Ethnographically speaking: Autoethnography, literature, and aesthetics* (pp. 35–43). Walnut Creek, CA: AltaMira Press.

———. (2004). *A methodology of the heart: Evoking academic and daily life.* Walnut Creek, CA: AltaMira Press.

Pelias, R. J., and J. Van Oosting. (1987). A paradigm for performance studies. *Quarterly Journal of Speech* 73, 219–31.

Piccalo, G. (2003, December 30). Authentic?: The search is on in our electronic society for connections to a more genuine life. *The Arizona Republic,* pp. E1, E4.

Pifer, D. A. (1999). Small town race: A performance text. *Qualitative Inquiry* 5(4), 541–62.

Pineau, E. (2000). *Nursing mother* and articulating absence. *Text and Performance Quarterly* 20(1), 1–19.

Pinkerton, J. (2002, July 14). "Anything goes" attitude looks like it's here to stay. *The Arizona Republic,* p. V2.

Pollock, D. (1990). Telling the told: Performing *Like a Family. Oral History Review* 18(2), 1–36.

Prendergast, M. (2001). *"Imaginative Complicity": Audience education in professional theatre.* Unpublished master's thesis, University of Victoria, Victoria, British Columbia, Canada.

———. (2003). I, me, mine: Soliloquizing as reflective practice. *International Journal of Education and the Arts,* 4(1) [On-line]. Available: http://ijea.asu.edu/v4n1.

Preisinger, M. A., C. Schroeder, and K. Scott-Hoy. (2000, February). *What makes me? Stories of motivation, morality and me.* Interdisciplinary arts performance at the 2000 American Educational Research Association Arts-Based Research Conference, Albuquerque, New Mexico.

Rex, L. A., T. J. Murnen, J. Hobbs, and D. McEachen. (2002). Teachers' pedagogical stories and the shaping of classroom participation: "The Dancer" and "Graveyard Shift at the 7–11." *American Educational Research Journal* 39(3), 765–96.

Rivera, J. (2003). 36 assumptions about writing plays. *American Theatre* 20(2), 22–23.

Roberts, C. (2002). *"I've needed a friend my whole life."* Unpublished manuscript.

Rogers, D., P. Frellick, and L. Babinski. (2002). Staging a study: Performing the personal and professional struggles of beginning teachers. In ed. C. Bagley and M. B. Cancienne, *Dancing the data* (pp. 53–69). New York: Peter Lang Publishing.

Rohd, M. (1998). *Theatre for community, conflict and dialogue: The Hope is Vital training manual.* Portsmouth, NH: Heinemann.

———. (2001). *Shadows and bricks.* Unpublished manuscript.

———— . (2002). *Passing glances: Mirrors and windows in Allen County.* Unpublished manuscript.

———— . (2004). *Witness our schools.* Unpublished manuscript.

Rohd, M., and L. Eason, (2002). *Hidden.* Unpublished manuscript.

Rollheiser, K. (2004). *Mohammed's mountain.* Unpublished manuscript.

Saldaña, J. (1998a). Ethical issues in an ethnographic performance text: The "dramatic impact" of "juicy stuff." *Research in Drama Education* 3(2), 181–96.

———— . (1998b). "Maybe someday, if I'm famous . . .": An ethnographic performance text. In ed. J. Saxton and C. Miller, *The research of practice, the practice of research* (pp. 89–109). Victoria, British Columbia: IDEA Publications.

———— . (1999). Playwriting with data: Ethnographic performance texts. *Youth Theatre Journal* 13, 60–71.

———— . (2002). Finding my place: The Brad trilogy. In H. F. Wolcott, *Sneaky kid and its aftermath: Ethics and intimacy in fieldwork* (pp. 167–210). Walnut Creek, CA: AltaMira Press.

———— . (2003). Dramatizing data: A primer. *Qualitative Inquiry* 9(2), 218–36.

Saldaña, J., S. Finley, and M. Finley. (2004). *Street rat.* Unpublished manuscript.

Saldaña, J., and H. F. Wolcott. (2001). *Finding my place: The Brad trilogy.* Unpublished manuscript.

Sallis, R. (2003). Ethnographic performance in an all-boys school. *NJ (Drama Australia Journal)* 27(2), 65–78.

Schechner, R. (1985). *Between theatre and anthropology.* Philadelphia: University of Pennsylvania Press.

Schreiber, R., P. Rodney, H. Brown, and C. Varcoe. (2001). Reflections on deconstructing Harry, or when is good art bad science? [Letter to the editor]. *Qualitative Health Research* 11(6), 723–24.

Schwartz, S., and N. Faso. (1978). *Working.* New York: Music Theatre International.

Seidman, I. E. (1991). *Interviewing as qualitative research.* New York: Teachers College Press.

Smith, A. D. (1993). *Fires in the mirror.* New York: Doubleday.

———— . (1994). *Twilight: Los Angeles, 1992.* New York: Doubleday.

———— . (2000). *Talk to me: Listening between the lines.* New York: Random House.

Snow, S. (2002, November). *Nightride in the city.* Performance at the Association for National Drama Therapy Conference, Albuquerque, New Mexico.

Sparkes, A. C. (2002). *Telling tales in sport and physical activity: A qualitative journey.* Champaign, IL: Human Kinetics.

Spore, M. B., and M. D. Harrison. (2000, April). *Stories of the academy: Learning from the good mother.* Performance at the 2000 American Educational Research Association Conference, New Orleans, Louisiana.

Spry, T. (2001). Performing autoethnography: An embodied methodological praxis. *Qualitative Inquiry* (7)6, 706–32.

————— . (2003). Illustrated woman: Autoperfomance in "Skins: A daughter's (re)construction of cancer" and "Tattoo stories: A postscript to 'Skins'". In ed. L. C. Miller, J. Taylor, and M. H. Carver, *Voices made flesh: Performing women's autobiography* (pp. 167–91). Madison, WI: University of Wisconsin Press.

Strauss, A. L. (1987). *Qualitative analysis for social scientists.* New York: Cambridge.

Stucky, N. (1993). Toward an aesthetics of natural performance. *Text and Performance Quarterly* 13, 168–80.

————— . (2002). Deep embodiment: The epistemology of natural performance. In ed. N. Stucky and C Wimmer, *Teaching performance studies* (pp. 131–44). Carbondale, IL: Southern Illinois University Press.

Sykes, H., J. Chapman, and A. Swedberg. (2002, April). *Wearing the secret out.* Performance presented at the American Educational Research Association Conference, New Orleans, Louisiana.

Talen, B. (2003). *What should I do if Reverend Billy is in my store?* New York: New Press.

Taylor, J. (2003). On being an exemplary lesbian: My life as a role model. In ed. L. C. Miller, J. Taylor, and M. H. Carver, *Voices made flesh: Performing women's autobiography* (pp. 192–214). Madison, WI: University of Wisconsin Press.

Taylor, P. (2003). *Applied theatre: Creating transformative encounters in the community.* Portsmouth, NH: Heinemann.

Terkel, S. (1974). *Working: People talk about what they do all day and how they feel about what they do.* New York: Pantheon.

————— . (1993). *Race: How blacks and whites think and feel about the American obsession.* New York: Anchor Books.

Thorp, L. (2003). Voices from the garden: A performance ethnography. *Qualitative Inquiry* 9(2), 312–24.

Tillmann-Healy, L. M. (1996). A secret life in a culture of thinness: Reflections on body, food, and bulimia. In ed. C. Ellis and A. P. Bochner, *Composing ethnography: Alternative forms of qualitative writing* (pp. 76–108). Walnut Creek, CA: AltaMira Press.

Toth, J. (1993). *The mole people: Life in the tunnels beneath New York City.* Chicago: Chicago Review Press.

Turner, V. (1982). *From ritual to theatre.* New York: PAJ Publications.

Turner, V., and E. Turner. (1982). Performing ethnography. *The Drama Review* 26(2), 33–50.

Van Maanen, J. (1988). *Tales of the field: On writing ethnography.* Chicago: University of Chicago Press.

Vanover, C. (2002). *Attunement.* Paper presented at the American Educational Research Association Conference, New Orleans, Louisiana.

Vanover, C. (2004, April). *Teaching the power of the word: Culturally-responsive pedagogy in a Chicago public high school.* Performance at the American Educational Research Association Conference, San Diego, California.

Vanover, C., and J. Saldaña. (2002). *Attunement.* Unpublished manuscript.

Wagner, J. (1986). *The search for signs of intelligent life in the universe.* New York: Harper and Row.

Walker, R., C. Pick, and B. MacDonald. (1991). "Other rooms: Other voices"—A dramatized report. In ed. C. Pick and B. MacDonald, *Biography, identity and schooling: Episodes in educational research* (pp. 80–93). Washington, DC: Falmer Press.

Welker, L. S., and H. L. Goodall, Jr. (1997). Representation, interpretation, and performance: Opening the text of *Casing a Promised Land. Text and Performance Quarterly* 17, 109–22.

Wolcott, H. F. (1994). *Transforming qualitative data: Description, analysis, and interpretation.* Thousand Oaks, CA: Sage.

———. (2002). *Sneaky kid and its aftermath: Ethics and intimacy in fieldwork.* Walnut Creek, CA: AltaMira Press.

Wolfe, T. (1979). *The right stuff.* New York: Farrar, Straus and Giroux.

Wright, D. (2004). *I am my own wife: Studies for a play about the life of Charlotte von Mahlsdorf.* New York: Faber and Faber.

About the Contributors

José Casas (scenes from *14*) is a playwright and actor from Los Angeles. He received an M.A. in theatre arts from California State University, Los Angeles, and an M.F.A. in creative writing/playwriting from Arizona State University. Other plays written include *the vine, all brown, freddie's dead, a bag of oranges,* and *the assassination of erik estrada,* just to name a few. Contact information for inquiries: chicano_power_14@yahoo.com.

Jennifer Chapman (*Wearing the Secret Out*) is a visiting assistant professor at Albion College in Albion, Michigan, where she teaches classes in theatre history, theory, literature, drama in education, and theatre for youth. Her recent dissertation, written for the Department of Theatre and Drama at the University of Wisconsin, Madison, investigates intersections between gender, sexuality, and high school theatre practices. Contact information for inquiries: jchapman@albion.edu.

Laura Eason (*Hidden*) has been an ensemble member with Chicago's Lookingglass Theatre Company (LTC) for twelve years and has served as artistic director for six of them. She has worked with LTC as an actor, writer, director, composer, musician, script consultant and/or acrobat for more than twenty shows. Lookingglass has produced three of her plays, *They All Fall Down: The Richard Nickel Story* (cowritten with Jessica Thebus), *28,* and *In the Eye of the Beholder* (Jeff Citation, Best New Work). She is the recipient of a National Endowment for the Arts artistic development grant and recently received a play commission from Middlesex School in Concord, Massachusetts. As an associate artist with Sojourn Theatre in Portland, Oregon, her work includes cowriting and codirecting *Hidden, Look Away,* and *Smash'd.* She is a graduate of Northwestern University's Performance Studies department and is a native Chicagoan. Contact information for inquiries: leason11@earthlink.net.

Macklin Finley (*Street Rat*) is a poet currently writing a novel, *Mutt,* about the construction of personal histories. He has inhabited the world of New Orleans's street rats, and the corridors of Detroit's emptied factories and boarded-up neighborhoods. To support his writing, he has worked as a cook, luggage salesman, dishwasher, waiter, and street poet. Contact information for inquiries: finley@vancouver.wsu.edu.

Susan Finley (*Street Rat)* is an associate professor of educational foundations, literacy, and research methodology at Washington State University. She bases her pedagogy and inquiry in arts-based approaches to understanding social and cultural issues in educational contexts. She is an activist who has implemented educational efforts with street youths and economically poor children, youths, and adults, housed, and unhoused. Contact information for inquiries: finley@vancouver.wsu.edu.

Elissa Foster (*Storm Tracking*) received her B.A. and a postgraduate honours degree in theatre from the Queensland University of Technology in Australia. She holds an M.A. (1996, University of Memphis) and Ph.D. (2002, University of South Florida) in communication. She currently works as an Assistant Professor in the Department of Communication at the University of Texas at San Antonio. Her fields of study include interpersonal communication, health communication, and interpretive research methods, with a particular interest in narrative ethnography as an approach to understanding difficult communication within close relationships. Contact information for inquiries: efoster@utsa.edu.

Michael Keck (scenes from *Voices in the Rain*) is an actor, writer, and composer based in New York. He facilitates workshops in various settings including schools, universities, community centers, and correctional facilities. Contact information for inquiries: mgkex@earthlink.net.

Matthew J. Meyer (*The Practice*) is an associate professor of education at St. Francis Xavier University's School of Education in Antigonish, Nova Scotia, Canada. A longtime dramatist and stage director, he teaches drama education and educational administration. He strongly believes that the visual and performing arts have been underutilized as teaching and issue-provoking devices in both in-service and pre-service teacher preparation and graduate programs. He has written a number of dramatic works that are used in such programs with remarkable success and fun. Contact information for inquiries: School of Education, Saint Francis Xavier University, PO Box 5000, Antigonish, Nova Scotia, Canada B2G 2W5; E-mail: mmeyer@stfx.ca.

Jim Mienczakowski's (*Baddies, Grubs & the Nitty-Gritty*) formative years were dominated by training and employment in the performing arts. Subsequently, as an educator, he continued to work in theatre and the development of understandings of performance research. He is currently deputy vice-chancellor (Research & Academic) at Central Queensland University. Contact information for inquiries: dvcar@cqu.edu.au.

Steve Morgan (*Baddies, Grubs & the Nitty-Gritty*) is a forensic psychologist in Queensland. He has collaborated on a range of ethnodrama projects with Jim Mienczakowski (and even performed in a couple), as well as offering evaluations of nationally endorsed guidelines for the presentation of drama on the subject of suicide. Steve is presently in private practice and has been appointed to the Queensland State Community Corrections Board. He formerly worked with Griffith University and the Australian Institute for Suicide Research and Prevention. Contact information for inquiries: stevemorgan@powerup.com.au.

Monica Prendergast (prologue: *the theatre*) is a sessional instructor, doctoral candidate, and the recipient of the Interdisciplinary Doctoral Fellowship at the University of Victoria, British Columbia. Her interdisciplinary work on theatre audience and curriculum studies appears in *Youth Theatre Journal*, the *Journal of Aesthetic Education*, and the *Alberta Journal of Educational Research*. Her work on research poetry appears in the *International Journal of Education and the Arts*, *Research in Drama Education*, and *Language and Literacy*. Contact information for inquiries: mprender@uvic.ca.

Michael Rohd (*Hidden*) is founding artistic director of Sojourn Theatre in Portland, Oregon, where his work as creator/director/performer includes the warehouse performance journey *7 Great Loves* (five 2003 Drammy Awards including Best Production and Best Director). He is a recipient of Theatre Communication Group's 2001 New Generations Grant, and their 2002 Extended Collaboration Grant (as a playwright) with Atlanta's Alliance Theatre. He is an associate artist with Cornerstone Theater Company in Los Angeles and an artistic associate with Ping Chong & Co. in New York City. He is also founding artistic director of Hope Is Vital, an international theatre and community dialogue resource, and author of *Theatre for Community, Conflict, and Dialogue* (Heinemann, 1998). For more information on Sojourn Theatre, go to www.sojourntheatre.org. Contact information for inquiries: mrohd@aol.com.

Johnny Saldaña (editor, *Chalkboard Concerto, Street Rat*) is a Professor of Theatre at Arizona State University's Katherine K. Herberger College of Fine Arts. He is the author of AltaMira Press's *Longitudinal Qualitative Research: Analyzing Change through Time* (2003), and his ethnodramatic adaptation of "The Brad Trilogy" is included in Harry F. Wolcott's *Sneaky Kid and Its Aftermath: Ethics and Intimacy in Fieldwork* (2002). He has published articles in *Youth Theatre Journal, Research in Drama Education, Multicultural Perspectives,* and *Qualitative Inquiry.* Contact information for inquiries: Arizona State University, Department of Theatre, PO Box 872002, Tempe, AZ, USA 85287-2002; E-mail: Johnny.Saldana@asu.edu.

Anne Swedberg (*Wearing the Secret Out*) is a doctoral candidate in theatre research at the University of Wisconsin, Madison and is the recipient of a 2004–2005 dissertation year fellowship from the American Association of University Women. Her dissertation explores the workings of power and privilege in community-based theatre. Contact information for inquiries: annekswedberg@yahoo.com.

Heather Sykes (*Wearing the Secret Out*) is an assistant professor at the Ontario Institute for Studies in Education at the University of Toronto, Canada. Her research focuses on issues of sexuality, gender, and the body in sport and education. One of her research projects involved gathering the life histories of lesbian, gay, and queer physical education teachers to explore how desire and homophobia impact both teachers and students in schools. She is currently using performed ethnography in a teacher education program to help students find ways to make schools safer for LBGTQ students. Her work has been published in the *Journal of Gay and Lesbian Issues in Education, Journal of Curriculum Studies,* and the *International Journal of Qualitative Studies in Education.* Contact information for inquiries: Department of Curriculum, Teaching and Learning, OISE/UT, 252 Bloor St. W., Toronto, Ontario, Canada M5S 1V6. E-mail: hsykes@oise.utoronto.ca.

Charles Vanover (*Chalkboard Concerto*) worked in the Chicago Public Schools for eight years. He is currently a doctoral candidate in educational administration and social policy at the University of Michigan, and holds a master's degree in school library science from Chicago State University, as well as a Certificate in the Liberal Arts from the University of Chicago's Basic Program. He works as a policy analyst for the Study of Instructional Improvement. Contact information for inquiries: cvanover@umich.edu.

Breinigsville, PA USA
05 November 2010
248725BV00002B/7/P